THE
INTERNET'S
COMING OF AGE

Committee on the Internet in the
Evolving Information Infrastructure

Computer Science and Telecommunications Board

Commission on Physical Sciences, Mathematics, and Applications

National Research Council

NATIONAL ACADEMY PRESS
Washington, D.C.

NOTICE: The project that is the subject of this report was approved by the Governing Board of the National Research Council, whose members are drawn from the councils of the National Academy of Sciences, the National Academy of Engineering, and the Institute of Medicine. The members of the committee responsible for the report were chosen for their special competences and with regard for appropriate balance.

Support for this project was provided by the National Science Foundation under contract No. ANI-9714374. Any opinions, findings, conclusions, or recommendations expressed in this material are those of the authors and do not necessarily reflect the views of the sponsor.

Library of Congress Cataloging-in-Publication Data

The Internet's coming of age / Committee on the Internet in the Evolving Information Infrastructure, Computer Science and Telecommunications Board, Commission on Physical Sciences, Mathematics, and Applications, National Research Council.
    p. cm.
    ISBN 0-309-06992-0
    1. Internet. I. National Research Council (U.S.). Committee on the Internet in the Evolving Information Infrastructure. II. Title.
      TK5105.875.I57 I5435 2000
      004.67'8—dc21

                                         00-012242

Additional copies of this report are available from:

National Academy Press
2101 Constitution Ave., NW
Box 285
Washington, DC 20055
800-624-6242
202-334-3313 (in the Washington metropolitan area)
http://www.nap.edu

THE NATIONAL ACADEMIES

National Academy of Sciences
National Academy of Engineering
Institute of Medicine
National Research Council

The **National Academy of Sciences** is a private, nonprofit, self-perpetuating society of distinguished scholars engaged in scientific and engineering research, dedicated to the furtherance of science and technology and to their use for the general welfare. Upon the authority of the charter granted to it by the Congress in 1863, the Academy has a mandate that requires it to advise the federal government on scientific and technical matters. Dr. Bruce M. Alberts is president of the National Academy of Sciences.

The **National Academy of Engineering** was established in 1964, under the charter of the National Academy of Sciences, as a parallel organization of outstanding engineers. It is autonomous in its administration and in the selection of its members, sharing with the National Academy of Sciences the responsibility for advising the federal government. The National Academy of Engineering also sponsors engineering programs aimed at meeting national needs, encourages education and research, and recognizes the superior achievements of engineers. Dr. William A. Wulf is president of the National Academy of Engineering.

The **Institute of Medicine** was established in 1970 by the National Academy of Sciences to secure the services of eminent members of appropriate professions in the examination of policy matters pertaining to the health of the public. The Institute acts under the responsibility given to the National Academy of Sciences by its congressional charter to be an adviser to the federal government and, upon its own initiative, to identify issues of medical care, research, and education. Dr. Kenneth I. Shine is president of the Institute of Medicine.

The **National Research Council** was organized by the National Academy of Sciences in 1916 to associate the broad community of science and technology with the Academy's purposes of furthering knowledge and advising the federal government. Functioning in accordance with general policies determined by the Academy, the Council has become the principal operating agency of both the National Academy of Sciences and the National Academy of Engineering in providing services to the government, the public, and the scientific and engineering communities. The Council is administered jointly by both Academies and the Institute of Medicine. Dr. Bruce M. Alberts and Dr. William A. Wulf are chairman and vice chairman, respectively, of the National Research Council.

Preface

In 1967, the President's Science Advisory Committee's Panel on Computers in Higher Education opened its report by noting that "after growing wildly for years, the field of computing now appears to be approaching its infancy."[1] This comment preceded by about 2 years the initial deployment of Internet nodes, but while computing developed and penetrated society in many ways over the succeeding decades, the Internet grew more slowly until its commercialization in 1995, which led to an explosion of growth that continues today. Extending the 1967 advisory committee's analogy, one might today view the Internet as having reached its adolescence. How it will grow up—and how its maturation can be fostered—is the subject of this report.

Motivated by two concerns—what would help the Internet mature to meet ever-rising expectations and how might that maturation be achieved—the National Science Foundation asked the Computer Science and Telecommunications Board (CSTB) to undertake a study of the Internet and the key challenges that will shape its maturation, focusing on the core technologies of the Internet. In response to this request, CSTB assembled the Committee on the Internet in the Evolving Information Infrastructure. This committee, made up of experts in technology and

---

[1]President's Science Advisory Committee. 1967. *Computers in Higher Education*. White House, Washington, D.C., February, p. 1.

policy, received briefings and conducted deliberations over a period of almost 2 years. Those 2 years were particularly turbulent. They witnessed enormous growth and diversification of the industries and nonprofit entities associated with the Internet and turned it into a cause célèbre: the Internet seems to be everyone's business today.

No matter how rapid the changes, the committee process does not lend itself to the reaching of consensus in "Internet time." Like most CSTB committees, this one, too, needed time to learn, deliberate, and converge—and also to see which trends endured and which seemed transient. Many parts of the report required little updating in the course of this work, as they speak to basic design or technical principles that have remained durable. But some elements in the landscape changed over the past year, and the committee strove to update its analysis accordingly. It sought to focus on guiding principles rather than on the more rapidly shifting details. The resulting integrated discussion and analysis is intended to help inform technical design, development, deployment, operation, and management decisions relevant to the evolving network of networks. It is also intended to guide policy makers as they seek to reconcile the Internet's unique features with the existing body of policies and practices that are touched by the Internet, such as telecommunications regulation.

The Internet's Coming of Age is the latest report in an influential series about the Internet issued by CSTB. The first report, *Toward a National Research Network* (1988), validated the concept of a comprehensive network to support communications among researchers across the country (and around the world), and it leveraged federal funding to support Internet research, development, and deployment in the late 1980s. The second, *Realizing the Information Future: The Internet and Beyond* (1994), addressed the Internet's transition from a network complex aimed at the research, education, and library communities to a complex serving all segments of the economy and society, noting potential impacts on those pioneering communities and covering a range of issues, from pricing to intellectual property protection, that would impinge on the commercial Internet. It explained the makeup of the Internet, relating its essential technology to the proliferation of uses and communications modes that accelerated in the 1990s. The third, *The Unpredictable Certainty: Information Infrastructure Through 2000* (1996), examined the different industries whose investments would be key to the Internet's growth and the evolution of user interests in Internet capabilities—the chemistry of supply and demand that would shape what the Internet looks like. This new report gives readers an inside look at today's thriving commercial Internet, identifying short- and long-term technical challenges as well as approaches to Internet-related public policy.

The committee wishes to thank the various members of the CSTB staff who helped to make this report happen. In particular, Jon Eisenberg, the staff officer responsible for this project, has played a central role throughout the entire project, coordinating all of the various elements of the report. The committee would also like to thank Suzanne Ossa for her assistance in organizing committee meetings and preparing the report. David Padgham contributed significantly to the editing and research done for this report. Liz Fikre was instrumental in editing the final manuscript.

David D. Clark, *Chair*
Computer Science and
Telecommunications Board

Acknowledgment of Reviewers

This report has been reviewed in draft form by individuals chosen for their diverse perspectives and technical expertise, in accordance with procedures approved by the NRC's Report Review Committee. The purpose of this independent review is to provide candid and critical comments that will assist the institution in making its published report as sound as possible and to ensure that the report meets institutional standards for objectivity, evidence, and responsiveness to the study charge. The review comments and draft manuscript remain confidential to protect the integrity of the deliberative process. We wish to thank the following individuals for their review of this report:

Geoff Baehr, Sun Microsystems, Inc.,
Edward Balkovich, Bell Atlantic,
Scott Bradner, Harvard University,
Hans-Werner Braun, University of California at San Diego,
Charles N. Brownstein, Corporation for National Research Initiatives,
Brian E. Carpenter, IBM,
William J. Dally, Stanford University,
Joseph Farrell, University of California at Berkeley,
Robert M. Frieden, Pennsylvania State University,
Reed E. Hundt, McKinsey & Company,
Geoffrey Huston, Telstra Internet,
Stephen T. Kent, BBN Corporation,
Hal Varian, University of California at Berkeley, and
Kevin Werbach, Release 1.0.

Although the reviewers listed above provided many constructive comments and suggestions, they were not asked to endorse the conclusions or recommendations, nor did they see the final draft of the report before its release. The review of this report was overseen by William H. Press, Los Alamos National Laboratory, appointed by the NRC's Commission on Physical Sciences, Mathematics, and Applications, who was responsible for making certain that an independent examination of this report was carried out in accordance with institutional procedures and that all review comments were carefully considered. Responsibility for the final content of this report rests entirely with the authoring committee and the institution.

Contents

Overview and Recommendations

OVERVIEW

The rhetoric of the Internet revolution surrounds us. The transformation of a research network used by a few tens of thousands of researchers into a global communications infrastructure vital to many aspects of life is celebrated as folk history and pointed to as the basis for a new economic order. Electronic commerce has transformed the way in which many individual consumers, companies, and governments buy and sell products and services. E-mail, chat rooms, and other forms of communication have become common in the workplace and many homes. The Internet provides near-instant access to a wide range of multimedia content and has become an important channel for software distribution.

Where is the Internet going, and how is it getting there? All indications are that the Internet revolution—given its impact, "revolution" seems the appropriate label—is not nearly over. Just during the course of the authoring committee's work, there were a number of developments that are likely to have long-lasting impact; salient among them are the widening deployment of broadband residential Internet service and the beginnings of commercial deployment of mobile wireless devices that have Internet connectivity. Other recent developments include the advent of new interconnection models and businesses and the widespread use of new content delivery mechanisms designed as overlays to the Internet. Meanwhile, innovation continues in the applications and services that run over the Internet, exemplified by the rise of interactive chat and games and various forms of Internet-based telephony. Napster and

1

its kin, which enable decentralized, peer-to-peer distribution of information, are challenging conventional business models and stimulating yet more applications and new businesses. The unprecedented speed at which software can be distributed over the Internet means that dissemination of an innovation is not limited by the production and distribution of a physical artifact.

Further complicating the picture is uncertainty about which developments will prove to be transient and which will have a lasting impact. While the World Wide Web has indeed had a great impact, mid-1990s hype about "push" technologies proved unfounded, given their comparatively limited impact on either Internet users or businesses. Just a few years ago, experts and pundits predicted that congestion of the Internet backbone was an imminent peril, a forecast that proved incorrect, thanks to improved backbone speeds. Such uncertainty means that the planning process—for businesses, policy makers, and others focused on the Internet and its uses—can easily be overtaken by events and that the importance of specific events is hard to appraise, especially in the short term. This uncertainty was a confounding factor in the project that culminated in this report—technical issues can be resolved in multiple ways in a dynamic environment, and the consequent diversity of opinion sometimes makes it hard to reach consensus.

The middle of a revolution is a difficult point from which to gauge long-term outcomes. Inherent uncertainty clashes with growing political pressures on policy makers to respond to apparent trends and to the side effects of Internet activities. The actions of the businesses that provide Internet services, content, and applications fill the daily news. Increasingly, these businesses are the subject of public scrutiny and governmental inquiry into the implications of their actions, which range from mergers involving Internet service providers to practices surrounding personal information gathered from people visiting Web sites. The public debate about the Internet often reveals significant gaps in understanding of the Internet, and those gaps can compromise the decisions and investments that should be made in order to gain the most from what the Internet has to offer.

To shed light on appropriate actions and responses to the Internet revolution, this report, written by a committee with an in-depth understanding of the Internet's technologies and its core businesses, undertakes an assessment of the Internet along several lines:

• Reviewing the fundamental technical design principles that have helped shape the Internet's success;
  • Considering the state of the art as Internet technology continues to

evolve, with an eye toward identifying technical issues that merit attention;

• Exploring operational and management issues that require attention by those who develop, operate, and use the Internet; and

• Developing guiding principles for governments to use as they confront the Internet-related issues that arise in different spheres.

With these tasks in mind, the committee's assessment focuses on five themes: (1) the Internet's basic design features; (2) its scalability, reliability, and robustness; (3) interconnection and openness; (4) collisions between the Internet and other communications-based industries, particularly those that long predate the Internet; and (5) broader social policy issues. This chapter covers the key points made in the main text and goes on to recommend where investment will be required to head off future problems and to maximize the economic and social benefits that can flow from the use of the Internet. It concludes by articulating some guiding principles for those who formulate Internet policy and regulation.

Success by Design

The Internet is a composite of tens of thousands of individually owned and operated networks that are interconnected, providing the user with the illusion that they are a single network. A customer who purchases Internet service is actually purchasing service from a particular Internet service provider (ISP) connected to this network of networks. The ISP in turn enters into business arrangements for connectivity with other service providers to ensure that the customer's data can move smoothly among the various parts of the Internet. The networks that make up the Internet are composed of communications links, which carry data from one point to another, and routers, which direct the communications flow between links and thus, ultimately, from senders to receivers. Communications links to users may employ different communications media, from telephone lines to cables originally deployed for use in cable television systems to satellite and other wireless circuits. Internal to networks, especially larger networks, are links—typically optical fiber cables—that can carry relatively large amounts of traffic. The largest of these links are commonly said to make up the Internet's "backbone," although this definition is not precise and even the backbone is not monolithic.

The networks that compose the Internet share a common architecture (how the components of the networks interrelate) and protocols (standards governing the interchange of data) that enable communication within and among them. The architecture and protocols are shaped by fundamental design principles adopted by the early builders of the Internet, including the following:

- *"Hourglass" architecture.* The Internet is designed to operate over different underlying communications technologies, including those yet to be introduced, and to support multiple and evolving applications and services. It does not impede or restrict particular applications (although users and ISPs may make optimizations reflecting the requirements of particular applications or classes of applications). Such an architecture enables people to write applications that run over it without knowing details about the configuration of the networks over which they run and without involving the network operators. This critical separation between the network technology and the higher-level services through which users actually interact with the Internet can be visualized as an hourglass, in which the narrow waist represents the basic network service provided by the Internet and the wider regions above and below represent the applications and underlying communications technologies, respectively.
- *End-to-end architecture.* Edge-based innovation derives from an early fundamental design decision that the Internet should have an end-to-end architecture. The network, which provides a communications fabric connecting the many computers at its ends, offers a very basic level of service, data transport, while the intelligence, the information processing needed to provide applications, is located in or close to the devices attached to the edge of the network.
- *Scalability.* The Internet's design enables it to support a growing amount of communications—growth in the number of users and attached devices and growth in the volume of communications per device and in total, properties referred to as "scale." Nonetheless, as is discussed below, the Internet currently faces and will continue to face scaling challenges that will require significant effort by those who design and operate it.
- *Distributed design and decentralized control.* Control of the network (from the standpoint of, for instance, how data packets are routed through the Internet) is distributed except for a few key functions, namely, the allocation of address blocks and the management of top-level domain names in the Domain Name System. No single entity (organization, corporation, or government body) controls the Internet in its entirety.

These design principles mean that the Internet is open from the standpoint of users, service providers, and network providers, and as a result it has been open to change in the associated industry base as well as in the technologies they supply and use. A wide range of applications and services, some leveraging the commonality of the Internet protocol (IP) and others also leveraging standards layered on top of IP, most notably e-mail and the Web interface, have flourished. Observations about these design principles have already begun to be introduced into regulatory proceedings, and the merit of sustaining them is recognized by principals in the Internet technical community, including the members of this committee.

Sustaining the Growth of the Internet

The power of the Internet's basic design is reflected in its ability to sustain vigorous growth in three dimensions—the number of users (and devices) connected, the amount of data that each user or device typically transmits, and the number of ways in which people use the network. While its rapid growth rate makes it difficult to determine the extent to which the Internet has become entwined in daily life, all indications are that the Internet plays a vital role that will only continue to expand. Widely understood to be a place to "live," work, and play, the Internet has reached mission-critical status for many individuals, businesses, organizations, and applications.

To meet the expected demands, the Internet will have to continue to scale up into the foreseeable future. While the fundamental design principles have so far proven durable in the face of growth, sustained growth—including support for faster communications and the ability for more devices to connect to the network—will pose challenges. But with growth come needs beyond simple support for more or faster connectivity. Making the Internet and its constituent components more reliable and robust and less vulnerable to system or component failures and attacks is also of increasing importance. A comprehensive, detailed compilation of all the challenges posed by the growth of the Internet would easily fill an entire report; in this report, the committee describes several of the challenges in some detail, aiming to provide sufficient information to allow experts and nonexperts alike to understand their essential features.

Scaling Challenges

Scaling challenges at all levels, from the Internet's core to the applications that run over the Internet, will require continuing, persistent attention by infrastructure operators, equipment vendors, application developers, and researchers. The research and development that underlie the Internet core's growth and the processes by which new protocols are developed, deployed, and modified in response to shortcomings have generally been satisfactory. The challenges described below are ones that especially need continued or heightened attention by researchers and Internet operators.

Past experience with application protocols that scale poorly, in combination with an appreciation of the ease and rapidity with which new application protocols can come into widespread use as a consequence of the Internet's open architecture, gives rise to expectations of future scaling surprises. Like the earlier versions of the Web protocol HTTP, new Internet applications are not necessarily well designed for widespread use, and some of them will encounter performance challenges as the Internet continues to grow. Reengineering popular applications so they continue to work well as the scale of their use expands is likely to be an ongoing challenge.

The Internet's Domain Name System (DNS) also faces scaling challenges. Two sources of pressure—the flat structure of much of the name system and the registration of millions of names—reflect market demands. They are generating a growing load and concentrating it on a small number of servers. Possible solutions include alternative server architectures that can cope better with the load or new naming architectures (in place of or on top of the DNS) that spread the load over a larger number of servers.

There are also scaling challenges that are less immediate, such as those associated with routing—the mechanisms by which the Internet passes around information about system addresses and locations. In fact, some of the addressing issues discussed in this report stem from routing issues. The Internet routing infrastructure threatens to become overwhelmed by the volume and complexity of information being distributed and perhaps by the volume of information that each router is required to maintain. Indeed, some believe that the current system that enables routers to decide where to send data packets as they move through the network will require a fundamental rethinking.

Scaling up the Address Space

The Internet's basic protocol, IP, was designed to provide only roughly 4.3 billion unique identifiers, a limitation that is becoming increasingly problematic as the number of computers attached to the Internet continues to grow. The seriousness and urgency attached to a potential or actual address shortage depend largely on one's vantage point. Overall, only roughly one-fourth of the total pool of Internet addresses is observed to be in use today, but about half of this pool has been delegated by the regional registries—the handful of organizations that assign addresses according to global region—to ISPs and other organizations. Large blocks of addresses are held by organizations, including ISPs, government, research and educational institutions, and businesses that claimed them in the early days of the Internet. The balance of the delegated addresses is allocated in smaller blocks by the regional address registrars to ISPs or other organizations.

Unlike many Internet scaling problems, where the challenge is to find a new solution, concerns about address scarcity have led to simultaneous moves down two different paths. One response has been the creation of a replacement to the current protocol, IPv4. Called IPv6, this new solution provides billions of billions of unique addresses. Support for IPv6 has been included in a number of hardware and software products and tools, and strategies supporting a transition to IPv6 have been developed. But the costs of moving to IPv6, reflecting the large number of components that would have to be modified, have dampened enthusiasm for it, and it has seen only limited deployment to date. The low deployment rate, in turn, diminishes the incentives for switching.

The other response has been the installation in many networks, including those of both customers and ISPs, of a work-around technology known as network address translation (NAT), which allows individual computers in a group to be assigned private addresses even as they share a single Internet address. This response offers some advantages, such as easier management of addresses on local area networks, but has significant architectural shortcomings. Where true end-to-end connectivity is less important, such as for ISPs supporting users who engage mainly in basic Web browsing, NAT may prove to be an adequate work-around, at least in the short term. On the other hand, if support is desired for peer-to-peer applications or users that run servers, then NAT, with its tricky work-arounds, is a much less attractive solution. Widespread use of NATs also brings new complications: when NATs are connected to NATs, basic connectivity and the proper operation of some protocols can be inhibited. NAT is also unattractive where it is desired to deploy large numbers of Internet-connected devices with globally unique identifiers. In light of recent activity and in anticipation of continued growth in the mobile Internet device market, where it is projected that the number of devices will exceed the available address space, there has been renewed interest in IPv6. Indeed, the developers of so-called third-generation (3G) wireless services have, at this stage, committed to using IPv6.

At present, many concerns stem less from a shortage of addresses than from the cost or hassle associated with obtaining an allocation in a climate where regional address registrars and ISPs are motivated to be frugal as they hand out addresses. Address assignments reflect needs that the requesting organization has been able to substantiate on the basis of current use or credible projections that it can make of future needs;

they also reflect the overall availability of addresses at the time that the assignment is made. Thus, organizations and regions that have already been allocated greater numbers of Internet addresses and thus do not face a looming shortage are less likely to find IPv6 attractive, particularly in the short run. In contrast, organizations that are building new networks and seeking to greatly expand the number of users (and thus IP addresses) face costs (fees and effort expended in justifying their requests) to obtain an allocation from a regional address registry or their ISP, and they are more likely to advocate IPv6 deployment. Disparities among organizations and geographical regions in address allocation, which tend to favor those who made earliest use of the Internet, also mean that address scarcity may be perceived as an equity issue associated with perceived disparities in control over the Internet.

While there has been no crisis thus far, there is still considerable risk associated with exhaustion of the IPv4 address space. In the short term, the costs and problems associated with address scarcity will not be imposed uniformly. If there is no migration to IPv6, address scarcity will be a serious problem for a subset of Internet users in the short term and a more pervasive problem in the long term. The number of computers attached to the Internet can be expected to continue to grow, reflecting both more users and more devices per user. This growth will be most pronounced and will come soonest in regions and countries where the Internet has made the fewest inroads today, where the number of potential users is large and penetration is expected to be great, and where providers are seeking to deploy very large numbers of devices with full Internet connectivity, such as would be the case if there were an explosion in the development and sales of Internet-capable appliances for the home and/or the 3G mobile phones discussed above. A key question is just how far off the "long term" is, when the impacts of scarcity will be widely and deeply felt. The answer depends on many factors that are difficult to project. And even with a substantial commitment to an eventual switchover to IPv6, the use of NAT and NAT-like IPv4-to-IPv6 translators will adversely affect the end-to-end transparency of the Internet in the meantime.

Robustness and Reliability

There is widespread acknowledgment that it is important to make the Internet as a whole—as well as its constituent networks and individual components—more robust and reliable. Reactions to a series of distributed denial-of-service attacks in 2000 illustrate the extent to which problems are viewed with concern by government officials and the public. Some challenges, including the need to fix known problems, are well understood today, but more information is needed to comprehend the full spectrum of risks and vulnerabilities. Because the Internet is composed of thousands of distinct networks run by different ISPs and because ISPs typically do not publicly report outages, much less their cause, little is known about the primary causes of Internet failures. Indeed, little is known about how often there are major failures that affect a large number of customers. In the absence of this sort of information, it is very difficult to start a program to improve the Internet's robustness and reliability.

Even with better information on risks and vulnerabilities, a better understanding of the underlying technologies for reliable and robust networks is needed to design and implement fixes, especially in the face of less predictable applications and traffic running over the Internet. A bright spot is that those who develop security technologies and practices have learned much about how the Internet's components can be attacked and have been working with vigor on techniques to make the Internet less vulnerable to attackers, efforts that can also suggest ways of improving the Internet's robustness to inadvertent failures. A number of technologies have been developed to improve robustness—to secure Internet systems, detect and prevent intrusion, and authenticate transactions. Implementation of these measures, however, has tended to lag behind the state of the art, and an array of management actions will be needed to better align practices with the technology.

Quality of Service

The Internet's best-effort quality of service (QOS) has been successful in supporting a wide range of applications running over the Internet. The debate over whether mechanisms supporting other forms of QOS are needed is a long-standing one within the Internet community. It has shifted from an original focus on mechanisms that would support multimedia applications over the Internet to mechanisms that would support a broader spectrum of potential uses, from enhancing the performance of particular classes of applications over constrained network links to providing ISPs with mechanisms for value-stratifying their customers. There is significant disagreement among experts (including the experts on this committee) on how effective QOS mechanisms would be and on the relative priorities that should be attached to, on the one hand, investing in additional bandwidth and, on the other, deploying QOS mechanisms. A key feature of this debate is differing opinion on the extent to which a rising tide of capacity in the Internet will alleviate most performance problems. Contributing to the debate is incomplete knowledge of the causes of performance problems within the best-effort network and the actual benefits that would be obtained by deploying various QOS mechanisms within operational networks. Another open issue is whether there is a role for Internet QOS on links that are inherently constrained (e.g., wireless) or on links where adding capacity may be much more expensive than adding capacity within the Internet backbone (e.g., the links between local area networks or residences and ISPs).

Service quality is a weak-link phenomenon. Providing end-to-end QOS requires ISPs to agree as a group on multiple technical and economic parameters, including technical standards for signaling, the semantics of how to classify traffic and what priorities the categories should be assigned, and the addition of QOS considerations to their interconnection business agreements. The reality of today's Internet is that end-to-end enhancement of QOS is a dim prospect. It may be that localized deployment of QOS, such as on the links between a customer's local area network and its ISP, is a useful alternative to end-to-end QOS, but the effectiveness of this approach and the circumstances under which it would prove useful are both poorly understood, as is whether such piecemeal deployment could contribute to a balkanization of the Internet.

QOS deployment has also been the subject of interest and speculation by outside observers. One view is that QOS would be an enabler of new applications and business models while another is that the introduction of QOS capabilities into the Internet would undermine the equal treatment of all communications across the network, irrespective of source or destination. Mechanisms that enable disparate treatment of customer Internet traffic have led to concerns that they could be used to provide preferential support for particular customers or content providers (e.g., those having business relationships with the ISP). What users actually experience will depend on multiple factors: what the technology makes possible, the design of marketing plans, preferences that customers express, and what capabilities ISPs opt to implement in their networks—which will depend in part on their determination of how effective particular QOS mechanisms would be.

Additional insights into the role of QOS mechanisms in the Internet will come through several avenues: better understanding of the factors that contribute to network performance, including the limits to performance that can be obtained using best-effort service; better understanding of the effectiveness of QOS approaches in particular circumstances; and greater experience with QOS in operational settings.

Keeping the Internet Interconnected and Open

One of the Internet's hallmarks has been its openness. This openness appears in a variety of distinct although related ways, including openness to new entrants and openness to innovation. Keeping the Internet open has a number of goals, including continuing innovation in Internet service, preserving access to the full set of content and services that are made available over the Internet, and fostering competition as a means of ensuring innovation, access, and affordability.

Access to the Local Loop

The first key openness issue is access to facilities in the local loop (the final communications hop into the premises), especially perceived advantages for those who already own links—today, the incumbent local telecommunications carriers and cable operators. In the local loop, openness issues are frequently linked to the term "open access," which refers to the ability of residential or small-office customers to have a choice of alternative ISPs and to have access to content and services that are made available over the Internet even when they are not supported directly by the customer's ISP (i.e., when there is no business arrangement between the ISP and the provider of the content or service). Because the local loop is the point of entry for many Internet users, outcomes here can have significant consequences for the shape of the Internet as a whole. It is unclear whether issues of open access will be resolved in the near term through regulatory action (e.g., new unbundling requirements), legal decisions, actions by industry itself (perhaps in response to consumer pressure), or consumer choice as a result of facilities-based competition, or whether they will become persistent features of the Internet policy debate. Another Computer Science and Telecommunications Board body, the Committee on Broadband Last-Mile Technologies, is currently investigating these and other issues related to broadband services for homes and small offices, so they are not considered in detail here. However, a number of points in this report are likely to help inform thinking about the issue, including the discussions of what constitutes transparent, open Internet service; related trends in the ISP business; and the likely roles for QOS technologies on the Internet.

Interconnection

The second key openness issue is the nature of the interconnection agreements whereby many independently operated networks are interlinked to create the Internet. To become an ISP, a new provider must have one or more agreements with other ISPs to ensure that its customers can communicate with the customers of all the other ISPs. Interconnection has three dimensions—physical (point-to-point or connection at a public exchange), logical (transit or peering routing), and financial (generally either a fee-for-transit or peer-to-peer barter arrangement). Interconnection involves costs to the parties to the agreement and requires bilateral agreement on financial terms. In a transit agreement, one (typically smaller) ISP pays another (typically larger) ISP to accept and arrange delivery for all data that leave the first ISP's network; in a peering agreement, two (typically similar size) ISPs agree that the value and costs of interconnecting to each other are roughly equal and they need not exchange payments. Unlike transit agreements, peering agreements only provide for the transport of data packets between one ISP's customers and the customers of another ISP and do not provide for the transport of communications across the ISP's network.

Clearly this market model has risks. It assumes a reasonably competitive environment, where competition among ISPs keeps transit agreement charges reasonable, where no one ISP is so dominant that it can refuse offers to peer with other networks and thus force all the other ISPs to pay for access to its customers, and where there is not pervasive vertical integration of backbone ISP and content and service businesses. While such threats are possible, none have emerged. The number of so-called "tier 1" Internet service providers, distinguished by both size and their peer interconnections with one another, is small, but they have, at least thus far, provided customers with choices. Of the ISPs that provide service to consumers and small businesses, one ISP—AOL—is clearly far larger than the others; however, contrary to analyst predictions, the number of customer-focused ISPs has not been shrinking precipitously, suggesting that the market is not closed.

While concerns have long been expressed about interconnection in the Internet, interconnection arrangements are continuing to evolve in ways that support the growing base of Internet users and their changing needs. There have been several areas of innovation in the nature of interconnection that provide alternatives to the conventional binary choice between attaining peer status or paying as a transit customer. Tier 1 providers have experimented with new forms of interconnection arrangements that might be thought of as somewhere between pure peering (where two ISPs agree to exchange traffic on a settlement-free basis) and transit (where the customer ISP pays fees to another ISP to handle its traffic). New entrants have also developed business models for interconnection. For example, the company InterNAP has established connections to top ISPs, including a number of the tier 1 providers, using a connection arrangement that lies halfway between peering and transit. It then sells the resulting Internet access to the ISPs and large businesses that are its customers. Other businesses have entered the market to provide more sophisticated revenue models than the traditional peering model in which ISPs set revenue-neutral boundaries at the Internet's center, where the major tier 1 ISPs connect, and in which transit service is sold to downstream providers on the basis of rough measures. For example, Akamai's content delivery model places servers within the networks of ISPs, which enables new financial arrangements such as payments by the content producer to the ISPs that serve end-user customers.

Another important observation with regard to interconnection is that the nature of ISPs is changing. The current interconnection model assumes that ISPs are all in the business of providing carriage of customer traffic. Recently, however, the ISP market has become far more complex, with the development of Web- and business-hosting ISPs and specialized ISPs providing only certain Internet services (e.g., instant message or telephony) and not others. There are also demands for ISPs to provide multiple levels of service (e.g., better service for customers who pay more) that span the networks of multiple ISPs. It is not clear that the current transit agreements, which are designed to assess charges for the delivery of data packets across a boundary, are consistent with the future business needs of these ISPs, suggesting that further evolution of interconnection in the Internet will be necessary.

Innovation and Transparency

The Internet is built on a set of open standards and on a process that seeks to encourage the development of new open standards as needs for new functionality arise. (The term "open standard" has a variety of meanings—as used here, an open standard is one that is made easily available to all interested parties and owned and controlled by a noncommercial party such that changes to the standard are not made capriciously.) Companies can combine standard protocols to create new services and applications, and, freed from the need to develop basic technologies to get data from one end of the network to another, they can focus their energies on developing new protocols that build on the existing system to offer new services.

The Internet has been served well by an insistence that there is often more than one right answer to a question. Although there may be a common standard, there are frequently several independent implementations of it, keeping any one company from cornering the market in good technology. Indeed, whenever one company has come close to a monopolistic position, the traditional Internet community has been critical of the results, citing the potential for inhibiting innovation. The concern is not the addition of features that can coexist with standard protocols but the emergence of a monopolistic position that would eliminate the benefits that accrue from having independent implementations available from multiple vendors. The Internet has also been characterized by both stability (standard protocols are modified only when there is consensus that changes are necessary) and adaptability (protocols and practices are updated to provide new capabilities and meet new challenges).

A significant feature of the Internet is that it becomes more valuable to each user as the size of the network grows, making it possible for a small advantage in market share to snowball into a much larger market share and a very large economic benefit. This small advantage is often associated with being first, but sometimes a sufficiently large investment of resources (or some other circumstance) allows a newcomer to trump the original innovators. On the Internet the ease and the negligible cost of distributing software through the network amplify these effects. These properties suggest a pattern of highly concentrated markets and market leaders who greatly outdistance their competitors but remain, in their turn, vulnerable to a motivated competitor with a better product.

In this environment, companies will seek to differentiate their products on the basis of features other than what the standard protocols themselves provide or on the basis of content or services. But if products are built on open standards, there is always a chance that a new company will develop a competing product based on the same open standards (or on a new standard that provides the same services) that cuts into a company's existing market. The tippy quality noted above means that in an open standards market, a company must always worry that the market will suddenly tip away from it. Thus it is not surprising that there are periodic attempts by major Internet-related companies to protect valuable products by declining to work on open standards or by making proprietary extensions to open standards. Nonetheless, as evidenced by the entire set of industries that have been built on top of open Internet standards, there is considerable value in the continued development and use of open standards for key Internet functionality.

Another issue closely related to openness is preservation of the Internet's end-to-end transparency, whereby the networks that make up the Internet do not tamper with or restrict data in flight between computers attached to it. With suitable software running at each end and no knowledge other than each other's Internet address, any two devices connected to the Internet are, in principle, able to enter into any type of communication, limited only by the existence of the requisite network capacity and sufficiently low or at least predictable latency (delay) to support the application. As a result, someone who develops a new application can place it on the Internet without any changes needing to be made to the Internet to make the application work. This is highly advantageous; in a world with thousands of ISPs, coordinating changes to the network for every new application would be a nightmare.

In the real-world Internet, a number of trade-offs affecting transparency are made. One is pragmatic actions taken in response to operational considerations (e.g., deployment of NAT to deal with address scarcity) that limit transparency. Transparency is also traded off against other attributes of Internet service. For example, organizations and individuals may install firewalls in order to better protect their network against unwelcome types of traffic (protection against attacks, for instance, or against use that is considered inappropriate) or they may take steps to enhance the performance of a network by controlling the use of applications that place particular demands on network resources. However, the Internet's design places limits on efforts by governments, ISPs, organizations, and network managers to filter content or applications. Attempts to block particular types of content or applications can trigger an escalating battle in which the authors of Internet applications make use of a variety of techniques to allow application communications to masquerade as other types of traffic. Also, widespread use of IP-layer encryption (e.g., the IPSec protocol) would preclude most blocking of applications or content. The likely consequence is that any user or ISP that seeks to fully block certain types of traffic can rapidly find itself forced to block any traffic that it does not know, a priori, to be acceptable (i.e., traffic would have to be assumed to be undesirable unless proven otherwise). Of course, such a practice would be antithetical to openness. The Internet's openness is best preserved when users are aware of the trade-offs and able to strike their own balance with respect to them.

Collisions Between Existing Industries and Emerging Internet Industries: Telephony As a Case Study

The provision of voice services over the Internet is an example of the kinds of industry and policy shocks that emanate from the collisions between the Internet and traditional industries. Telephony is a particularly salient example because its practices and regulatory approaches are deeply rooted at both the federal and state level, and as such it was selected as the industry-policy nexus to be examined in this report.

Some attention to definitions is required. The terms "IP telephony" and "voice over IP" are both used in this report to describe services that employ the Internet's underlying technology to provide voice telecommunications. IP telephony is a broad label covering a diverse set of architectures, service providers and transport media, end-user equipment, local access technology, and interfaces and gateways between IP and public switched network elements. Not all forms of IP-based telephony make use of the public Internet; the term "Internet telephony" refers to the particular case of using the public Internet to carry telephone calls.

While IP telephony holds only a small share of the total telephony market today, it is growing rapidly. As IP telephony becomes more widespread and reaches more consumers, voice, data, and multimedia offerings will increasingly be linked. Telephony is now provided primarily in one of two forms: (1) the conventional managed form, where a single entity controls both the service and the communications infrastructure (including the public switched telephone network, PSTN) or (2) an unmanaged form of IP telephony, such as pure Internet telephony. In the future, however, IP telephony services will also include amalgams of managed and unmanaged networks. As they mature, these new services will provide a flexible and robust service creation platform for a range of new voice and multimedia services.

In contrast to the PSTN, IP telephony permits the data packets carrying voice to be transported by a different entity from the one providing application services (e.g., call agents and directory services). Also, like other packet data, traffic associated with a phone call over the Internet will transit one, two, or many providers depending on which networks the calling parties are attached to and how the networks are interconnected. IP-based telephony also does not necessarily provide the same functionality as the PSTN. For example, once a call has been set up, the data stream associated with it may flow directly between the two end points rather than through a central facility. The general-purpose nature of the Internet also means that IP telephony can introduce novel services and features that do not parallel those offered by classic telephony.

Such differences signal impending conflicts between the new services that IP telephony enables (and the companies that provide those services) and the practices and assumptions of the current regulatory system. As IP telephony gains market share, its amenability to innovation and its apparent cost advantage are provoking calls for voice over IP to be subject to regulation like that to which existing PSTN services are subject. At the same time, the inconsistencies between the Internet technology and the regulatory framework will frustrate this goal. For instance, in Internet telephony there are no meaningful distinctions between local and interexchange carriers. Furthermore, because the functions of moving voice packets between parties and control functions such as call setup are completely separable, the regulatory assumptions that control and transport are necessarily performed by the same party are not valid.

In contrast to the Internet, the PSTN evolved in a highly regulated environment over much of the past century. Design and regulation are closely coupled; today's regulations reflect the technologies and design choices underlying the PSTN, but at the same time the regulatory environment has itself helped shape the PSTN's architecture. To the extent that Internet telephony becomes a significant force in voice services, design differences will pressure the existing regulatory regime and the existing players. There are difficult choices to be made on how and whether to apply existing definitions and rules to new technologies and services.

The inconsistencies between the architecture assumed in the current regulatory regime governing the PSTN and the architectures for IP telephony suggest that PSTN regulation should not be transferred as is simply because the new services appear to constitute telecommunications. The committee recognizes that there are pressures for regulation precisely because of that appearance. Acknowledging (1) that the processes for developing the relevant laws and the regulations that implement those laws may be separate, (2) the uncertain prospects for major legal reconsideration (given the recentness of the 1996 Telecommunications Act), and (3) the awkward fit of regulations designed for the PSTN to Internet telephony, both the legal framework—the rationale for regulation—and the design of specific regulations may need to be reconsidered. The analysis should start by reconsidering the old rationales for regulation rather than by looking for ways of accommodating existing regulation. As the same technologies and service offerings are introduced in the PSTN, the challenge posed by mismatches between regulation and technology will no longer be confined to new players.

In addition to basic telephony service, the PSTN provides some services, such as 911 emergency services, that are not necessarily provided (or readily realizable) in today's IP telephony offerings. The PSTN also is mandated to provide certain facilities for interconnection among networks and to provide universal service. While legislators, regulators, and consumers are sure to expect certain functions now provided by the PSTN to be maintained, it is currently unclear how those functions will be implemented and maintained as PSTN and IP telephony evolve. Also, as the shape of telephony evolves in an Internet environment, so, too, will expectations and requirements for these capabilities. A 911 emergency service in the future might not be limited to a simple voice channel; it could, for instance, be implemented with text messaging or a Web page. Nor will life-critical services necessarily be confined to simply summoning assistance.

The Internet and Broad Social Policy

By providing a network with lower costs and increased functionality, the Internet represents a disruptive force across domains that have separate bodies of well-established law. It will surely continue to raise many societal issues and questions about the need for additional governmental laws and regulations. The committee's examination of IP telephony and the PSTN provides one important illustration of how an existing industry and its associated policy framework come into collision with competing new Internet-based industries. The committee also explored several other places where the Internet is challenging social policies. Many of the concerns existed in other contexts before the emergence of the Internet, but the Internet, by virtue of its support for comparatively easy information access and distribution and the relative speed with which new applications of it can be developed and deployed, amplifies these concerns. The subset of issues explored by the committee—privacy, anonymity, and identity; authentication; taxation of commerce transacted over the Internet; and universal service—is not comprehensive (nor could it be so in a study of this size). Rather, these issues were chosen as significant points of interaction between the Internet and the broader society.

RECOMMENDATIONS

The Internet's coming of age has been marked by increased attention across the board. The businesses and organizations that design, build, and operate the Internet's constituent networks are working to shape that network to meet the demands of users. The work being done on the inside has been changing in character, reflecting the Internet's increasing importance to customers, growth in the number and kinds of applications, and changes in the nature of the business itself (e.g., while they are interdependent, ISPs are also competitors). Accompanying these efforts are increased attention and heightened expectations from the outside—individuals, organizations, corporations, and government bodies—that reflect the importance of the Internet as an infrastructure for society. The assimilation of the Internet into society and the economy involves a growing role for a second business community in addition to the businesses that design, build, and operate networks: these are the businesses that provide content, applications, and services that run over the Internet. In some cases, of course, the same entity may be involved in both kinds of business, but overall, this second community tends to be distinct, larger, and more differentiated, and it raises a wider range of concerns. However, although much of the attention now being paid to the Internet relates to the behavior (as regards, for example, online privacy and other consumer protection issues) of these businesses that leverage the Internet, the committee concentrates its recommendations on the businesses that design, build, and operate the Internet.

The committee's overview of social policy concerns completes the picture by illuminating actions that leverage the Internet and that, directly or through policy responses, may influence future decisions about how the Internet develops. Sound recommendations that respond to the particulars of these social policy concerns—unlike the general principles articulated below—would require further examination of the contexts and behaviors associated with each concern.

The principal conclusion of the committee, which underlies the discussion below, is that the Internet is fundamentally healthy and that most of the problems and issues discussed in this report can be addressed and solved by evolutionary changes within the Internet's current architectural framework and associated processes. Multiple actors—the research community, industry, government, and the users themselves—have important roles to play in ensuring the Internet's continued well-being and progress. The recommendations provided here cover both the general and the specific, reflecting overall principles as well as more targeted opportunities.

The Technology Base

Exhortations about the importance of research and development on scaling, reliability, and the like are not new, but the committee makes recommendations in these areas to underscore their importance at this point in time. Research and development have enabled the Internet to become a mainstream infrastructure, but the job is far from done: use of the Internet and dependence on it can be expected to grow. Staying on the Internet growth curve, so frequently projected by pundits and analysts and expected by the Internet's users, will require continued, sustained effort in many places. Some of the challenges are shorter term: these the research community and industry infrastructure seem well placed to solve, as they have in the past, through sustained effort and incremental enhancements. Others are longer-term, enduring challenges and will need more fundamental breakthroughs. Many research advances would provide benefits to all who operate and use the Internet, not just a single player. This outcome argues for using public funds to support such work even in the face of considerable private investment in the Internet, particularly where self-interest or near-term gains are insufficient motivators for industry investment.

Research and development that address scaling challenges and enhance reliability and robustness should continue to receive support from both industry and federal research funding agencies. Priority scaling issues include the continuing need to improve the scalability of applications deployed over the Internet, scaling issues associated with the DNS infrastructure, and long-term scaling issues related to addressing and routing in the Internet. Key research and development areas related to reliability and robustness include (1) the development of improved trust models that better describe the business relationships of organizations and what sessions and relationships they authorize; (2) research on technologies to cope with attacks—such as technologies for intrusion detection and isolation, including capabilities that would provide faster and more focused isolation of attacks in a manner that scales to the Internet's increasing speeds and complexity; (3) the design of mechanisms and protocols that better protect one part of the Internet from attacks and operational errors in other parts and from damage to components without disrupting the basic requirement for global connectivity; and (4) fast link and node failure detection and healing mechanisms as well as interdomain routing protocols that provide greater recovery speed.

Researchers, research funders, and network operators should work together to find opportunities that would allow more network research to be done in realistic operational settings. A common theme across the technical challenges discussed in this report is that they have to do with properties of the Internet as a system, including how it scales or how it handles failures or deliberate attack. These challenges are hard to study in small-scale systems, which are what researchers generally have to work with, and hard to study through simulation, because both theory and models pertaining to the operation of very large networks such as the Internet are weak. The need for researchers to have better access to real-world artifacts has been noted in earlier studies.[1] The payoff from better access to Internet networks would be an improved understanding of network behavior, particularly behavior related to large scale and high congestion, that could lead to insights that would enable improvements in operational networks. For example, research aimed at better understanding where and how quality-of-service mechanisms would best benefit a particular class of applications needs to be done on a network with realistic congestion and cannot be done through simulation unless one has good models of how a congested network behaves. Implementing this recommendation will require overcoming the reluctance of ISPs to make their networks available because they fear that researchers may induce malfunctions or disclose proprietary information when they "play around" in ISP backbones. It will also require attention to the lag in capabilities between research instrumentation and the equipment found in high-capacity ISP networks. These inhibiting factors are not confined to commercial networks operated by ISPs; they also arise in research net-

---

[1]Computer Science and Telecommunications Board (CSTB), National Research Council (NRC). 2000. *Making IT Better*. Washington, D.C.: National Academy Press; Computer Science and Telecommunications Board (CSTB), National Research Council (NRC). 1994. *Academic Careers for Experimental Computer Scientists and Engineers*. Washington, D.C.: National Academy Press.

works that are used in operational modes, such as for applications research.

Industry and researchers should continue to investigate the economics of interconnection and technologies to support interconnection. Improved understanding of the economics that underlie interconnection in the Internet may be useful for better understanding how the Internet's interconnection arrangements are evolving and may lead to new models that improve the overall interconnection of the Internet or that help address concerns such as barriers to entry. Key topics include how to best approach the value relationships that exist across the Internet; identifying economic alternatives beyond simple peering and transit; and exploring the organizational dimension of interconnection and openness issues, including the implications for industry structure and performance. At the same time, industry should continue to explore new business models for interconnection and for fostering a commercial environment that encourages competition and innovation. There are also challenges on the technical side: research on routing could provide better control and protection of interconnecting providers, thus increasing the range of possible interconnection alternatives available to ISPs.

Government, industry, and other stakeholders should continue to foster the development of open standards for the Internet. Each Internet player will be tempted to diverge from the common standard if it looks like it might be able to capture the entire market (or a large portion of it) for itself. However, a common, open standard maximizes overall social welfare as a result of the network externalities obtained from the larger market. When competent open standards are made available, they can be attractive in the marketplace and may win out over proprietary ones. The government's role in supporting open standards for the Internet has not been, and should not be, to directly set or influence standards. Rather, its role should be to provide funding for the networking research community, which has led to both innovative networking ideas as well as specific technologies that can be translated into new open standards.

Where there are societal expectations associated with particular existing industries, such as expectations for 911 emergency service as part of telephony, analogous capabilities for the Internet should be developed and demonstrated through research and experimentation in the marketplace rather than by mandating particular technical solutions. Whether, when, and how regulation is introduced can affect innovation in this area because the underlying telephony technologies and service offerings are themselves evolving rapidly and have yet to prove themselves in the marketplace. For example, the interoperation of PSTN and Internet telephony systems raises longer-term questions: How should number portability be implemented? How can customers be provided with numbering and naming? Both research and market-based experimentation will be important in developing the best and most efficient means of implementing telephony services.

Designers and Operators

The Internet's developers and operators have devised technologies and processes that will do much to keep the Internet healthy and growing. However, improvements in scalability, reliability, and robustness will involve more than technical advances per se; questions of implementation are also important and in many cases require collective action by many thousands of entities. Business imperatives generally motivate individual organizations and companies to act in ways that promote their individual business success, but such actions do not necessarily provide broad-based, global benefits for the Internet as a whole. Indeed, there are many places where long-term, overall benefits for the Internet as a whole are traded off for shorter-term, local benefits to particular subsets of Internet users and operators. For example, while the Internet industry and its customers stand to gain in the long term from a shift to IPv6, the costs for individual organizations will, at least in the short term, probably outweigh the benefits they themselves obtain. Another example is the scalability of applications: applications whose deployment adversely affects the performance experienced by all Internet users may, nonetheless, provide local benefits (because a short time to market can yield more immediate returns) and result in the capture of a greater market share (because the Internet is what economists call a tippy market). One possible driver of collective action is the prospect of governmental regulatory intervention. But the extent to which enlightened self-interest can be a motivator will depend on the specific issues and circumstances.

Several private, nonprofit organizations play critical roles with respect to the Internet, including the principal standards bodies (the Internet Engineering Task Force and the Internet Architecture Board); organizations that deal with operational issues (e.g., the North American Network Operators Group); and the Internet Corporation for Assigned Names and Numbers (ICANN), which has assumed overall responsibility for managing the Internet's addresses and names. The absence here of recommendations for these organizations should not be taken as an indication that the actions and evolution of these organizations are not important. The committee's lack of commentary on them should not be read as either critical of or supportive of either side in debates such as that surrounding the role of ICANN. While the committee has not examined these issues in depth, it believes that these institutions make important contributions to the operation and development of the Internet, notwithstanding the unstable circumstances.[2] Because the committee's membership includes several individuals who work closely with these organizations, the committee decided not to issue conclusions related to the specifics of the organization's work but urges continued, close attention by Internet operators, users, and policy makers alike.

As a first step to improving robustness, the ISP industry should develop an approach for reporting outages and make the information available for studying the root cause of failures and identifying actions and technologies that would improve the Internet's robustness. While anecdotal reports of failures are available from both the popular press and various Internet community forums, these sources generally lack sufficient detail and are not systematically collected, making it hard to assess Internet reliability and robustness trends or conduct root-cause analysis. The availability of these data will make it possible to properly analyze the robustness of the Internet, identify key related issues, and provide the information needed for research into how to make the Internet more robust. The committee recognizes that there is currently no consensus on what data ought to be reported and that there would be strong resistance to a mandated reporting of irrelevant information. It also anticipates that some form of reporting of outages is likely to become a requirement, at least in the United States, which suggests that the industry should work to devise a program that represents a balance of interests as an alternative to the imposition of government-developed reporting standards; the voluntary program initiated by the Network Reliability and Interoperability Council is a first step. Cooperative consideration of an approach for reporting outages and failures should determine what information ought to be collected as well as to whom it should be reported. Since the primary purpose of collecting this information is to inform industry activities as well as research aimed at improving reliability and robustness, it will not be necessary that all of the information be reported publicly—the operators themselves and the research community would be the main beneficiaries of some of the detailed information. A process for gathering systematic data on failures should be understood to be distinct from independent monitoring of ISP performance, which is best performed by independent organizations that gather data on behalf of consumers.

---

[2]Another CSTB committee is expected shortly to begin an examination of issues surrounding the assignment of domain names in the Domain Name System such as conflicts between DNS names and trademarks.

Internet service providers, content and service providers, and users should continue to adopt technologies and practices that improve the reliability and robustness of the Internet as a whole. The Internet's trust model distributes responsibility for robustness across many actors, including ISPs, network operators, and end users, placing responsibility on each to adopt the best practices and technologies. Also, the Internet's composite nature and international scope mean that no one can impose overall requirements for such things as reporting problems, minimum operational standards, or controls on malicious actions. This limitation makes it even more important to develop industry agreements addressing robustness that are international in scope, and it underscores the importance of developing technical mechanisms that permit one piece of the Internet to protect itself from another.

NATs (and the somewhat NAT-like IPv4-to-IPv6 translators) are a necessary short-term measure but should not substitute for a long-term transition to IPv6. Investment in the development and deployment of IPv6 technology, along with promotion of the long-term benefits of IPv6 for customers and ISPs alike, should be continued. In addition, there should be a concerted effort to address other pressing issues that IPv6 does not now completely address. IPv6 alone does not resolve other, related issues faced by the Internet. For example, while it does provide some aids for automatic configuration, it does not adequately simplify the management of internal networks interfaced to the Internet. Nor does it solve the scaling problems mentioned above with respect to the computational complexity of updating routing tables as the number of addresses increases. Also, while it includes stronger authentication and confidentiality safeguards than IPv4, it does not respond to other security considerations that may be critical to minimizing vulnerability to attack.

Decisions made by industry, government, and consumers should all take into account the significant long-term benefits of open, transparent IP service. The preservation of open IP service would have a number of benefits for both ISPs and customers. Because of its critical role in the continued dynamism and growth of the Internet, government should include considerations of openness in its inquires relating to the Internet and should favor policy decisions that are consistent with maintaining open IP service. Government also has a role to play in convening dialog and supporting research about openness issues. By the same token, concerns about the vertical integration of the data transport and content businesses and about content control, as seen in recent debates about access to cable broadband Internet systems, could be eased if ISPs committed to providing their customers with open IP service. From this standpoint, the continued delivery of open IP service would be an enlightened move in the long-term interest of the industry.

ISPs should make public their policies for filtering or prioritizing customer IP traffic. Many filtering and traffic prioritization policies work to the mutual benefit of both the provider and the customer. But given their subjectivity, all would benefit from an environment in which such policies are publicly disclosed, allowing customers to understand the nature of service offerings and reducing the likelihood that ISPs will be perceived as manipulating the nature of their services—such as favoring their own content—behind the scenes, against the interests of consumers. Further, such disclosure might foster a market in which ISPs compete on the terms of their policies and in which a particular ISP offers different service options so as to better meet the needs of its customers. Also, those who monitor the industry or rate the quality of ISPs could use such information to inform consumers about the advantages and disadvantages of the various ISP service offerings.

Government Policy Responses

By lowering the cost of communications and increasing the functionality and utility of the communications infrastructure, the Internet has enabled significant changes. Experiencing a revolution on Internet time is extraordinarily challenging. Changes come quickly and unpredictably. Fads appear suddenly and fade away just as rapidly. Nor is the speed of events the only challenge. The distributed nature of the Internet, with its thousands of ISPs and software vendors and its millions of individual users all contributing to the overall shape of the network, makes it very difficult to understand what is happening. The technology is changing swiftly, and in many cases the perceived problem may fix itself or evolve into an entirely different problem. In such a dynamic environment, flexibility is essential and regulatory caution is a virtue. This should be a period of watchful waiting.

The present policy of nonregulation of the Internet should be accompanied by close monitoring of the Internet's structures and operation by government, the Internet industry, and Internet users to ascertain enduring trends and identify what problems, if any, are due to persistent—as opposed to transient—phenomena. While this recommendation is intended to apply across the structure and operation of the Internet as a whole, the committee sees several important places where it should be applied:

• Absent evidence of abusive control over Internet interconnection, regulation here would be premature. However, as interconnection is so important to the health of the Internet, all players, including government, should continue to monitor the evolution of interconnection carefully to ensure that it remains competitive and innovative.

• In view of the importance of the various organizations that help to coordinate various aspects of the Internet, as well as the uncertain impact on them of the constellation of changing conditions relating to the Internet, the activities and operations of these coordinating organizations merit continued close attention.

• Regulation of IP telephony at this point in time would be premature because it is a newly emerging alternative to traditional telephony that is evolving along multiple paths; further maturation and observation are needed to yield a realistic sense of the shape of the markets and the industry. Any regulation applied in the future to IP telephony should be technology-neutral and minimally constrain innovation. In order to not inhibit growth of and innovation in IP telephony and Internet services, regulatory intervention associated with IP telephony should take into account the different architecture of the Internet and the diverse set of telephony technologies and designs being developed and deployed for use on the Internet and PSTN. A technology-neutral approach would allow this diverse set of technologies and designs to be accommodated, particularly during this period of experimentation and rapid change, and would permit emerging technologies to continue to evolve. A similar approach should be applied to other Internet-based alternatives to existing industries.

Monitoring should be supported by a broad-based research effort (including research in social science) to promote objective, methodologically sound measurements and analysis and should be complemented by efforts to understand what might one day be potential triggers for intervention. Examples of technical information that would inform decision making include information on the growth of the Internet (in terms of users, traffic, and range of uses), its reliability, and its socioeconomic impacts. Federal efforts to collect technical and socioeconomic data on the Internet should be given adequate resources, and options for leveraging complementary private data collection should be explored.

The following principles, derived from the committee's examination of the broad social policy issues—privacy, anonymity, and identity; authentication; taxation of commerce transacted over the Internet; and universal service—should be used to guide the development of policy issues arising from the use of the Internet.

Principle 1. Focus laws and regulations on the activities and behaviors of concern rather than on the network architecture or its constituent networks. Use existing laws and regulations first, provided they are consistent with the capabilities and design of the relevant technologies. In many cases, existing laws are adequate to address Internet-related issues, and they should be the default approach. One risk posed by Internet-specific legislation or regulation is that of measures whose implementation would force modifications to the Internet's architecture. The adverse effects of new laws and regulations on that architecture should be weighed against their usefulness for addressing a particular problem. Indeed, requiring enforcement of a particular policy within the network could entail breaking the hourglass transparency of the Internet. Existing laws and regulations will not prove adequate in all circumstances, however; the salient instance at present is Internet telephony.

Principle 2. Where Internet-specific government intervention is required, laws and regulations should establish the framework and overall parameters, while industry and other nongovernment stakeholders should devise appropriate implementations. The rapid evolution of the Internet and its interactions with societal interests argue for caution in setting rules and crafting legislation. The extent to which specific actions are required today is unclear, in part because it is unclear which circumstances will endure or to what extent voluntary actions in response to public and government pressures are at least in part addressing some concerns. However, today's heated national and international debate in areas such as privacy and anonymity illustrates that not all stakeholders believe status quo approaches will prove satisfactory, so governmental institutions will surely be monitoring progress and may, at some stage, intervene through new regulation or laws. The committee does not recommend where government intervention should or should not be undertaken. As noted above, it finds too many of the elements of the situation to be too dynamic, and it in any case did not conduct a complete assessment of social policy issues. But if it is determined that voluntary action alone is not sufficient, a legislative or regulatory approach should be adopted that reflects the dynamic, evolving nature of Internet applications and services and the Internet marketplace. Legislative and regulatory actions should establish a framework for desired outcomes and define the principles and parameters that bound online conduct. A flexible approach also helps create an environment that fosters alternative solutions, both in terms of new practices and new technologies, and that can both satisfy the established principles and provide additional benefits such as easier implementation, decreased costs, and greater investment in innovation.

Principle 3. Keep a broad geographic perspective when thinking about Internet issues. Over the Internet, it can be as easy to interact with a person, organization, or company thousands of miles away as with someone in the next town. Issues surrounding sales tax collection have shown how the Internet weakens geographical boundaries and how local and national social and economic interests and concerns come into play as political institutions attempt to address the geographical challenge. Commerce is but one of many instances where the Internet's global nature raises issues and stresses existing regimes; another instance is cultural as well as community identity. The global nature of the Internet also means that many issues will have to be addressed in international forums, in the interest of harmonizing approaches to transborder problems and establishing reciprocity and other arrangements in the event of transborder responses to problems. In accordance with principle 1, Internet-related issues are best resolved, wherever possible, by the established law of the relevant domain or established rules for handling cross-border activities. Pursuant to principle 2, solutions that seek to establish performance objectives rather than specify implementation details are preferable. In some areas, existing national and multilateral frameworks (and adaptive processes) will be sufficient to address concerns. Harmonization will, however, present an ongoing challenge, and resolution may necessitate countries making compromises on the specific approaches; global scope implies, among other things, a need to frame U.S. policy in the context of policy in other parts of the world, which can affect the design and enforceability of measures taken in the United States.

1

Introduction and Context

WHAT IS THE INTERNET?

The Internet is a diverse set of independent networks, interlinked to provide its users with the appearance of a single, uniform network. Two factors shield the user from the complex realities that lie behind the illusion of seamlessness: the use of a standard set of protocols to communicate across networks and the efforts of the companies and organizations that operate the Internet's different networks to keep its elements interconnected.

The networks that compose the Internet share a common architecture (how the components of the networks interrelate) and software protocols (standards governing the interchange of data) that enable communication within and among the constituent networks.[1] The nature of these two abstract elements—architecture and protocols—is driven by the set of fundamental design principles adopted by the early builders of the Internet. Because an appreciation of these principles is important to understanding what makes the Internet what it is, several of them are discussed at length below. Those who design and operate the Internet generally characterize the Internet in terms of these principles, which is not surprising given that the Internet derives from work done by researchers

---

[1]Some would argue that the term "Internet" embraces the entire interconnected data world rather than just the IP-based infrastructure. That broader definition includes networks using other protocols that interface with the IP-based Internet.

in computer science and engineering—fields that rely on abstraction as a technique for managing the complexity of what computer scientists study or build.

The success of the abstracted interface through which users encounter the Internet contributes to the Internet illusion. Software such as Web browsers makes use of names for things attached to the Internet— www.example.com, for instance—that hide the nature of the networks to which both they and the user are connected. This, of course, has enormous advantages for users, who need not worry about the complexities of the networks they are making use of. Making things appear simple, however, can lead to unmet expectations. For example, a user who attempts but repeatedly fails to connect to a Web site—say, www.example. com—will look to the Internet service provider (ISP) to resolve the problem. However, the odds are good that the computer named www.example.com will turn out not to be attached to the network of the user's provider. The provider, in fact, may not have a direct connection to the provider servicing www.example.com and may not be able to even tell the user what the problem is, where the problem is located, and the likelihood of its happening again. If a user considers connecting to that site to be mission-critical, such a response is likely to be very frustrating. Advances in technology and services can, however, improve the quality of the illusion substantially, as can a better understanding by users of how the Internet is constructed. We will return to the technological, economic, and policy issues surrounding interconnection in Chapter 3.

One consequence of the Internet illusion is that the ordinary Internet user is likely to assume that a connection to the Internet via a given provider of Internet services amounts to a direct connection to the totality of the Internet. But in reality, the user has only contracted for Internet service with one of a number of ISPs—enterprises that provide Internet connectivity to end users or other ISPs. Each ISP controls and operates only a fraction of the global network system. To reach all of the end destinations, content, or services that a user wishes to reach, an Internet service provider may have to forward the user's communication through several other networks, none of which it controls. Interconnections are made largely though network links that are bilaterally coordinated between ISPs.

It is important to distinguish between the public[2] Internet, which is

---

[2]"Public" is used here in the same sense it has in the context of the public telephone network. It does not denote public ownership; it denotes instead a network to which anyone can connect and in which any customer can exchange traffic with any other. The line between private and public is not always sharp; in particular, the physical networks they use are not necessarily distinct.

normally what is meant when "Internet" is written with a capital I, and the Internet's core technologies (standard protocols and routers), which are frequently called "IP technology" in reference to the key protocol used on the Internet. Throughout this report, these terms—Internet and IP—will be used in this way. The public Internet is distinguished by global addressability (any device connected to the Internet can be given an address and each address will be unique) and routing (any device can communicate with any other). In practice, however, as a consequence of interventions imposed by ISPs and local network managers—such as the deployment of firewalls and other technologies for filtering communications traffic—not all data are allowed to pass to all devices and not all devices are assigned public addresses. IP technologies are also employed in private networks that have full, limited, or even no connectivity to the public Internet; the distinction between public and private blurs because to the extent that private networks acquire connections to the Internet, they by definition become part of it.

If one looks at the elements that physically make up the Internet, one sees two categories of objects. The networks that make up the Internet are composed of communications links, which carry data from one point to another, and routers, which direct the communications flow between links and, ultimately, from senders to receivers. Communications links may use different kinds of media, from telephone lines to cables originally deployed for use in cable television systems to satellite and other wireless circuits. Internal to networks, especially larger networks in more developed parts of the world, are links that can carry relatively large amounts of traffic, typically via optical fiber cables. The largest of these links are commonly said to make up the Internet's "backbone," though this definition is not precise and even the backbone is not monolithic.[3] Links closer to users, especially homes and small businesses, typically have connections with considerably less capacity. Large organizations, on the other hand, tend to have high-capacity links. Over time the effective capacity of links within the network has been growing. Links to homes and small businesses—the so-called "last mile"—have until recently, with the emergence of cable modem, digital subscriber line (DSL), and other technologies, been largely constrained to the relatively low speeds obtainable using analog modems running over conventional phone lines. Analog modems remain the dominant mode of home access.

---

[3]There is no easy way to specify which networks comprise the Internet backbone. For instance, in some countries a rather modest link may serve as the local backbone. Nor do all connections between providers take place through the backbone—there is no assurance that any particular data packet will flow through any part of the Internet's backbone.

Routers are computer devices located throughout the Internet that transfer information across the Internet from a source to a destination. Routing software performs several functions. It determines the best routing paths, based on some set of criteria for what is best, and directs the flow of groups of data (packets) through the network. Path determination at each step along the way depends on information that each router has about the paths from its location to neighboring routers as well as to the destination; routers communicate to one another some of this path information. A number of routing algorithms that determine how routers forward packets through the network are in use; routing protocols mediate the interchange of path information needed to carry out these algorithms.

The Internet can be divided into a center, made up of the communications links and routers operated by Internet service providers, and edges, made up of the networks and equipment operated by Internet users. The line between center and edge is not a sharp one. Users who connect via dial-up modems attached to their computers clearly sit at the very edge. In most business settings as well as in an increasing number of homes, LANs sit between the ISP and the devices that the Internet connects. These LANs, and the routers, switches, and firewalls contained within them, sit near the edge, generally beyond the control of the ISP,[4] but not at the very edge of the network.

Software applications running on these computing devices—today, typically PCs—use Internet protocols to establish and manage information flows that support applications over the Internet. Much as a common set of standard protocols lies at the core of the Internet, common standards and a common body of software are features of many applications, the most common being those that make up the World Wide Web (the Web). The Web adds its own protocols for information exchange that build on top of the fundamental Internet protocols, and it also provides a standard way of presenting information, be it text or graphics. More specialized software, which also makes use of the Internet's basic protocols and frequently is closely linked to Web software, supports such applications as real-time audio or video streaming, voice telephony, text messaging, and a whole host of other applications. In light of the prominence of the Web today, Web-based applications and the content and services provided by them are sometimes viewed as synonymous with the Internet; the Internet, however, is a more general-purpose network over which the Web is layered.

---

[4]Though ISPs do sometimes provide firewalls for their customers.

Following usage from the telecommunications industry, the essential physical components—communications links and routers—of the network (including links that are parts of other networks, such as the telephone lines used by dial-up modems or DSL or the high-capacity fiber-optic cables shared among Internet, other data, and voice communications services) can be referred to as "facilities." Internet service providers use these facilities to provide connectivity using the Internet protocols. What is done with the facilities and basic connectivity comes under the heading "services." These services, which include such things as access to content (e.g., viewing Web sites, downloading documents, or listening to audio), electronic commerce (e.g., shopping, banking, and bill paying), or telephony, are enabled by both devices and software in the hands of users and service providers. Some services are enabled merely by installing software on user computers, while others rely on functionality implemented in computers and software attached to the Internet by a third party. In either case, the general-purpose nature of the Internet has meant that there does not have be any arrangement between the Internet service provider and the provider of a particular service. While this statement generally holds true today, we are seeing the emergence of exceptions to it in the form of application-specific delivery networks (e.g., Akamai) that employ devices located throughout the network, generally near the edges. Chapter 3 discusses these trends and their implications for the future development of the Internet.

A multitude of businesses are based on selling various combinations of these elements. For instance, many Internet service providers (ISPs) integrate connectivity with content or services for their customers. Some ISPs rely in part or in toto on access facilities (e.g., dial-up modem pools) owned and operated by other providers, while others operate most or all of these facilities themselves. Also, ISPs may opt to own and operate their own communications links, such as fiber-optic cables, and networks or they may run Internet services over links and networks owned and operated by other communications companies (just as companies have resold conventional voice telephony services for years).

The tale is well told about how, over the past decade, the Internet evolved from a novel, but still developing, technology into a central force in society and commerce,[5] and the committee will not belabor the point here. Suffice it to say that the transformations resulting from the Internet along with expectations for continued growth in its size, scope, and influ-

---

[5]See, for example, Computer Science and Telecommunications Board (CSTB), National Research Council. 1996. *The Unpredictable Certainty: Information Infrastructure Through 2000*. Washington, D.C.: National Academy Press.

ence, have given rise to widespread interest and concern on the part of government and society. A more realistic and better-informed appraisal of Internet issues has become imperative now that governments at all levels seek to control its evolution and use and dedicated issue-advocacy groups have begun to proliferate. This report, written by a group of experts in a number of areas—technologies, operation, and management of the Internet; associated communications infrastructures, such as the public switched telephone network; and related policy and social issues—is intended to explain key trends in the Internet's evolution and their implications for policy. It focuses on trends that are often misunderstood or incompletely treated by the mass media and it highlights specific areas of policy that warrant more or better consideration. The remainder of this chapter characterizes the Internet's special design attributes and outlines several key trends in facilities and services.

SUCCESS BY DESIGN—
ABSTRACT FEATURES AND PRINCIPLES

Why has the Internet been so successful? Much of the answer lies in the combination of two factors—functionality and lower costs. The new functionality stems from the Internet's unique design principles and features that make connection, interconnection, and innovation in both facilities and services relatively easy. The Internet's characteristics have also made it possible to use the underlying communications infrastructure more efficiently, thereby setting a lower price point for the communications it enables. Both factors have generated a pattern of innovation in Internet technologies and uses.

Its relatively rapid responsiveness to users and other design attributes distinguish the Internet from other parts of the information infrastructure, such as the public switched telephone network (PSTN) or the television networks (cable and broadcast). The design of those other networks is more focused on the center, and greater functionality is located within the networks. They have been more centrally developed and managed and historically have limited what users can do with them. In contrast, as detailed below, the Internet's design is effectively neutral to what services operate across the network. This enables a relatively unrestricted set of applications to run over it without the need for changes to be made within the network.

Much of the design of the Internet can be traced to the principles adopted by the research community that undertook its early development. These principles and the resulting architecture have been codified in research papers and in a special set of documents describing the Internet's design known as requests for comments (RFCs), a name reflecting the interactive and iterative nature of Internet technology development. Especially notable are the articulation of the end-to-end argument[6] and RFC 1958.[7]

These and other documents embody some value judgments and reflect the fundamental political and ethical beliefs of the scientists and engineers who designed the Internet: the Internet architecture reflects their desire for as much openness, sharing of computing and communications resources, and broad access and use as possible. For example, the value placed on connectivity as its own reward favors gateways and interconnections over restrictions on connectivity—but the technology can be used permissively or conservatively, and recent trends show both. Another value underlying the design is a preference for simplicity over complexity.

These values have been advanced through the architectural view embodied in voluntary standards set by such bodies as the Internet Engineering Task Force (IETF),[8] which has been the dominant standards-setting body. Within this body, there has been open competition between compatible implementations. Other standards-setting bodies have also contributed to the establishment of key standards. One such body is the World Wide Web Consortium, which has worked on standards related to the Web. Another is the International Telecommunication Union (ITU). To date, Internet standards generally tend to be developed on a perceived-need basis and respond to technological developments; they also continue to be linked to the activities of the network research community.

The design values of the Internet have been reinforced by the environment in which the Internet was developed. In its early years as a cooperative research project, it was isolated from some of the stresses and strains associated with commercial marketplace interactions. Today the IETF, like other organizations associated with the Internet, must respond to the economic forces of a robust marketplace. Whether and how the traditional Internet design values will be maintained is an important issue for the future of the Internet.

---

[6]See J.H. Saltzer, D.P. Reed, and D.D. Clark. 1984. "End-to-End Arguments in System Design," *ACM Transactions on Computer Systems* 2(4):277-288, November.

[7]Internet Architecture Board. 1996. *Architectural Principles of the Internet*, Brian Carpenter, ed., Request for Comments (RFC) 1958, June. Available online at <http://www.ietf.org/rfc/rfc1958.txt >.

[8]While the IETF does apply an architectural view to the development of Internet standards, it does not have anything to do with controlling how the networks that make up the Internet are actually built and configured.

The Internet's "Hourglass" Architecture

As an open data network,[9] the Internet can operate over different underlying technologies, including those yet to be introduced, and it can support multiple and evolving applications and services. In this layered architecture, bits are bits and the network does not favor by its design or effectiveness any particular class of application.[10] Evidence of this openness lies in the fact that the Internet's essential design predated a number of communications technologies (e.g., LANs, ATM, and frame relay) and applications and services (e.g., e-mail, the World Wide Web, and Internet radio) in use today—and that within the Internet all of these technologies and services, both new and old, can coexist and evolve. The shape of an hourglass inspired its selection as a metaphor for the architecture—the minimal required elements appear at the narrowest point, and an ever-increasing set of choices fills the wider top and bottom, underscoring how little the Internet itself demands of its service providers and users.[11]

As a consequence of this hourglass-shaped architectural design, innovation takes place at the edge of the network, through software running on devices connected to the network and using open interfaces. By contrast, the PSTN was designed for very unintelligent edge devices—telephones—and functions by means of a sophisticated core that provides what are termed "intelligent facilities." Edge-based innovation derives from a fundamental design decision made very early in the development of the Internet and embodied in what is called the end-to-end argument in systems design.[12] Aimed at simplicity and flexibility, this argument says that the network should provide a very basic level of service—data transport—and that the intelligence—the information processing needed to provide applications—should be located in or close to the devices attached to the edge of the network.

Underlying the end-to-end argument is the idea that it is the system

---

[9]Computer Science and Telecommunications Board (CSTB), National Research Council. 1994. *Realizing the Information Future: The Internet and Beyond.* Washington, D.C.: National Academy Press.

[10]The layering principle is a powerful one and appears in other contexts. One sees operating system application interfaces such as those provided by Windows or Unix that allow a large number of application programs to run on diverse computing platforms as well as bus protocols (e.g., PCI or USB) that allow a large number of peripheral devices to work with a variety of different computing platforms.

[11]Some caution is needed in interpreting the hourglass metaphor. The narrow "waist" at the middle of the hourglass is a metaphor for the minimally specified choice of technology at this point and is not intended to convey any sense of a choke point or bottleneck.

[12]This was first expressed in J.H. Saltzer, D.P. Reed, and D.D. Clark. 1984. "End-to-End Arguments in System Design," *ACM Transactions on Computer Systems* 2(4):277-288.

or application, not the network itself, that is in the best position to implement appropriate protection. If the network or network provider tries to take on this task it is likely to implement something that is too heavy-handed and performance-inhibiting for some applications and too light for others. Both the sender and receiver are held ultimately responsible for assuring the reliability of communications services (e.g., making sure that what is received is complete and in order), so as to protect end users against the vagaries of the networks that lie between them.[13] End systems are also responsible for protecting themselves—an end system must be able, for example, to authenticate the sender of a message requesting, say, the deletion of a file located on the system.[14]

The original architects of the Internet made a key design decision to use the principle of layering to separate applications from the underlying transport infrastructure of the Internet. By hiding the realities of how the Internet is constructed—for instance, the topology of the network or the physical configuration of its elements, how routing is performed within the network, or how particular data transport services are implemented— the architecture enables people to write applications that run over it without having to possess any knowledge of these realities. In fact, without using specialized diagnostic tools, there is very little way for application software that makes use of the Internet to discover the detailed characteristics of the underlying networks. In general, even a poorly designed application can be added in a few sites at the edge of the network without putting the network at risk; this is how new applications can be experimented with, tested, and improved.

This manifestation of the Internet illusion discussed above has been key to the explosion of new services and software applications of the Internet. The combination of a standardized interface to the network and the location of intelligence at the edges means that developers can write and field new devices or new software without any coordination with network operators or users or any changes in the underlying transport

---

[13]One counterexample is denial-of-service attacks at the network level (i.e., "storms" of IP packets sent to a network or router), which can be argued to deserve remedy within the network itself.

[14]One can think of the result of combining the end-to-end argument and the hourglass architecture in another way. By providing an unreliable datagram delivery service in which the network attempts to deliver a given datagram (piece of information) but does not guarantee such delivery, the Internet makes minimal assumptions about the characteristics of the underlying transmission networks and passes a minimal set of functions up to higher levels of the protocol. This design allows complex networks of connectivity to be overlaid across a highly diverse collection of communications elements.

network. Nor do new applications or changes need to be deployed all at
once. Even though many developers of network applications do not understand or appreciate the technical and management challenges confronting those who build and operate Internet networks, they are still able
to succeed in developing all kinds of popular new applications.

Thus, not only do we see PCs and larger computer systems attached
to the Internet, we now see televisions (e.g., WebTV), telephones, personal digital assistants (PDAs), and other devices being attached as well;
the future is likely to see many other devices emerge (e.g., music appliances directly connected to the Internet). Of course, not all such applications represent improvements (and many will fade away over time), but
the Internet supports rapid feedback and the evolution of new and improved features and function, both of which are associated with the
Internet's culture of cumulative knowledge building.

The corollary to ease of innovation at the Internet's edges is that
innovation at the center of the network is difficult and can be very slow
because building new features into the network requires the coordinated
actions of many providers and users. The problem is exemplified by the
difficulties of deploying new network-level features such as enhanced
quality of service or IP multicast (both discussed further in Chapter 2).

This is not to say that an increasing number of sophisticated things
are not being implemented inside the Internet to optimize the delivery of
various services. For example, algorithms for filtering and load balancing
are found in some routers because they provide benefits in terms of service quality for certain traffic (perhaps at the cost of raw switching speed).
Web caching entails adding devices throughout the network to improve
network performance. Such caching is achieved by moderating or redi-
recting specific types of network traffic in ways that can avoid congestion
by making use of temporary local copies of frequently accessed information.   Also, businesses that are building applications that require a great
deal of network capacity or low-latency delivery of information—requirements not met very well on today's Internet—are coping by building their
own application-specific delivery networks, which employ devices located throughout the edges of the network as a work-around. Installation
requires cooperation (and may require colocation) with particular ISPs.
These technologies are controversial from an architectural and robustness
standpoint as they disturb the end-to-end model. Robustness implications are discussed in Chapter 2 and architectural implications are discussed in Chapter 3.

The Robustness Principle

The robustness[15] principle is arguably the single most enabling characteristic of the Internet.[16] It was initially adopted for the ARPANET in order to accommodate the unpredictably changing topologies anticipated for defense applications (i.e., dynamic network reconfiguration) and then for the Internet in order to accommodate interconnecting a diverse set networks built by multiple implementors out of components using multiple implementations (i.e., heterogeneity of devices and technologies). In accommodating both requirements, the Internet accommodates decentralized management, growth, and—accordingly—evolution.

In practice, this robustness principle has taken several forms. One way of viewing robustness is that the rule for interpreting standards (and other specifications) that are not quite as precise as they might be in a perfect world should be for the sender to take the narrowest interpretation (i.e., the intersection of all possible interpretations) and for the receiver to be prepared for the broadest possible interpretation (i.e., the union of all possible interpretations).[17] Robustness also entails conservative and careful design at the transport level that is able to deal with a

---

[15]The robustness being discussed here should not be confused with the same term used elsewhere in this report, especially Chapter 2, where it denotes lack of vulnerability to failures or attack.

[16]This principle was written down by Jon Postel in the 1979 Internet protocol specification: "In general, an implementation must be conservative in its sending behavior, and liberal in its receiving behavior" (Jon Postel. August 1979. *Internet Experiment Note (IEN) 111* (the IP specification), p. 22). The same text appears in September 1981, in RFC 791, p. 23, and a variant appears in the TCP specification, under the heading "robustness principle": "TCP implementations should follow a general principle of robustness: be conservative in what you do, be liberal in what you accept from others" (Information Sciences Institute, University of Southern California. 1980. *DOD Standard Transmission Protocol*, RFC 761, January. Available online at <http://www.ietf.org/rfc/rfc0761>). A conservative approach in Internet protocol design appeared earlier in Internet Engineering Note 12. However, that paper falls short of enunciating a "robustness principle." See Lawrence L. Garlick, Raphael Rom, and Jonathan B. Postel. 1977. *Issues in Reliable Host-to-Host Protocols*. Internet Engineering Note (IEN) 12. Augmentation Research Center, Stanford Research Institute, Menlo Park, Calif., June 8. Available online from <http://www.isi.edu/in-notes/ien/ien-12.txt.2>.

[17]It should also be noted that the robustness principle can be (and has been) cited as a justification for non-interoperability. For example, a vendor can release protocol elements that, by a narrow (or even reasonable) reading of the standards, are not compliant with the standard, and then claim that other implementations that do not interoperate with them are inadequate because they are not robust enough. The most literal interpretation of the robustness principle could also be taken as a requirement that each application or system must protect itself against any behavior whatsoever by others, but the general assumption is that others will behave in acceptable ways.

wide range of behavior such as packet loss, delay, and out-of-order delivery.

Another facet of robustness is the use of soft state within the Internet. Here "state" refers to the configuration of elements, such as switches and routers, within the network. Soft state, in contrast to hard state, means that operation of the network depends as little as possible on persistent parameter settings within the network. Basic transmission of data over the Internet takes this to the extreme—routing of packets is done in a completely stateless manner so that each packet transmission is a separate event that takes place without reference to previous or following packets. There is no explicit establishment of a particular network path through which information will flow. This principle underpins the robustness of the Internet because it allows the network to dynamically reconfigure its routing state continually (including routing around links that have failed) yet still deliver packets.[18] The manner in which routers receive their routing information is also based on soft state. A router is able to discover necessary routing information from its neighbors, allowing a router that fails and then restarts to resume operation without intervention.

Other network services that provide for explicit allocation of network resources for a particular communications session (e.g., some forms of quality of service) require state to be retained within the network. In these cases, robustness dictates that this be done in accordance with the principle of soft state, meaning that the state must not be persistent. For example, if an application requests network resources, that request will time out if not rerequested periodically, ensuring that network resources are not tied up if the application fails.[19]

Scalable, Distributed, and Adaptive Design

The Internet's design, in particular the design elements listed above, make it able to support a growing amount of communications—growth in the number of users and attached devices and growth in the volume of communications per device and in total. The capacity of communications links has been one element of Internet scaling. Roughly a decade ago, the Internet passed its first scaling hurdle with the replacement of 56-kbps lines with higher capacity, 1.5-Mbps (T1) lines throughout much of the

---

[18]Stateless transmission also leads to the interesting property that a packet can be removed from an arbitrary location in the Internet and reinjected at any other point in the network and it will continue on the shortest path to its addressed destination.

[19]This stands in contrast to the use of hard state for telephone call setup in the PSTN, in which the network is requested to allocate the necessary circuits to complete a call and the circuits are held until a request to "tear down" the call is issued.

NSFNET backbone. Subsequently, it passed successive scaling hurdles and a decade from now will have passed several more. Growth in the number of devices attached to the Internet gives rise to other scaling pressures such as the size of the routing table and the processing and distribution of routing information (see Chapter 2 for a further discussion). Yet a risk remains that solutions will be deployed that work for the moment but fail at the next bandwidth or memory scale, which guarantees that the crisis that precipitated the 1988 T1 deployment will be repeated. Other scaling issues arise outside the network itself and relate to the scalability of the systems put in place to implement a particular service (e.g., a content server or an e-commerce site). If the service is designed in such a way that it can support only, say, a half-million Internet users, it will fail if the service becomes popular with users. The lesson to learn from history is that scaling must be considered in every decision, and that lesson is increasingly important as there are more pressures driving innovations that may not scale well or at all (see Chapter 2 for further discussion).

Reflecting its architecture and design and the associated reliance on a multitude of organizations to operate its constituent networks, the Internet is more distributed and adaptive than other information networks. The Internet protocol (IP) enables distributed control of the network (e.g., decisions made about routing) except for the allocation of address blocks and the management of top-level domain names in the Domain Name System. This distributed control, enabled by the hourglass architecture, provides for the more rapid development and introduction of innovative applications and services.

From Internet Technology to Internet Marketplace

In large part as a reflection of these design principles and features, the Internet has come to possess a set of attributes different from those of other networks. These unique attributes include the following:

- *Multiple and evolving pricing models.* Internet businesses offer many pricing models and do not necessarily stick with any one. The norm for consumer Internet access today in the United States is a flat-rate monthly charge,[20] which encourages use of the Internet by eliminating uncertainty

---

[20]From the standpoint of users, Internet access is not flat rate in many countries because the local telephone call required for dial-up access is metered rather than flat rate, as is common in the United States. This results in significantly higher total costs for Internet access and is a significant deterrent to increased Internet use. In some countries the local calling charges for Internet access have been reduced; in other countries, the cost of Internet access has been absorbed into the per-minute charges for local calls.

about monthly charges. The level of charge may vary according to provider promises of service quality. Other factors affecting price include the ISP's dependence on advertising as a source of revenue, the bundling of sales of equipment and Internet service (e.g., "free PC" deals), and the bundling of Internet access with content and special services. Business clients of ISPs follow a variety of pricing models, frequently based on usage. Pricing for interconnection within the Internet itself—that is, the charges that ISPs pay to other ISPs—also follows a variety of pricing models, ranging from flat (traffic-insensitive) rates for interconnection to barter arrangements with peers; these models are in flux. Notably, unlike the PSTN, very few pricing models are based on either distance or the exact volume of traffic carried. Interconnection prices are often privately negotiated rather than based on fixed rates. Internet interconnection contrasts with the PSTN, where terms for interconnection and financial settlement are well established and the subject of regulation.

• *Low barriers to entry for innovation.* Consistent with the "Criteria for an Open Data Network,"[21] the Internet is designed to be open from the standpoint of users, service providers, and network providers, and as a result it has been open to change in the associated industry base as well as in the technologies they supply and use. A wide range of applications and services, some leveraging the commonality of IP and others additionally leveraging standards layered on top of IP, most notably the Web interface, have flourished. As that industry base grows and matures, questions arise about whether innovation will face other kinds of entry barriers.

• *Tippy markets.* The Internet is the epitome of a network market. By definition, participation in a large network market is more rewarding; the larger the network, the larger the number of users. A small initial advantage in market share, often associated with being first, can snowball into a large advantage. These snowball effects are amplified on the Internet by the ease and negligible cost of distributing software through the network, which can promote much faster change than is typical for a product with physical distribution—on a scale of months or a couple of years rather than several years or a decade. The desire to tip the market, seen in many competitive markets, is epitomized by the struggle to build a leadership position in streaming audio and video. This tippiness of the Internet marketplace suggests a pattern of highly concentrated markets and market leaders who greatly outdistance their competitors—an outcome that

---

[21]Computer Science and Telecommunications Board (CSTB), National Research Council. 1994. *Realizing the Information Future: The Internet and Beyond.* Washington, D.C.: National Academy Press.

would be at odds with the historic expectation of heterogeneity in technology implementation. Indications are, however, that these positions of leadership are unstable. At least sometimes, a sufficient investment of resources or other circumstances can allow newcomers to trump the incumbents and tip the market in another direction.[22] In recent years, for example, Microsoft acquired much of the market for Web browsers, a market that was once dominated by Netscape Communications. Whether these patterns prove enduring and sustainable remains to be seen.

The Internet has been well served by an insistence that there is often more than one "right" answer to a question. Its designers argue that no single technology solves all the problems well, or even well enough, so that no single technology should be considered as the sole solution. Thus, when there is a common standard, there are frequently multiple independent implementations of it. No single vendor has cornered the market in good technology, and when one has gotten close to a monopolistic position, the traditional Internet community has been critical of the situation because of its potential for inhibiting continued innovation. It is not that developing proprietary extensions or protocols to implement optional features (which can generally coexist with standard protocols) is a problem per se. Rather, a monopolistic position would preclude the significant benefits of having the essential elements of the infrastructure (hardware or software) exist in multiple, independent implementations, available from multiple vendors. Competition has served the Internet well.

Internet Organizations

Several private, nonprofit organizations play critical roles with respect to the Internet. These include the Internet's principal standards-setting bodies: the Internet Engineering Task Force (IETF), the Internet Architecture Board (IAB), and the Internet Engineering Steering Group (IESG). Along with the ever-growing number of other organizations involved in setting Internet standards, they are grappling with a growing number and diversity of stakeholders and with the ever-larger commercial stakes associated with the outcomes of their work. Another class of organizations deals with operational issues: for example, the North American Network Operators Group (NANOG) provides a forum for troubleshooting and exchanging technical and operational information.

---

[22]For an overview of network economics, see Hal Varian and Carl Shapiro. 1998. *Information Rules: A Strategic Guide to the Network Economy.* Boston, Mass.: Harvard Business School Press.

Most visible recently has been ICANN, a newly formed body that has assumed overall responsibility for managing the Internet's addresses and names. Its work has received considerable attention and been the subject of vigorous debate as address and name management become more contentious and controversial activities. And, while the Internet Corporation for Assigned Names and Numbers (ICANN) was not established to take on the broader mission of Internet governance, it has not been able to avoid some international governance questions in the course of its work, leading observers to see its potential to play a larger role in the ambiguous arena of Internet governance. Regional address registries have responsibility for managing the pool of addresses delegated to each region of the world.

KEY TRENDS IN INTERNET DEVELOPMENT

The Internet has already gone through several iterations. New routing protocols have been deployed in bounded administrative domains, for example, and replaced with other protocols as technology has matured. IP addresses at one time had to be given out in blocks of fixed size, whereas today they are assigned in blocks defined by demonstrated needs. What has worked over a period of some 25 years has been continual, generally gradual change, characterized in most cases by continued interoperation between newer and older hardware and software. Sudden revolutionary changes—for instance, the sudden phasing out of one protocol in favor of another—have not worked as well.[23] For this reason, it is unrealistic to believe that major infrastructure components, whether hardware or software, can be changed without a significant period of coexistence and interoperation. The history of the Internet argues for an expectation of change from time to time and for design choices that at each step include the ability to transition to the next step.

Advancing the Internet is about improvements in three areas: (1) the nature and business of supplying network facilities; (2) Internet connectivity; and (3) applications, content, and services. One of the things that is special about the Internet is that its architecture allows an Internet business to separate these three areas or to combine them in different ways.

---

[23]One notable "flag day" transition occurred in the ARPANET on January 1, 1983, when all hosts had to simultaneously convert from NCP to TCP. The transition, which came at a time when the Internet was far smaller, nonetheless required careful advance planning (Barry M. Leiner et al. 1998. *A Brief History of the Internet.* Version 3.1, February 20. Available online from <http://www.isoc.org/internet/history/brief.html>).

Growth in Backbone Capacity

The heart of the Internet grows through the interactions of ISPs and major equipment manufacturers (principally router vendors and communications circuit suppliers). Increased capacity—speed, performance, and the accommodation of more users and more connections—is the watchword. In terms of fundamental communications, ever-increasing exploitation of optical fiber facilities has been the trend. Growth in Internet traffic (by a factor of roughly 2 every year) has been outstripping growth of computing speed (by the Moore's law factor of 2 every 18 months).[24] To maintain this trend, equipment manufacturers are constantly challenged to improve the performance of communications equipment nearly twice as fast as the PC and PC-component manufacturers improve PCs. For staying on this curve, the equipment industry is highly dependent on the help of innovations from both industry- and government-funded research (the latter comes chiefly from the Defense Advanced Research Projects Agency (DARPA) and the National Science Foundation (NSF)).

It is generally believed that given current technology and some sustained research support, equipment manufacturers should be able to continue to improve performance in the time frames required to keep on this performance trajectory. In 2005, if current trends persist, the fastest link will be roughly 2 terabits per second (Tbps), requiring routers that can move data at 100 Tbps rates internally, and 5 years later, links will be approaching the 100 Tbps level. At that point, routers that can handle petabits (1000 Tb) per second will be required, and the requirement for extremely fast routers becomes a major challenge. Some predict that all-optical networking—unlike the networks today, which combine optical fiber with routers based on electronics—will provide a solution. However, the channel switching speeds of today's optical technologies are far slower than the speeds of today's routers, suggesting that optical switching's importance may come from automating and speeding up the management of aggregated traffic flows.[25]

---

[24]See Lawrence G. Roberts. 2000. "Beyond Moore's Law: Internet Growth Trends." *Computer* 33(1):117-120.

[25]One thing that appears crucial is further development of optical multiplexing. One particular technique, known as wavelength division multiplexing (WDM), allows one to pack a great deal of data into a single fiber by using multiple lasers operating at different colors in parallel (it is much harder to use one laser to signal at very high bandwidths). One approach will be the use of link management techniques, whereby routers aggregate traffic to different destinations, so that traffic is placed onto a switched flow, bypassing intermediate routers. These large aggregates, not individual packets, would be switched optically. To switch a packet, the existing router technology works well. In this approach, different colors would be configured on a timescale of minutes to days to carry these aggregates from source to destination routers, bypassing intermediate routers and switches.

Growth and Diversification of the ISP Market

The several thousand Internet service providers differ widely in size, type of service they provide, and type of interconnection they have with other service providers. As the market has grown in overall size, it has evolved to comprise both very large players—the tier 1 providers that constitute the Internet's backbone and the large, consumer-oriented ISPs—and many smaller players that focus on particular segments of the market. Some serve particular markets (e.g., consumers or businesses) while others provide such specialized services as hosting Web servers for other companies. Peering, transit, and other interconnection arrangements—which have both technical and economic dimensions—have played a vital role in enabling the interlinking that defines the Internet, and several issues related to these arrangements and their evolution are covered in Chapter 3.

Upgrading the Local Access Infrastructure

Today most home users access the Internet through narrowband connections made by modems using the public switched voice network. This approach has led to fairly ubiquitous access services from multiple providers that offer very similar pricing and features. Such access achieves relatively low data rates compared to what the telephone company's copper loops can provide and does not provide the continuous connectivity that Internet protocols were designed to take advantage of. The approach required little investment in new access infrastructure and could make use of the existing voice infrastructure fairly straightforwardly.

Now, however, dial-up access, with its low bandwidth and need to complete a telephone connection each time access is desired, is increasingly seen as limited, though it remains the least common denominator for residential service today. At the same time, a range of new applications that require higher bandwidth and/or continuous connectivity are being developed.

Broadband access enables services that, because they require high capacity and limited delay, cannot be provided via dial-up access to the Internet; it also makes many existing services much faster and more responsive. Broadband also enables multiple applications to be run, such as simultaneous telephony and Web browsing. Software or music downloads that require minutes or hours over a dial-up connection take as little as a few seconds via a broadband connection. Another benefit of broadband Internet connections is that, rather then requiring a phone call and connection to be set up, they can be online all the time. This has two significant implications. Routine monitoring tasks can easily occur continuously (e.g., notifying users that they have new mail), and network interactions can take place immediately (without waiting the minute or two required to establish a dial-up connection), reducing the overhead required to retrieve information or conduct a transaction. Looking up a telephone number online, for example, instead of in a phone book, is a viable option when one does not need to wait for an Internet connection to be established; similarly, other activities become possible with better connectivity. While these advantages are compelling, it remains easier at this early stage of deployment to posit likely benefits than to quantify with confidence actual consumer demand.

While the wireline and wireless telephone companies still dominate the provision of voice services and broadcast entertainment still uses radio signals delivered over the airwaves or via cable, delivery of voice, video, and other services over the Internet is emerging. As an increasing number of users have broadband Internet connections, it is reasonable to project that the use of various IP-based telephony services is likely to increase substantially and that video applications will probably grow as well. A number of services that compete with existing broadcasting and entertainment businesses are emerging that are likely to increase in use, including Internet delivery of music and Internet "radio" broadcasting. Another emerging trend is the use of distributed, peer-to-peer applications (Napster and its offspring, particularly those that operate without any centralized server facility) to exchange content among Internet users, capabilities that harken back to the early days of the Internet, which was designed to support peer-to-peer connectivity. These developments will have several implications, including a change in the value consumers place on Internet access (especially broadband service) and potential stresses on the Internet itself.

As an increasing number of people become familiar with broadband and its implications, the rate and patterns of broadband deployment as well as the types of services being offered have become the subject of public debate today, with congressional and multilevel regulatory scrutiny in the United States and political activity by organizations representing consumer and industry perspectives.

Deployment is a nontrivial undertaking; it will require billions of dollars in investment to deploy broadband pervasively. Broadband technologies are being deployed at varying rates by a number of companies. Cable companies are deploying two-way hybrid fiber/coax infrastructures capable of providing high-speed Internet services. Both incumbent and competitive local exchange carriers are also investing in broadband access, primarily through a family of DSL technologies, which leverage existing copper wiring to provide high-speed Internet services. As with cable, the solution of leveraging copper plant is generally considered an interim step on the path to providing very high bandwidth connections to the home using fiber-optic cable, although the time line for this is both uncertain and likely to vary according to local circumstances.

Because two major facilities for broadband—cable and the incumbent local exchange carrier's copper loops—are owned by incumbent players in regulated industries and the third option today—wireless—depends in part on spectrum allocation, deployment issues are tightly coupled to both the interests of incumbents and the evolution of the regulatory regimes that apply to these players. Thus, for example, cable's move into Internet access and telephony have led to increasing political activity and government scrutiny of the terms and conditions of its Internet service offerings and associated competitive conduct.

The 1996 Telecommunications Act[26] sought to promote competition and consumer choice as key enablers of high-quality, affordable broadband local access to the Internet. Efforts to enhance consumer choice fall into two general classes: facilities-based competition and unbundling of network elements through regulation. Facilities-based competition is competition among multiple access providers each of which operates its own infrastructure. In such a regime, competition would exist, for example, between the copper pair infrastructure owned by the local exchange carriers, the hybrid fiber/coax infrastructure being deployed by cable operators, and wireless services. The premise of facilities-based competition is that a multiplicity of facilities-based providers and their heterogeneous business models will keep any one provider from dominating and creating a bottleneck for innovation and control of content on the Internet.

Another approach to ensuring consumer choice included in the 1996 act is to use regulation to unbundle the elements of the incumbent carrier's networks, thereby enabling the entry of competitors. For example, incumbent local exchange carriers are required to resell their copper lines to subscribers—the so-called "local loops"—to other telecommunications providers, allowing these entrants to offer competitive voice service or other services such as DSL over these lines. More recently, there have been calls for various forms of unbundling of the cable infrastructure, an idea generally referred to as "open access" (Box 1.1). The architecture of the Internet fundamentally supports unbundling—the issues that arise with respect to unbundling include what particular approaches work technically in the context of particular access technologies, as well as a complex set of economic and policy issues.

---

[26]Telecommunications Act of 1996, Public Law No. 104-104, 110 Stat. 56 (1996).

BOX 1.1 Open Access and Cable

Cable operators have tended to select a single ISP to provide Internet service over their facilities, and the service has typically been bundled with at least some content or services aimed specifically at their own customers. Several concerns appear to have prompted attention to cable open access. First, there are concerns stemming from cable operator assertions of control over what television content is transmitted over their systems. Some fear that cable operators will seek analogous control over the Internet content available to their subscribers—that they will favor particular content or create a "walled garden" service in which outside content is difficult or impossible to access. There are also concerns that those cable operators who are in a monopoly position in their market, which is the case in many but not all markets, will be able to charge other ISPs access fees that are higher than the costs charged to the ISP affiliated with the cable operator, giving the latter an unfair competitive advantage. On the flip side, open access requirements could deter cable operators from investing in system upgrades to support broadband. The debate over open access has also been accompanied by debate over how to implement open access, the actual extent of proposed technical difficulties, and the additional costs of supporting competitive ISP access over cable facilities. Several pilot efforts aim at demonstrating the feasibility of technical approaches that support access by multiple ISPs. It is unclear whether these concerns will be resolved as a result of moves by industry or regulatory action or legal decisions, or whether they will persist.

A detailed exploration of unbundling or open access policies and practices and of other specific complex technical, social, and economic considerations that underpin the regulation of broadband local access is largely outside the scope of this work. The present report, therefore, does not recommend policy on regulating local access, whether by DSL, cable, wireless, or other technologies. Another CSTB body, the Committee on Broadband Last-Mile Technologies, is currently investigating these and other issues related to broadband services for homes and small offices. However, several elements of the present report are likely to inform thinking about the issue, including its discussions of what constitutes transparent, open Internet service; trends in the ISP business; and the likely roles for quality-of-service technologies on the Internet.

Growing Role for Wireless Services

At the same time as cable and DSL technologies are starting to be deployed, there have been considerable interest and investment in building competitive Internet access via high-speed wireless networks. One can also expect the development and deployment of wireless services to provide mobile access. Deployment has benefited from FCC efforts to open up radio-frequency spectrum for such services, and it remains contingent on the ability to make spectrum available and to resolve issues related to the siting of transmission towers in local communities. Additionally, new satellite ventures are planning to deploy broadband communications delivered from space; these will be a boon to sparsely populated areas where any sort of terrestrial infrastructure deployment is problematic.

In addition to providing access in competition with wired technologies or access where terrestrial infrastructure is not cost-effective, wireless Internet can be expected to play a key role for a wide range of mobile applications. There are many instances, such as when a user is in a car or in a public space, where being connected through a wire is simply not a practical option. IP connectivity in such situations could lead to all sorts of new applications (and businesses), some of which have not yet been thought of and which might turn out to be as popular as normal e-mail or Web surfing itself. The popularity of the i-mode phone service provided in Japan by DoCoMo shows the potential for rapid adoption of wireless data services elsewhere.

Voice and Data Services

Many industry analysts predict that the rapid growth of data networks, particularly the Internet, will result in voice traffic increasingly being carried using IP technology (voice over IP or IP telephony). While the time frame for completing such a transition is unclear today, it is clear that many service providers, equipment manufacturers, and customers are moving in this direction. The public switched telephone network (PSTN) is itself evolving to a more data-centric architecture, and the landscape of equipment suppliers is also rapidly changing. As use of these services grows, they will have significant impacts on the traditional, regulated voice service providers and may provoke calls for IP telephony to be subject to regulation akin to that in place for circuit-switched voice services. Chapter 4 examines these issues, as well as the more general question of what happens when Internet-based services compete with other communications industries.

Rise in the Use of Single-Purpose Devices

Today the majority of devices connected to the Internet are general-purpose computers. Most users access the Internet through general-purpose computers that are used for a multitude of tasks, and the servers used by providers of content and services over the Internet are also generally based on general-purpose computing systems. However, single-purpose devices offer several advantages for both uses. First, a carefully designed, single-purpose device can often be made much less inexpensively, with prices more in line with prices of other consumer electronics devices than those of general-purpose computers. Second, single-purpose devices are likely to have fewer failure modes and harmful interactions with other devices. Third, single-purpose devices lend themselves to simpler interfaces and greater ease of use.[27]

For those providing content and applications over the Internet, possible single-purpose devices include network-attached file servers and specialized audio or video servers. For end users, a single-purpose device running a standard protocol can interact with any service that supports that protocol (e.g., consumers wishing to listen to music could use simple devices that stream audio or simple stand-alone music players that download music).

Looking ahead, it is reasonable to project that networked systems will include a diverse set of embedded systems in homes and commercial settings, and computers used in other infrastructures, such as electric power, will also be networked. International Data Corporation, for example, has forecast that the number of devices connected to the Internet will more than double every year for the foreseeable future and that non-PC devices will account for nearly half of Internet devices shipped by 2002.[28] Acknowledging the limitations of market research, it is nonetheless reasonable to plan for their widespread use.

Such a future can have several significant implications for the Internet infrastructure. Widespread use will, for example, increase the draw on the IP address space. The existence of large numbers of more specialized devices aimed at narrower applications also may put pressure on the Internet model of using a single, standard protocol (as illustrated by the introduction of the Wireless Access Protocol as a solution for the mobile, wireless space). Finally, because they could be used for passive monitoring, deployment of a large number of smaller networked devices also raises privacy concerns, including the question of informed consent.

FUTURE EVOLUTION AND SUCCESS

Reflecting its widespread deployment and adoption,[29] substantial commercial investment,[30] and broad societal awareness, the Internet has become a mainline piece of the communications infrastructure. Expan-

---

[27]Conversely, a proliferation of single-purpose devices, especially in the absence of standardized interfaces, could complicate the user's experience.

[28]International Data Corporation (IDC). 1999. *Death of the PC-Centric Era* (IDC Executive Insights). Boston, Mass.: IDC. Available online at <http://www.idc.com/F/Ei/gens19.htm>.

[29]Nielsen Media Research and CommerceNet reported in June 1999 that the number of U.S. and Canadian Internet users aged 16 and older was 92 million, an increase from 79 million in the preceding year's study (Associated Press, June 18, 1999).

[30]One measure comes from a Cisco-sponsored study conducted at the University of Texas

sion into the foreseeable future appears inevitable, and new technologies and new applications that leverage these technologies and new opportunities will continue to emerge. The Internet's design principles and the values that underlie these principles have been critical to the spectacular success of the Internet. However, from today's vantage point of relative maturity, there are questions that need to be asked about the underlying structures that have brought us to this point—the looseness of the Internet's internal coordination mechanisms, of the process by which Internet standards are developed, and of the interconnection arrangements that tie it together—and questions about the Internet's scalability and reliability. Because of the prominence of the Internet, as well as its potential for disruptive effects on both business and society, there are pressures for government to act in these and many other areas related to the Internet. Thus far, telecommunications regulators have been reluctant to intervene. Government involvement with the operation of the Internet has largely been limited to places where it was already involved, such as transitioning the administration of the Domain Name System, or places where Internet and more traditional telecommunications issues overlap, such as within the PSTN local exchanges. On the other hand, there have been both regulatory attention and legislative activity aimed at consumer protection, such as protection of personal privacy and protection against junk e-mail or spam, as well as measures aimed at content and conduct over the Internet (e.g., the Communications Decency Act and gambling) and measures aimed at enhancing Internet-based applications, such as legislation governing digital signatures.

Underlying this hands-off approach has been the belief that the Internet will continue to expand, mature, and evolve and that intervention could threaten that success. Indeed, indications are that much of this evolution can be expected to occur naturally, without recourse to remedial action by government or other players. However, the technical and policy challenges alluded to above raise questions about whether existing mechanisms are up to the task of supporting increasing demands and pressures and what the role of government should and should not be. In addressing these questions, this report seeks to distinguish the issues that will probably be self-resolving from those whose resolution will require greater attention and/or new approaches.

---

at Austin (Anitesh Barua et al. 1999. *Measuring the Internet Economy: An Exploratory Study*, Technical report. Austin, Tex.: Center for Research in Electronic Commerce, Graduate School of Business, University of Texas. Available online at <http://cism.bus.utexas.edu/>), which found that the revenue of companies in the Internet infrastructure business (ISPs, including backbone providers, network hardware and software companies, manufacturers of computers and servers, suppliers of security products, and manufacturers of optical fibers and associated hardware) totaled nearly $115 billion annually in 1998.

2

Scaling Up the Internet and Making It More Reliable and Robust

BUILDING A BETTER INTERNET

The Internet has become a place where many live, work, and play. It is a critical resource for many businesses that depend on e-commerce. Indeed, when attacks are made on Internet infrastructure or commonly used Web sites like CNN, Yahoo! and the like, they become front-page news.[1] As a consequence, the Internet must become and remain more robust and reliable. Reflecting demand for its capabilities, the Internet is expected to grow substantially worldwide in terms of users, devices, and applications. A dramatic increase in the number of users and networked devices gives rise to questions of whether the Internet's present address-ing scheme can accommodate the demand and whether the Internet community's proposed solution, IPv6, could, in fact, be deployed to rem-edy the situation. The 1990s saw widespread deployment of telephony and streaming audio and video. These new applications and protocols have had significant impacts on the infrastructure, both quantitatively in terms of a growing level of traffic and qualitatively in terms of new types of traffic. The future is likely to see new applications that place new demands on the Internet's robustness and scalability. In short, to meet the potential demand for infrastructure, the Internet will have to support

---

[1]For example, Matt Richtel. 2000. "Several Web Sites Attacked Following Assault on Yahoo." *New York Times*, February 9, p. A1; and Matt Richtel. 2000. "Spread of Attacks on Web Sites Is Slowing Traffic on the Internet," *New York Times*, February 10, p. A1.

a dramatically increasing number of users and devices, meet a growing demand for network capacity (scale), and provide greater robustness at any scale.

SCALING

"Scaling" refers to the process of adapting to various kinds of Internet growth, including the following:

- The increasing number of users and devices connected to the Internet,
- The increasing volume of communications per device and total volume of communication across the Internet, and
- The continual emergence of new applications and ways in which users employ the Internet.

While details of the growth in Internet usage are subject to interpretation and change over time, reflecting the dynamic nature of Internet adoption, it is only the overall trends that concern us here. In the United States, a substantial fraction of homes have access to the Internet, and that number is likely to eventually approach the fraction of homes that have a personal computer (a fraction that itself is still growing). Over 100 million people report that they are Internet users in the United States.[2] Overseas, while the current level of Internet penetration differs widely from country to country, many countries show rates of growth comparable to or exceeding the rapid growth seen in the United States,[3] so it is reasonable to anticipate that similar growth curves will be seen in other less-penetrated countries, shifted in time, reflecting when the early adoption phase began.

Perhaps a more important future driver for overall growth is the trend toward a growing number and variety of devices being attached to the Internet. Some of those devices will be embedded in other kinds of equipment or systems, and some will serve specific purposes for a given user. This trend could change the number of devices per user from the current number, slightly less than 1 in developed countries, to much more than this—10 or even 100.

---

[2]Data from *Computer Industry Almanac*, available online at <http://www.c-i-a.com>.

[3]For an analysis based on OECD data, see Gonzaolo Diez-Picazo Figuera. 1999. *An Analysis of International Internet Diffusion*. Master's Thesis, MIT, June, p. 83.

Scaling of Capacity

The basic design of the Internet, characterized by the elements discussed in Chapter 1, has proved remarkably scalable in the face of such growth. Perhaps the most obvious component of growth is the demand for greater speed in the communications lines that make up the Internet. As was noted in Chapter 1, the first major scaling hurdle was seen about a decade ago when, in response to growing demands, many of the 56-kbps lines in the NSFNET backbone were replaced with higher capacity 1.5-Mbps lines (also known as T1 lines).[4] Doing so required developing higher performance Internet routers and some retuning of protocols and software. Since then, the Internet has passed many scaling hurdles and increased its capacity many times over. The fastest lines in the Internet were 2.5 Gbps (OC-48) in 1999, almost 50,000 times faster than the original lines, and the deployment of 10-Gbps lines (OC-192) is under way.

All expectations are that more such growth will be seen in the coming decade. There is a persistent and reasonable fear that demand for capacity will outstrip the ability of the providers to expand owing to a lack of technology or capital. The 1990s were characterized by periodic scrambling by ISPs, equipment providers, and researchers to develop and deploy new technologies that would provide the needed capacity in advance of demand. The success of those efforts does not, however, guarantee continued success into the future. Furthermore, efforts to expand capacity may not be uniformly successful. Regional variations in the availability of rights of way, industry strategies, and regulation could slow deployments in particular areas.

Better use of existing bandwidth also plays a role in enhancing scalability. A recent trend has been to compensate for the lack of network capacity (or other functionality, such as mechanisms for assuring a particular quality of service) by deploying servers throughout the Internet. Cache servers keep local copies of frequently used content, and locally placed streaming servers compensate for the lack of guarantees against delay. In some cases, innovative routing is used to capture requests and direct them to the closest servers. Each of these approaches has side effects that can cause new problems, however. Their implications for robustness and transparency are discussed elsewhere in this report.

---

[4]An abbreviation for bits per second is bps; kbps means thousands of bits per second, Mbps means millions of bits per second, Gbps means billions of bits per second, and Tbps means trillions of bits per second. The use of a capital B in place of lower case b means the unit of measurement is bytes (8 bits) rather than bits.

Scaling of Protocols and Algorithms

A more difficult aspect of growth is in design of new or improved protocols and algorithms for the Internet. The ever-present risk is that solutions will be deployed that work for the moment but fail as the number of users and applications continues to grow—today's significant improvement may be tomorrow's impediment to progress. Scaling must thus be considered in every design. This lesson is increasingly important as there are many pressures driving innovations that may not scale well or at all.

The IETF processes through which lower-level network protocols are developed involve extensive community review. This means that the protocols undergo considerable scrutiny with regard to scaling before they are widely deployed. However, particularly at the applications layer, protocol proposals are sometimes introduced that, while adequate in such settings as a local area network, have been designed without sufficient understanding of their implications for the wider Internet. Market pressures can then lead to their deployment before scaling has been completely addressed. When a standard is developed through a forum such as the IETF, public discussion of it in working groups helps. However, a protocol can nonetheless reach the status of a "proposed standard," and thus begin to be widely deployed, with obvious scalability problems only partially fixed.

The Web itself is a good example of scaling challenges arising from particular application protocols. It is not widely appreciated that the "World Wide Wait" phenomenon is due in part to suboptimal design choices in the specialized protocol used by the Web (HTTP), not to the core Internet protocols. Early versions of HTTP relied on a large number of short TCP sessions, adding considerable overhead to the retrieval of a page containing many elements and preventing TCP's congestion control mechanisms from working.[5] An update to the protocol, HTTP 1.1, adopted as an Internet standard by the IETF in 1999,[6] finally fixed enough of the problem to reduce the pressure on the network infrastructure, but the protocol still lacks many of the right properties for use at massive

---

[5]Though it took some time to launch an update, the shortcomings of HTTP 1.0 were recognized early on. See, for example, Simon E. Spero. 1994. *Analysis of HTTP Performance Problems*, Technical report. Cambridge, Mass.: World Wide Web Consortium, July. Available online at <http://www.w3.org/Protocols/HTTP/1.0/HTTPPerformance.html>.

[6]R. Fielding et al. 1999. *Hypertext Transfer Protocol — HTTP/1.1*. RFC 2616. Network Working Group, Internet Engineering Task Force, June. Available online at <http://www.ietf.org/rfc/rfc2616.txt>.

scale. The challenge posed by this lack of scalability has been significant given HTTP's large share of Internet backbone traffic.[7]

The case of IP multicast demonstrates the interplay between protocol design, the Internet's routing system, and scaling considerations. Multicast is a significant example because it allows applications to simultaneously and inexpensively deliver a single data stream to multiple delivery points, which would alleviate Internet scaling challenges. Multicast can be used in numerous applications where the same data are to be sent to multiple users, such as audio and audiovisual conferencing, entertainment broadcasting, and various other forms of broad information dissemination (the delivery of stock quotes to a set of brokers is one example). All of these applications are capable of running over today's Internet, either in the backbone or within corporate networks, but many operate via a set of individual, simultaneous (unicast) transmissions, which means that they use much more bandwidth than they might otherwise.

Despite its promise of reducing bandwidth requirements for one-to-many communications, multicast itself presents scaling challenges. By definition, an Internet-wide multicast group needs to be visible throughout the Internet—or at least everywhere where there is a group's member. The techniques available today require that routers track participation in each active group, and in some case for each group's active senders. Such participation tracking requires complex databases and supporting protocol exchanges. One might reasonably assume that the number of groups grows with the size of the Internet or with the growth of applications such as Internet radio broadcast, and that the footprint of each group (the fraction of the Internet over which the group information must be transmitted) will grow as the size of the Internet. However, the two factors multiply, meaning that under these assumptions, the challenges posed to providers will grow as the square of the Internet's size. Resolving this situation requires not merely defining an appropriate protocol but also researching a hard routing question—how to coalesce routing information of multiple groups into manageable aggregates without generating too much inefficiency.

---

[7]For example, Internet traffic statistics for the vBNS, a research backbone, show that about two-thirds of TCP flows were HTTP. See MCI vBNS Engineering. 2000. *NSF Very High Speed Backbone Network Service: Management and Operations Monthly Report*, January. Available online at <http://www.vbns.net:8080/nettraff/2000/Jan.htm >.

Scaling of the Internet's Naming Systems

Growth in the number of names and an increasing volume of name resolution requests, both of which reflect Internet growth, are placing scaling pressures on the Internet's name-to-address translation service, the Domain Name System (DNS).[8] There is broad consensus as well as a strong technical argument that a common naming service is needed on the Internet.[9] People throughout the world need to be able to name objects (systems, files, and facilities) correctly in their own languages and have them unambiguously accessible to authorized people under those names, which requires a common naming infrastructure. People also need naming services to allow them to identify applications and services provided by particular companies and organizations.

The DNS is instrumental in hiding the Internet's internal complexity from users and application developers. In the DNS, network objects such as the host computers that provide Web pages or e-mail boxes are designated by symbolic names that are independent of the location of the resource. The name provides an indirect reference to the network object, which allows the use of names instead of less mnemonic numbers and also allows the actual address to which the name points to be changed without disrupting access via the name. Because the computer associated with a particular named service can be changed without changing the IP addresses of that machine (only the address associated with the name in the DNS needs changing), indirection provides users with portability if they wish to switch Internet providers. While most users receive IP address allocations from their ISP and thus have to change address if they change ISP, DNS names are controlled by the user—a change of provider requires only that the address pointed to by the DNS entry be changed. The significance of DNS names was greatly increased as a result of the decision by the original developers of the World Wide Web to use them directly to identify information locations. The importance attached to DNS names is reflected in the contention surrounding the system's management (Box 2.1)

The DNS is organized as a hierarchy. At the very top of the hierarchy, the "root servers" record the address of the top-level domain servers, such as the .com or .uk servers (Figure 2.1). The addresses of these root

---

[8]The DNS was first introduced in P. Mockapetris. 1983. *Domain Names – Concepts and Facilities*, RFC 882. November. Available online at <http://www.ietf.org/rfc/rfc0882.txt>.

[9]Internet Architecture Board. 2000. *IAB Technical Comment on the Unique DNS Root*, RFC 2826. May. Available online at <http://www.ietf.org/rfc/rfc2826.txt>.

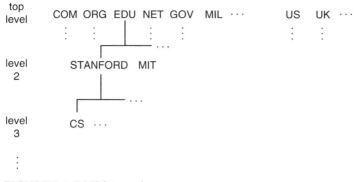

FIGURE 2.1 DNS hierarchy.

servers are known locally to every name server of the Internet, using information provided by ICANN (in practice, coded into the DNS software by the vendor). Each top-level domain server records the addresses of the domain name servers for the second-level domains, such as example.com. These secondary servers are responsible for providing information on name-to-address mappings for names in the example.com domain. The hierarchical design permits the secondary servers to point themselves to third-level servers, and so forth. To access named objects, Internet sessions start with a transaction with a name server, known as name resolution, to find the IP address at which the resource is located, in which a domain name such as www.example.com is translated into a numerical address such as 128.9.176.32. Assuming that the local name server has not previously stored the requisite information locally (see the discussion of caching, below), three successive transactions are generally required in order to find the address of a target server such as www.example.com: (1) to learn the address of the .com server from the root server, (2) to learn the address of the example.com server from the .com server, and (3) to learn the address of the target web server, www.example.com, from the example.com name server.

The situation in practice may, in fact, be more complicated. If example.com is a very popular service, it is useful to be able to distribute the load among multiple servers and/or to direct a user to the server that is closest to him. To do either of these, the name servers run by example.com may make use of a clever trick: requests for the address corresponding to www.example.com, for example, may produce replies pointing to

---

BOX 2.1 Managing the Domain Name System

Providing a single, authoritative mapping between names and addresses requires Internet-wide coordination.[1] The management of Internet names was until recently provided by several organizations with little formal status—a group of regional registries, a U.S. government contract supporting the Internet Assigned Numbers Authority,[2] and a U.S. government contract with Network Solutions. Network Solutions has had responsibility for assignments of names in the generic (i.e., non-country-specific) .com, .net, and .org top-level domains; regional Internet registries coordinated by IANA have had responsibility for allocation of names in country-specific domains (e.g., .uk for the United Kingdom or .fi for Finland).[3] The regional registries have also been responsible for allocating blocks of numerical addresses to Internet service providers. As a result of the Clinton Administration's efforts to end the U.S. government's direct involvement with Internet address registration, responsibility for top-level domain name administration was assigned in 1999 to the Internet Corporation for Assigned Names and Numbers (ICANN), a new nonprofit corporation established to assume responsibility for the management of the DNS and the root server system (which forms the basis for all the domain name servers distributed throughout the Internet) as well as IP address space allocation and protocol parameter assignment. ICANN was charged with establishing a system in which multiple competitors would be able to provide name registration services. Network Solutions remains the keeper of the root database.

---

[1]Names are not the only thing that require Internet-wide coordination. Other, less visible value assignments (technical parameters), such as TCP ports or application parameters, which are also important to the Internet's operation, need coordination. Such coordination has been provided by the IANA for the IETF, a process that has worked well. The relationship between IANA and the new ICANN organization remains to be resolved in detail. In addition, where appropriate, other standards organizations have established their own registration processes, and again, these mechanisms seem to be working well.

[2]IANA, now incorporated into the new ICANN, was located at the University of Southern California's Information Sciences Institute, where it was led by the late ISI computer scientist Jon Postel, supported by contracts from DARPA and NSF.

[3]While a majority of U.S. institutions make use of the generic top-level domains, some also use a .us domain. The .us domain has been managed by IANA.

---

one of a number of different servers that, presumably, contain copies of the same information.[10]

The rules governing DNS names would seem to permit millions of naming domains each containing billions of names,[11] which would seem adequate to support scaling demands. However, with the number of top-

---

[10]Another non-DNS trick for load distribution makes use of so-called transparent proxies or interception proxies. These intercept and divert data packets going to a particular address to one of a number of servers that contain the same content. Because it interposes information processing outside the control of either the user's computer or the server he is

Managing the DNS has also come to mean dealing with tensions resulting from the use of DNS names in commerce and society at large. Because the Internet never developed a true directory system, Internet users frequently use domain names as their key to navigate the Web and connect to a specific organization's servers, usually of the form www.company-name.com. Businesses may also register domain names for brand name products; there are entries for Ivory soaps (www.ivory.com) and Crest toothpaste (www.crest.com) as well as for the manufacturer, Procter & Gamble, (www.pg.com). Domain names are known explicitly by many consumers, are used in commercial advertising, and even used as the name of some companies. Limited look-up capabilities are provided by the category-based directories established by Internet portals such as Yahoo! or alternative naming systems provided by companies such as RealNames or AOL with its keywords, but none of these alternatives has, at least thus far, taken the place of the DNS.

The allocation of Internet names and addresses has been the subject of intense public debate during the last 3 years, especially the conflict of interest between domain name owners and trademark holders. Two organizations/companies that wish to use the same name on the Internet cannot both obtain a name in a single generic top-level domain—there can, for instance, be only one example.com. There can be a distinct example.org and example.net in the .org and .net generic top-level domains, respectively, but companies that want to protect their trademarks may well register names in all the top-level domains. Also, with only one generic top-level domain generally used for commercial entities, two companies with the same name that have established protection for their names (trademarks) in a particular geographical area or industry sector cannot both obtain this name in the .com domain. Following a World Intellectual Property Organization study, ICANN adopted a dispute resolution process to address conflicts related to the use of particular domain names, a move that has itself not been without controversy. Another issue is that the growing popularity of .com makes it increasingly difficult to come up with short, readable names that are not already taken. These considerations have given rise to proposals that would alleviate the situation by expanding the number of generic top-level domains. As of this writing, ICANN has proposed doing just that, but the details of such an expansion are under discussion and the proposal remains to be implemented.

level domains currently limited to one national domain per country (e.g., .fr for France), plus a limited number of global domains (e.g., .com and .org), many domains are organized with a very large number of names contained at the next level rather than by distributing names further down

connecting to, this technique runs counter to the end-to-end principle and can sometimes have the side effect of delivering inconsistent information to the user.

[11]Each DNS name can be composed of up to 256 characters and up to 64 naming elements, each of which can be made of up to 64 characters (letters, digits, and hyphen).

in the hierarchy (e.g., using product.example.com instead of product. com). This can cause scaling problems, and there are concerns that the performance of the DNS will worsen over time.

The multistage process required to find the address of a target, repeated for many Web page accesses by millions of Internet users, can result in a heavy load on the servers one level down from the top of the tree. If the name servers were to be overwhelmed on a persistent basis, all Internet transactions that make use of domain names (i.e., virtually all Internet transactions) would be slowed down, and the whole Internet would suffer.

Today's DNS design relies on two mechanisms to cope with this load—caching and replication. These mechanisms have been effective in alleviating scaling pressures, but there are signs that they may not be sufficient to cope with the continuing rapid growth of the network. DNS caching is a technique whereby the responses to common queries are stored on local DNS servers. Applications such as Web browsers also may perform DNS caching.[12] Using caching, a local DNS server need only request the addresses of the .com server from the root servers infrequently rather than repeatedly. Similarly, once a request has been made for the address of the example.com server, the local name server need not ask for this information again—for a period of time known as the "time to live." Because of the dynamic nature of DNS information, name servers return not only an address but a time-to-live parameter selected by the administrator of the name server for the relevant domain, usually on the order of days or hours, which indicates how long the name-to-address mapping can be considered valid, helping ensure that servers do not retain outdated information.

Caching works well when the same request is repeated many times. This is the case for high-level queries, such as requesting the address of the .com name servers, and also for the most popular Web servers, the search engines, and the very large sites. (It works even better for very frequently accessed services like a file server on a local area network.) However, the efficiency of caching decreases as the number of names that

---

[12]Why do applications also need to cache DNS names? Good DNS performance depends on having local access to DNS information. Because the target platform was a tiny, diskless machine, the earliest implementations of TCP/IP software for the IBM PC lacked DNS cache functionality and depended on local LAN access to a DNS server for all name resolution requests. This resolver-only design has persisted in a number of machines today. Not only does this force the application designer to implement DNS caching, but there are performance costs as well. Since an application cannot determine whether the host it is running on supports a caching server, application-layer caching makes it possible for caching to be carried out twice, potentially yielding inconsistent results.

are kept active by a given user or domain name server increases. When millions of names are registered and accessed in the DNS, only a small fraction can be present in any given cache. Requests for the names of less frequently requested sites, which in total will represent a significant fraction of all requests, will have to be forwarded to the DNS. Even if user queries are concentrated mostly on large sites or queries from the same local group of hosts are concentrated on the same group of sites, which may or may not be the case, the remaining fraction still constitutes an important and growing burden for the DNS. The effect of cache misses is made even worse by the concentration of names in a small number of popular top-level domains, such as .com, .net, and .org. Consequently, an inordinate fraction of the load is sent to these domains' servers (a load that could be alleviated if the hierarchical design of the DNS were used to limit the number of highest-level names). These servers need to scale in two ways. They must support an ever-growing name population, which means that the size of their database keeps increasing very quickly, and they must serve ever more frequent queries. The growth of the database implies increased memory requirements and an increased management load.

Replication, whereby name databases are distributed to multiple name servers, is a way of sharing the load and increasing reliability. With replication, the root server is able, for example, to provide the addresses of several .com servers instead of one. The volume of name resolution inquiries could be met by splitting the load across a sufficiently large number of replicated servers. Unfortunately, current DNS technology limits this approach because the list of the names and addresses of all the servers for a given domain must fit into a single 512-byte packet. (Even after efforts were made to shorten host names, the number of root servers remains limited to 13.) Once the maximum number of servers that will fit within the single-packet constraint has been deployed, increased load in that domain can only be dealt with by increasing the capacity and processing power of each of the individual .com name servers. While the performance of the most widely used DNS software, BIND, lags that of modern high-performance database systems and root servers' software can almost certainly be improved to handle much higher loads, Internet growth rates suggest that the demand on the root servers is likely to be growing faster than their processing speed is increasing and that in a few years the root servers could nonetheless be heavily overloaded.

One proposal for addressing issues ranging from scaling to DNS name-trademark conflicts is to move toward a solution that makes use of directories as an intermediate layer between applications and the DNS. A directory might help resolve conflicts between DNS names and registered trademarks because a particular keyword could be associated with multiple trademarks. It also would help alleviate pressures on the DNS by freeing companies from the necessity of registering separate domain names for each of their brand names (as well as all possible variants). For example, Procter & Gamble would not need to register domains for ivory.com and crest.com and so forth to ensure that customers would be able to locate Web pages describing these products. Directories would also support the association of a particular resource with multiple computers without resorting to clever tricks in the DNS server. A directory can be aware of the source making an inquiry and respond to a query by providing the address of the nearest server that has the requested information.

A number of directory proposals have been floated, many of which might prove adequate. The combination of rivalry among proponents of various systems (many of them at least partially proprietary) and the Internet community's traditional resistance to changing something that is working—although only poorly—is probably responsible for impeding deployment of any one of these proposals. There is reason to hope that rising pressure for new capabilities that the DNS cannot easily accommodate, such the ability to support non-Roman alphabet characters in domain names, could unlock the problem and speed deployment of a directory-based solution that would alleviate scaling pressures.

SCALING UP THE ADDRESS SPACE

Achieving global connectivity requires not only that every part be interconnected but also that the constituent parts use common labels—the numerical addresses (of the form 144.171.1.26) that permit any connected device to communicate with any other. Provisioning these numbers to users who need them to connect their computers to the Internet raises a number of technical, organizational, and management challenges. This section briefly discusses organizations and management issues related to addresses and then focuses on the scaling challenges associated with the complexity of Internet routing and the threat that a likely explosion in the number of devices attached will exhaust the address space. Both raise questions about what technical measures will help alleviate the situation and how such measures can be implemented pervasively. In addition, the challenge of scaling up the address space exemplifies the technical complexity, the interplay between problems and solutions, and the organizational deployment challenges that arise in scaling up the Internet infrastructure overall.

Managing Addresses

The overall concern with the allocation of Internet addresses is that the address pool may be exhausted by the growing number of users and attached devices. The Internet is not the only infrastructure facing scaling challenges associated with its addresses.[13] For traditional telephony, these challenges are being addressed in an established (if evolving) context of global and regional numbering administrations and government scrutiny by federal and state regulators. By contrast, addressing functions in the Internet have been provided by a group of organizations with less formal status. These include a group of regional registries and the Internet Assigned Numbers Authority[14] and Network Solutions (supported by a U.S. government contract). In 1997, the responsibility for network address allocation in North America was shifted from Network Solutions to ARIN, a nonprofit organization funded by North American ISPs. In 1999, under arrangements coordinated by the U.S. Department of Commerce to replace and expand on IANA, the overall responsibility for management of address space was assumed by ICANN. Under the current rules, regional registries such as ARIN receive large blocks of addresses from ICANN (formerly IANA). They, in turn, distribute smaller blocks of addresses to Internet service providers. Customers generally receive their addresses from these service providers, though in some instances large organizations are able obtain addresses directly from the registries.[15]

The rules that determine how many addresses are allocated, and to whom they are allocated, are debated within the regional registries, within ICANN, and within the IETF. These rules are often contentious, as there is an obvious tension between ensuring that there are enough addresses to go around and meeting the desire of users to be assigned the quantity and type of address blocks that they feel best meet their needs. Addresses are considered scarce today, and network managers' initial requests for address space are often turned down and renegotiated. Because the enforcement of address allocation rules has significant consequences, the registries and ICANN must obtain and maintain the trust of all the orga-

---

[13]A growing tide of cell phones, fax machines, and second lines for dial-up Internet access have all put pressure on the pool of available telephone numbers. Responses to this demand have included the allocation of phone numbers to local exchange carriers, implementation of local number portability, and establishment of new area codes.

[14]IANA, now incorporated into the new ICANN, was located at the University of Southern California's Information Sciences Institute under the technical leadership of the late ISI computer scientist Jon Postel, supported by contracts from DARPA and NSF.

[15]The assignment of a number of very large address blocks to individual institutions (companies and universities) predates the practice under current rules.

nizations that make up the Internet; ICANN will probably be under pressure to develop appropriate processes, including appeal procedures, to make the allocation process as fair as possible.

Routing Table Scaling and Address Aggregation

The first part of an Internet address, known as the "routing prefix," is used to direct the routing of each packet from the source to the destination end point. Just as a telephone number contains a country code, area code, central office selector, and individual phone portion, IP addresses contain hierarchically organized topological identifiers that identify an address as belonging to a particular topological segment of the Internet, a subset (e.g., a corporate network) within that region, a local area network within that, and finally an individual interface connected to a particular computing device. In contrast to area codes and central office locators, which typically map to particular geographic regions, Internet identifiers map to logical regions which may or may not coincide with geographical regions. To route packets through the Internet successfully, each router must store a table that provides a mapping between each known routing prefix and the correct routing decision for that prefix. At one extreme, within the network of a customer, this routing table can be very simple, and a "default route" can be set to map all nonlocal prefixes to the customer's ISP. At the other extreme, in the backbones of tier 1 providers, the routing table must contain a complete list of all prefixes. Today this requires tables that hold on the order of 75,000 entries.[16]

As the Internet grows, the routing tables are sure to grow, but the limited capabilities of today's routers dictate that this growth must be constrained. The first and most obvious consideration is that the size of the table cannot exceed the memory available in the routers. Even the latest switching equipment used in the Internet can only accommodate a couple of hundred thousand routing entries, and older equipment as well as new, low-end equipment can store many fewer. Routers could be redesigned so that their memory could be increased to store more routes, but this is nontrivial. High-performance routing typically requires that the routing table be stored either in memory located directly on the chip or in memory connected at very high speed to the chip to avoid delays. While large amounts of memory are widely viewed as something cheap, very fast memory remains expensive and places severe constraints on the

---

[16]As of May 2, 2000, 76,265 entries had been reported in Tony Bates. 2000. *The CIDR Report*. Available online at <http://www.employees.org/~tbates/cidr-report.html>. The precise number of entries varies depending on where in the Internet the measurement is made, but this number gives the right sense of scale.

hardware design. Furthermore, as the Internet moves to supporting quality of service and various forms of filtering, router memory will be required for more than just holding routing tables. So despite continuing improvements in the capabilities of microelectronic devices, the amount of high-speed memory available in routers remains a limiting factor.

And router memory is only one of the factors that limit the size of the routing table. Each of the routing entries in the table describes the path from the router to a given network corresponding to a particular routing prefix. Each entry must be updated in all routers across the network whenever that path changes. Route update messages have to be carried throughout the Internet; because each backbone router must maintain the full table, each must receive and process each update. Given that the network is always changing (owing, for example, to installation, reconfiguration, or failure of network elements), the frequency of updates will increase as the size of the table grows. The updates today are already so frequent that many routers can hardly keep up, and network operators have to resort to "update damping" techniques to limit the rate of update that they accept from their peer networks, slowing the rate at which routing information is distributed. Recent data show that it often takes several minutes for route updates to propagate throughout the Internet.[17] This results in long transition periods during which the routing tables are incorrect and information cannot be routed to portions of the Internet. If the size of the table were to be further increased without increasing the processing power of the routers, the processing of updates would have to be further slowed down, and the whole Internet could be plagued by routing failures.

The explosive growth of the Internet address structure from 1993 to 1995 led to a routing table scaling crisis, when it was feared that the capabilities of routers would be overwhelmed. This pressure resulted in remedial actions starting with the rapid deployment of Classless Interdomain Routing (CIDR). CIDR controls the number of routes that a router must remember by assigning addresses in a hierarchical manner that forces addresses to be assigned in blocks. This involves, for example, Internet service providers consolidating address space allocations into fewer, larger routing prefixes, which are then allocated to customers (these, in turn, may include smaller Internet service providers) out of the service provider's block of addresses. In addition, to reduce pressures on the size of the global routing table, the address registries were also forced

---

[17]Craig Labovitz et al. 1999. *Analysis and Experimental Measurements of Internet BGP Convergence Latencies.* Presentation to the NANOG conference, Montreal, October. Available online at <http://www.nanog.org/mtg-9910/converge.html>.

to adopt a very restrictive policy whereby small, independently routable address blocks would not be allocated to individual organizations. Instead, the registries decided to require organizations to obtain address allocations from their service providers. More recently, tensions surrounding address allocation were heightened when a few large backbone providers, in an effort to force reluctant network operators to aggregate their routing information into larger blocks, refused to pass routing information about prefixes that were smaller than a certain size. This caused some address blocks that had been allocated independently to small providers and companies to lose global connectivity, since the global routing system would filter out their topology information and not allow many destinations on the Internet to be able to pass traffic to their networks. These networks generally were reconfigured into larger prefixes and the crisis was resolved without widespread service outages. The overarching interest of the players in maintaining the Internet's interconnection led to self-correction of the problem.

Deployment of CIDR, together with the adoption of a restrictive address allocation policy by the registries and the use of network address translation, has contained the growth of the routing tables, and the growth in the global routing table has by and large been slow and linear (Figure 2.2). Note, however, that the most recent data displayed in this figure suggest that CIDR and restrictive allocation policies have not entirely alleviated pressures on the routing table size and that table size has recently grown faster than linear.

Whatever pain the new rules created, uncontrolled growth of the routing tables would have caused even greater pain by rendering the whole Internet unusable. Without proactive aggregation, the table would have grown exponentially, like the Internet, and the routers would have been overwhelmed long ago. Provider-based addressing also helps each ISP limit the growth in its routing table by eliminating the necessity of knowing individual prefixes in other service provider domains. It should be noted, however, that the switch to CIDR has had a price. When an organization is given aggregatable addresses by its Internet service provider, it must relinquish these addresses and renumber its network if it changes providers.[18] Note that this is more an issue of ease of network management than of portability of identity; the more familiar names by which the organization is known to the outside world are portable and can remain the same when an organization switches ISP. Large users,

---

[18]For organizations that outsource management of their DNS service to their ISP, there are two barriers to switching: transferring DNS functions and renumbering.

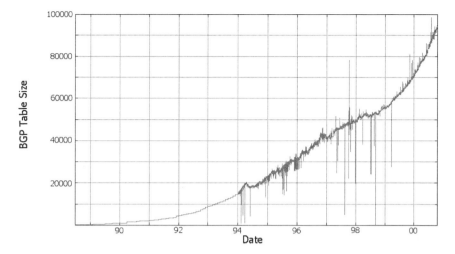

FIGURE 2.2 Border Gateway Patrol (BGP) route advertisements as reported by Telstra in April 2000, showing an overall linear increase in the routing table size but with a recent upward inflection in 1999-2000. SOURCE: Geoff Huston. 2000. *BGP Table Size.* Technical Report, Telstra Corporation, Ltd., Canberra, Australia. Data from April 12.   Available online at <http://www.telstra.net/ops/bgptable.html>.

who had in the past been able to manage their own address space, have felt constrained by the new rules. The limited availability of address space would make it harder to design management-friendly addressing rules within their network, while the provider-supplied addressing rule meant that they would have to renumber whenever they changed provider. Despite the emergence of better tools for renumbering networks, this remains an involved, expensive operation that may inhibit organizations from seeking better deals from competing providers. As a result, there have been calls for users to be provided again with portable addresses so as to minimize switching costs. However, because addresses would no longer be aggregated within the blocks assigned to an ISP network, allocating portable addresses in small blocks to small networks would trigger a dramatic increase in the size of the routing tables. With the current state of routing technology, such a policy could destabilize the whole Internet.

The desire of users, CIDR notwithstanding, to retain the ability to manage their own address space led to the development of a technology known as network address translation (NAT) (see Box 2.2). NAT permits users to use and manage a large amount of private address space independent of the allocation policies of the registrars, giving the network

---

BOX 2.2 Network Address Translation

Network address translators (NATs) are devices that sit between a private network and a network connected directly to the public Internet. They may be stand-alone devices (sometimes referred to as NAT boxes) or included along with other capabilities in computers that serve as gateways between internal networks and the Internet. In a small office/home office environment, they may run on a general-purpose computer that does double duty as the local area network's gateway to the Internet. NATs enable edge networks in homes, companies, and other organizations to use private address spaces and share a smaller set of global addresses among devices using those private addresses on an as-needed basis.

NAT uses a set of global addresses to give devices on a private network a window on the global Internet. In essence, NATs work by detecting what appears to be a data flow from a machine within the private network (e.g., a TCP/IP connection) and allocating one of the external IP addresses on demand to support the flow. Of course, if many machines within the private network are active at any given time, that alone does not conserve many IP addresses. Generally, in addition to the mapping between private and global addresses, NATs perform another mapping that makes use of port numbers, which are, in effect, another set of addresses that are local to each machine. Many of these ports are associated with particular services (e.g., Web servers listen by default on port 80), while others are assigned on demand. Because each data flow has not only an address but also a port associated with it, a single global address and group of ports can be mapped to a set of individual local addresses and single ports. When NATs perform this port-number multiplexing, a smaller set of global addresses is able to serve a larger number of machines with local addresses.[1]

---

[1]For an overview of NATs and a more in-depth discussion of the technical nuances, see P. Srisuresh and M. Holdrege, eds. 1999. *IP Network Translator (NAT) Terminology and Considerations*, RFC 2663. Internet Engineering Task Force. Available online from <http://www.ietf.org/rfc/rfc2663.txt>.

---

manager great latitude in assigning addresses because he or she need not worry about doing so in an efficient manner, unless the private network is so large as to push up against the limit set by the size of the private address blocks. The expectation was that NAT use would be a short-term phenomenon that would be obviated by the deployment of a next-generation Internet Protocol, IPv6. But NAT had an unintended side effect—the explosion of private addressing. This widespread use had the effect of letting the wind out of IPv6's sails, as the perception of crisis requiring a wholesale replacement of the Internet Protocol faded. Instead, it began to be debated whether IPv4 needs to be replaced at all.

Efforts to improve the aggregation of addressing notwithstanding, the number of address blocks that must be stored in the core routers of the Internet can be expected to continue to grow, suggesting that new approaches to routing may be important in the future. Specific problems that deserve exploration include modifications to the current global routing scheme (Border Gateway Protocol, or BGP) to better support controlled peering. Further, while there is by no means consensus within the Internet community on this point, there are some who view routing concerns as stemming fundamentally from the approach taken in today's interdomain routing protocol, BGP4. Routing in BGP depends on each backbone or backbone node having a complete and fairly precise picture of the Internet. As the Internet grows, this need to have complete knowledge of the system presents scaling problems. Many other complex problems, such as ambulance routing, airplane routing, and chess games, have been solved using an approach where in place of complete knowledge, one starts things off in the right general direction, looks ahead a limited distance at each step, and keeps adjusting as the objective comes nearer. Such algorithms have much better scaling properties in very large, complex systems than complete-knowledge approaches.

Running Out of Addresses?

In addition to scaling issues raised by constraints on the structure of addresses and their allocation, there exist concerns about running out of numbers altogether. The present Internet protocol, IPv4, provides 32-bit-long addresses, which translates into an address "space" of about 4.3 billion unique addresses. For historical reasons, about seven-eighths of this address space is available for use as addresses for connecting devices to the Internet; the remainder is reserved for multicast and experimental addresses. While more than 4 billion addresses was considered more than sufficient in the Internet's early days, widespread Internet adoption means that this seemingly large number is becoming a constraint. There is evidence today of pressures on the address space, but using this evidence to predict long-term trends is difficult. Clearly, while there has been no crisis thus far, there is still considerable risk associated with exhausting the IPv4 address space, particularly over the longer term. But just how long is "long term"? Estimates vary wildly, from "never" to 10 to 20 years to as few as 2 or 3.

Estimating Address Use and Demand

How much of the IPv4 address space is used? Huitema reports that about half of the address space has now been allocated by the address registries, which along with the rate of address allocation, suggests that exhaustion is relatively near.[19] However, not all the addresses that have been allocated are in active use. Another measure is the sum of the size of all the blocks of addresses (addresses with a common prefix) that are made known ("advertised," in Internet lingo) through BGP to the routers that lie within the core of the network. NLANR reports that 22 percent of the address space is advertised in BGP. This number is smaller than the allocation figure would indicate, reflecting the fact that not all allocated addresses are in use. The NLANR data also indicate relatively rapid consumption: the advertised address space increased by roughly 6 percent from November 1997 to May 1999.[20] Interpretation of these data is further complicated because not all the addresses that are advertised are actually assigned to an active host. A provider using an address block for a set of devices will generally advertise the whole block (since there is no cost to it in doing so, and doing otherwise would result in many more routing table entries) and then assign the unused addresses from the block as necessary. In most cases, ISPs do not reveal whether they have many or few unused addresses in their active blocks, an uncertainty that confounds determination of the immediacy of address space pressures.[21]

The advertised address space reported by NLANR is sufficient to address over 960 million hosts. How does this figure compare to what we can learn from other sources of information about the number of Internet users and computers attached to the Internet?   The Computer Industry Almanac estimates that in the year 2000 there are about 580 million computers in use worldwide. [22] If all of the 580 million deployed computers were attached to the Internet all the time, we would surely exhaust at least the advertised addresses. This is because the addresses are allocated in a hierarchical fashion, in fairly large blocks. Each computer must therefore be assigned an address from a block associated with the part of the Internet it is attached to, so that not all 960 million addresses could, in practice, be used.

Data on computers attached to the Internet suggest a much smaller number. Estimates from Telcordia's Netsizer project, for example, are

[19]Christian Huitema. 1999. *Evaluating the Size of the Internet*. Technical Report, Telcordia. Available online at <ftp://ftp.telcordia.com/pub/huitema/stats/global.html>.

[20]National Laboratory for Applied Network Research (NLANR). 1999. *18 Months in the Routing Life of the Internet*. Technical Report, Measurement and Network Analysis team, NLANR. University of California at San Diego, May 27. Available online at <http://moat.nlanr.net/IPaddrocc/18monthSequel/>.

[21]For an examination of the inherent inefficiencies in addressing, see C. Huitema. 1994. *The H Ratio for Address Assignment Efficiency*, RFC 1715. Internet Engineering Task Force. Available online at <http://www.ietf.org/rfc/rfc1715.txt>.

[22]Data obtained from <http://www.c-i-a.com/>.

that there were more than 86 million active Internet hosts[23] in July 2000. The Internet Software Consortium estimates that there were over 72 million hosts in January 2000 (the Telcordia data show a slightly smaller number for that date).[24] If these numbers are accurate, fewer than 10 percent of the addresses within the advertised blocks are actually in use today, suggesting that pressures are, on average, not as great as one might conclude based on other measures.

Another relevant piece of information is the number of Internet users. According to Nua Internet Surveys, there were an estimated 332 million users online as of June 2000.[25] Today this number exceeds the number of active Internet hosts. If each of these users were to have an active connection to the Internet, the resulting consumption of addresses would be a significant issue.   The ratio of users to hosts today is greater than 1, reflecting the fact that not all computers are attached to the Internet at any given time (especially dial-up connections) and that many computers are shared by more than one individual, particularly in the developing world. However, both of these factors are likely to lessen with time, and it is reasonable to project that in the long run the ratio of users to hosts will drop below 1, meaning that there will be more hosts than users.

Latent demand further complicates the prediction of address consumption rates. Available data reflect the outcome of the present address allocation regime, in which addresses are tightly rationed for fear of depleting the address space. Consequently, the address consumption statistics, even to the extent that they are accurate, do not reflect the actual demand for addresses. Nor do they reflect the degree of hardship experienced by customers as a result of this rationing. Unique addresses would probably be more widely used if they were not so tightly rationed, but how much more widely is a matter of speculation.

A further challenge is that today's rate of consumption may greatly underestimate demand in the future. One source of potentially large growth is the predicted emergence of many new IP devices.[26] For example, it is reasonable to assume that within a few years individuals who currently have one or two IP-addressable devices will have five or ten

---

[23]Data obtained from <http://www.netsizer.com/daily.html>.

[24]Data obtained from <http://www.isc.org/ds/WWW-9907/report.html>.

[25]Data from <http://www.nua.ie/surveys/how_many_online/index.html>.

[26]Various forecasts project that the number of such networked devices will vastly exceed the number of individual Internet users within the next decade. See, for example, Frank Gens. 1998. *Death of the PC-Centric Era*, International Data Corporation (IDC) Executive Insights, Technical report. Framingham, Mass.: IDC. Abstract available online at <http://www.itresearch.com/alfatst4.nsf/UNITABSX/W16276?OpenDocument>.

(considering pagers, phones, PDAs, etc.). The need for IP-addressability will also increasingly extend beyond human-held and -operated devices, to devices that are embedded in our physical infrastructures. While nationwide deployment of such systems would take many years, the next 3 to 5 years could see explosive growth of this sort of instrumented environment in office buildings, factories, hospitals, etc.[27] In the longer term (beyond 5 to 10 years), the size of the realizable devices will continue to decrease to the point where we might have hundreds or thousands of devices per person. Some will be freestanding devices while others will be embedded in the user's environment.

Current research and development efforts on the part of government and industry are addressing a number of technical issues such as power consumption and wireless communication; progress on these issues will help propel deployment of new networked devices. The IEEE 802.11 standard for wireless local area networks and other efforts to standardize physical layer communications are evidence of the readiness of the technology and market.

Not all devices need to be individually and globally addressable and not all IP addresses in use are public (i.e., visible in the global address space). These private address spaces are used for a variety of reasons, including reducing the number of public addresses required and enhancing security.[28] In many instances where the system is "closed"—such as when a number of computers operate elements of a manufacturing facility—it may be perfectly adequate to give individual devices local, network-specific addresses. Data transfer into and out of a system or facility can be mediated by a special computer that acts as a gateway or external interface between a group of computers and the outside network.

The number of computers currently assigned private addresses could be a significant factor in estimating future demand for global addresses. Many provide access to the Internet in some way, but most often through a private address space indirectly attached to the Internet. Because any device with a private IP address may, with appropriate modifications to a network's connectivity to the public Internet, be connected to the Internet,

---

[27]More examples of possible applications and environments: medical (operating rooms, hospital beds, injected in-body monitoring), scientific (environmental monitoring, physiological data collection), office and home (tracking and coordinating people and objects, implementing sophisticated security systems), and industrial (factory floors, hazardous operations, distributed robotics).

[28]The security afforded by NAT is limited. In particular, it suffers from all of the limitations associated with perimeter defensive measures, as discussed later in the chapter.

its owner may at any time seek an address for it on the public Internet. This latent demand is found in home networks as well as the networks of large organizations. In the home, some users today share a single provider-supplied IP address among multiple home devices using NAT running on a home gateway (which may be in the form of software running on one of the computers in the home).[29]   However, many computers will be used in applications that require devices to be capable of external interrogation in a flexible manner and thus not via explicitly configured gateways—meaning that they will need to be assigned unique global IP addresses.

International Pressures for Addresses

Address availability and consumption rates are not uniform from country to country. Demand from regions of the world where Internet use can be expected to continue to grow steeply—not surprisingly, these are often places that historically have not had many computers connected to the Internet—could rapidly exhaust their existing global address space allocations. Forecasts for the next decade suggest, for example, that although there are relatively few computers and users in China today, by the end of this decade that country may have more computers and users on the Internet than the United States.[30] The present disparity in address allocation is illustrated by the observation that a number of organizations and businesses, including several U.S. universities, were each allocated 2^{24}, or 16,777,216, addresses many years ago under a different regime (about 40 class A networks were allocated that way), whereas the 1.3 billion people in China have far fewer. Because of the shortage of addresses, Stanford University undertook a project, completed on May 1, 2000, to consolidate its use of addressees for its roughly 56,000 computers and return the more than 15-million-address block for reassignment by

---

[29]IP address scarcity as seen by home users is not just a reflection of an overall shortage of addresses. Many ISPs restrict residential customers to a single IP address on the assumption that a site that needs more than one address is really a commercial site, for which a higher rate can be charged.

[30]For example, a 1999 study from BDA (China Ltd.) and the Strategis Group projects that total Internet users in China could exceed 33 million by the end of 2003. (See PRC Information Technology Review. 1999. "Internet Users in China to Reach 33 Million by 2003." 1(26), July 2.) More recently, the Boston Consulting Group forecast that, based on projected growth of 25 to 35 percent per year, the number of Internet users in Asia is likely to grow more than fivefold, to nearly 375 million, by 2005. (See Agence France Presse. 1999. "China to Propel Asian Internet Users to 375 Million in 2005." November 2.)

the organization that allocates addresses in North America.[31] The comparison between addresses assigned to these organizations and China provides an extreme example of the dominant factor behind these allocation disparities—address assignments reflect needs that the requesting organization has been able to substantiate on the basis of current use or through credible projections of future needs and reflect the overall availability of addresses at the time that the assignment is made.

Network Address Translation

As described above, CIDR and NAT were adopted to alleviate address scaling-related challenges. In addition to offering capabilities for local address management, NAT enables reuse of global addresses. The technology is widely employed and is included in a number of current and planned operating system releases.[32] Not just a technology used by larger organizations, NAT is being used in home and small office networks to allow a single IP address connection (e.g., through a dial-up, DSL, or cable modem connection) to be shared by multiple computers on the home network.

However, the NAT approach has significant shortcomings. To start with, the growing support for NAT and NAT-like facilities delivers the wrong message to anyone trying to resolve the address space shortage by deploying IPv6 technology rather than NAT. NAT is viewed by many as a rather ugly, simplistic fix that is cheaper to deploy (something that might be referred to as a "kludge") than an architectural model backed by long-term analysis. NAT devices, which are computers where large numbers of data streams come through in one place, also are attractive targets for man-in-the-middle attacks that can listen in on or redirect communications. NAT is also not a satisfactory solution for some very large networks because the size of the address blocks designated for use in private networks (i.e., blocks of IPv4 addresses that are not allocated for global addresses) is finite. These blocks would be, for instance, too small to permit an ISP to provide unique addresses for each of potentially tens of millions of customers (e.g., set-top boxes or wireless Internet phones), although some ISPs, such as China's UNINET, have been forced to make

---

[31]See Networking Systems Staff. 2000. *IP Address Changes at Stanford*. Stanford University. Available online at <http://www.stanford.edu/group/networking/ipchange/> and Carolyn Duffy Marsan. 2000. "Stanford Move Rekindles 'Net Address Debate.'" *Network World*, January 24. Available online at <http://www.nwfusion.com/news/2000/012ipv4.html>.

[32]For example, both Windows 98 SE (as part of the Internet connection software) and Windows 2000 include NAT functionality.

use of NATs to cope with address shortages. As an architectural approach, NATs are seen by some as self-contradictory. NATs have the advantage that they provide some degree of security by hiding private addresses behind the address translator, but the protection afforded is limited. Another difficulty with the model is that it presumes that the Internet is limited in design to a finite set of edge domains surrounding a single core network, each of which contains a number of machines sitting behind a NAT. This model is inadequate because there are, in fact, many parts to the Internet core.

Another difficulty is that because NAT requires devices to in effect have two addresses—the external address (and port number) seen by the global Internet and the internal address (and port number) used to connect to the device within the local network—it breaks the transparency of the network. This difficulty is discussed in detail in Chapter 3; the essential point is that globally unique addresses are an important design attribute of the Internet and that applications are supposed to be able to rely on them without any knowledge of the details of the network between source and destination. If a NAT is being employed, the address the device knows about (the local address) will differ from the address by which the device is known in the global Internet (the external address). Also, the mapping between local and external address is dynamic, depending on the actions of the NAT.

IPv6: A Potential Solution to Addressing and Configuration

The specter of an address shortage drove the development of IPv6, a recommended follow-on to today's IPv4 protocol. The Internet Engineering Task Force (IETF) produced specifications[33] defining a next-generation IP protocol known variously as "IPng," "IP Version 6," or "IPv6." IPv6 was designed to improve on the existing IPv4 implementation, tackling the IP address depletion problem as well as a variety of other issues. Its major goals were the following:

- Expand addressing capabilities, eliminating the IP address depletion problem;
- Incorporate quality-of-service capabilities, particularly for real-time data;
- Reduce the processing time required to handle the "typical" packet and limit the bandwidth cost of the IPv6 packet header;

---

[33]S. Deering and R. Hinden. 1998. *Internet Protocol, Version 6 (IPv6) Specification.* RFC 2460. December. Available online from <http://www.ietf.org/rfc/rfc2460.txt>.

• Provide routing improvements through address autoconfiguration, reduced routing table sizes, and a simplified protocol to allow routers to process packets faster;
• Provide privacy and security at the network layer supporting authentication, data integrity, and data confidentiality;
• Improve network management and policy routing capabilities;
• Allow a transition phase by permitting the old (IPv4) and new protocol to coexist;
• Allow the protocol to evolve further by imposing less stringent limits on the length of options and providing greater flexibility for introducing new options in the future; and
• Improve the ability of the network manager to autoconfigure and manage the network.

The request for proposals for a next-generation Internet Protocol was released in July 1992, and seven responses, which ranged from making minor patches to IP to replacing it completely with a different protocol, had been received by year's end. Eventually, a combination of two of the proposals was selected and given the designation IPv6. The essential improvement offered by the new protocol is the expanded address. It is 16 bytes long with 61 bits allocated to the network address, compared to the 32 bits provided by IPv4. IPv6 addresses support billions of billions of hosts, even with inefficient address space allocation.

The new standard offered a number of additional features, including the following:

• *Increased efficiency and flexibility.* Some IPv4 header fields were dropped, so that the header now contains only 7 mandatory fields as opposed to the 13 required in IPv4. IPv6 also offers improved support for extensions and options.
• *Enhanced autoconfiguration.* IPv6 offers improved autoconfiguration or negotiation of certain kinds of addresses. Possible approaches include (1) using the Ethernet or other media address as the "host selector" part of an address otherwise learned from the local router, (2) procedures for creating local addresses on point-to-point links, and (3) improvements to the Dynamic Host Configuration Protocol (DHCP) that may allow partial autoconfiguration of routers.[34]

---

[34]Recently, there have been concerns that using a unique identifier as part of the IPv6 address would facilitate the tracking of users on the networks and could therefore pose a privacy risk. This risk is in fact inherent in any system where the connection to the Internet is always "on," a characteristic of most broadband services. This concern, while widely expressed, is not necessarily valid; there exist ways to limit the ability to isolate addresses

- *Enhanced support for quality of service (QOS)*. QOS functionality is potentially enhanced through the addition of a new traffic-flow identification field. QOS products based on this flow identifier are still in the planning stage.

Deploying an IPv6 Solution

The technical viability of IPv6 has been demonstrated by a number of implementations of IPv6 host and router software as well as the establishment of a worldwide IPv6 testing and preproduction deployment network called the 6BONE, which reaches hundreds of academic and commercial sites worldwide. However, to date, IPv6 has not seen significant deployment and use. This is not a surprise; IPv4 has been adopted by a very large number of users, and there are significant costs associated with a transition to IPv6. Reflecting their perception that the gain for switching to IPv6 is not sufficient to justify the pain of the switch, customers have not expressed much willingness to pay for it, and equipment vendors and service providers are for the most part not yet providing it. An important exception is the planned use of IPv6 for the so-called third-generation wireless devices now being developed as successors to present mobile telephone systems.[35]

For many, the devil they know is better than the one they don't know. Until an address shortage appears imminent, incremental steps—restrictions on address growth or use, or the use of NATs or some other (painful but understood) kludge—will appear less painful than switching to IPv6. Indeed, some believe that address exhaustion is not a problem meriting deployment of a new solution, arguing that CIDR makes the Internet's core a stable enough addressing domain that private address spaces around the periphery of that domain can effectively serve demands for the foreseeable future. On the other hand, as discussed in the previous section, this approach could have serious drawbacks: an Internet in which NATs become pervasive is an Internet in which the assumption of transparency no longer holds (see Chapter 3 for more on this issue). Moreover,

---

to machines, and since many machines are used by more than one person, the identifier doesn't track back to a person. Full protection requires the use of explicit services, such as anonymizing relays. The specific IPv6 problem has been addressed by the IETF, which has devised a way to derive the address from the unique identifier without exposing the identifier itself.

[35]See, e.g., Nokia. 2000. *Nokia Successfully Drives Forward IPv6 As the Protocol for Future 3G Networks*. Press release, May 26. Available online at <http://press.nokia.com/PM/782371.html>.

it ignores the needs of potentially large consumers for address space for devices such as IP-based mobile telephones.

Transition to IPv6 requires the development and deployment of new networking software (Internet Protocol stacks) on all the devices that are connected to networks running IPv6, updated software (and even hardware) in routers within these networks, and translation gateways between networks running IPv4 and IPv6. Also, many applications running on computers connected to IPv6 networks will probably also need to be adapted to use the longer address. Desktop support alone is not enough to trigger industry adoption, because IPv6 is not something that can take place as a result of actions taken at the edges of the network alone.[36] Implementations of many of the requisite elements exist today; the hurdle is largely not one of developing the required technology but of making the investments needed to deploy it.

There are various strategies by which IPv6 could be deployed. No one believes that a scheduled, "flag-day" transition would be effective, given the absence of incentives for players to comply and, worse still, the prospect that an abrupt shift to IPv6 could go awry catastrophically. (No one in the industry wants to wake up to news reports like "Major ISP Backbone Melts After Messing with IPv6.") The difficulty of making a switch has long been recognized, along with the idea that deployment will need to be incremental. Transition is complicated because an IPv4-only system cannot communicate directly with an IPv6 system, meaning that either the IPv6 device must also speak IPv4 or it must have a translator. A transition period is foreseen in which IPv4/IPv6 translators (somewhat like NATs) sit between systems running different protocol versions, enabling a piecemeal deployment of IPv6 from the Internet's edge toward its core, and a model known as "6 to 4" is emerging in which every IPv4 site automatically inherits an IPv6 prefix with the IPv6 traffic encapsulated in IPv4.

Finally, it should be noted that many of the addressing issues discussed here arise, in part, from routing scaling considerations. CIDR was a measure to control the number of routes that a router must remember. It assigns addresses in a hierarchical manner that forces them to be assigned in blocks (and also forces most Internet subscribers to obtain their addresses from their ISP). It is, however, viewed as a burden for the subscriber, because it means that to switch from one ISP to another, it is necessary to renumber all the attached machines. With NAT, this is not an issue, because subscriber machines are assigned private addresses,

---

[36]Another example of this is multicast, which, although it is supported in major operating systems such as Windows, is not widely used.

and only the single addresses of the NAT boxes need to be changed, a much smaller number. However, if IPv6 were to be deployed and all machines were to revert to the original architectural model of globally unique, public addresses, this problem would resurface on a large scale. While it would not be fully automatic, IPv6 would provide for much simpler renumbering. Still, while the current situation is generally adequate, the difficulties associated with assignment and renumbering suggest that continued research on new approaches to addressing and routing would be worthwhile.

RELIABILITY AND ROBUSTNESS

The proliferation of devices and applications discussed above is symptomatic of growing use and an expectation that the Internet can be depended on. This expectation translates into a requirement for greater reliability, robustness, and predictability. As more and more critical functions are moved to the Internet, there is increasing pressure for reliable and continuous service, even when things go wrong. As the uses of the Internet expand, the stakes—and thus the visibility of reliability and robustness concerns—will rise.

There are also public safety considerations, some of which will derive from expectations associated with conventional telephony; telephone users expect a high level of availability for normal calling and demand availability for making emergency (911) calls. It is reasonable to assume that such expectations—including, for instance, the capability for automatically notifying authorities of the geographical location of a 911 caller—will transfer to Internet telephony services. As Internet use becomes more widespread, it is conceivable, or even likely, that other, new life-critical applications will emerge. For example, Internet-connected appliances could be used to monitor medical conditions, e.g., remote EKG monitoring.[37]

Concerns about the Internet's robustness and vulnerability to attack are reflected in the attention given to these matters by the national security/emergency preparedness (NS/EP) community. This community traditionally relied on the PSTN for 911 emergency services and priority restoration and service delivery during designated crises. It promulgates guidelines that are then codified in regulations and builds on years of experience and personnel training as well as the cost structures of regu-

---

[37]Computer Science and Telecommunications Board (CSTB), National Research Council (NRC). 2000. *Networking Health: Prescriptions for the Internet.* Washington, D.C.: National Academy Press.

lated telephony. NS/EP organizations, with public and private sector elements, have expanded their missions and compositions to embrace nontelephony service providers and the Internet, and they have begun to study and make recommendations regarding the Internet's robustness.[38] Discussions between the NS/EP community and ISPs are in their early stages, and what form any agreements between the two would take remains to be seen.

Designing for Robustness and Reliability

While the terms are often used interchangeably, reliability, robustness, and predictability refer to different aspects of the communications service. *Robustness* refers to the ability of a system to continue to provide service even under stress (e.g., if some of the system's components or capabilities are lost to failure or it is subject to malicious attack.) A robust system is, essentially, one that is not subject to catastrophic collapse; instead, it degrades gracefully, providing the level of service that would be expected from the available resources. *Reliability* is a measure of whether a system provides the expected level of service For example, a system designed for 99.999 percent reliability would fail not more than 5 minutes per year. Reliability is typically achieved by the combination of component reliability, component redundancy, and a robust system design. An important distinction between robustness and reliability is that while a robust system typically provides a reliable service, a reliable system need not be robust. For example, many companies run certain vital functions on a single computer that is very well maintained. This computer and its services are reliable (because the system is carefully maintained, the service is almost always available) but they would not be considered robust (if the computer fails, the service is not available). *Predictability* refers to the user's expectations about the availability and quality of service routinely being met. While a service can, in theory, be predictably poor (e.g., telephone service in some developing countries), when most users speak of a predictable service they mean a reliable service whose occasional periods of degraded service can be anticipated (e.g., the difficulty of making long-distance phone calls on Mother's Day due to the volume of calls).

The Internet's design is based on a world view different from that of the PSTN on how to provide the qualities of reliability, robustness, and predictability. The choice to base the Internet on richly interconnected

---

[38]See, for example, National Security Telecommunications Advisory Committee (NSTAC). 1999. *Network Group Internet Report: An Examination of the NS/EP Implications of Internet Technologies.* Washington, D.C.: NSTAC.

components stems from two observations that have their origins in research in the early 1960s.[39]   First, although the PSTN depends on the reliability of its components, neither the overall system nor any of its components are perfectly reliable.   Second, with the right design, the reliability of a network does not depend on all its components working; it only requires that there are enough working components to connect any two end points.   Each component is itself reasonably reliable, but the design relies on the network's ability to adapt, i.e., to reconfigure itself when a component fails so as to make efficient use of the remaining components.   Consequently, it is able to recover from local outages of components by simply requiring the computers communicating across it to retransmit the messages that were in transit at the time of the failure. The result is a robust service built of components that are far less reliable than those of the PSTN.

In contrast, the PSTN's design emphasizes building a network out of highly reliable components and using them reasonably well.   The PSTN achieves its reliability in part by working very hard to make sure that every important component of the PSTN is, in and of itself, reliable.   The result is a system that may not be robust in all circumstances, because if a critical component of the PSTN fails, the system fails.   Typically these failures are minor (e.g., a few phone calls get prematurely disconnected) but some can be spectacular (e.g., the multiday loss of phone service as a result of a fire at a central office in Hinsdale, Illinois, in 1990).   Also, in the PSTN the viability of a given call is viewed as secondary to the reliability of the total infrastructure—individual calls need not be reliable in an infrastructure failure. Rather, user applications are required to be robust in the presence of failure, and the PSTN concerns itself with restoring service quickly when an outage occurs so that the application can restart. Following service restoration, applications restart—the caller places a new call, and interrupted file transfers restart from the beginning or from a saved checkpoint.   Any resource optimization that might result from dynamic rerouting is viewed as secondary to the predictability of the call itself.   The routing path for a connection through the PSTN is established at call time; this routing does not change during the life of a call.

While the Internet is sometimes unreliable, it generally operates as the underlying design presumed it would.   There are a number of reasons why the Internet is viewed as unreliable despite its robust design; the discussion below outlines several of these as well as possible remedies.

---

[39]See, for example, Leonard Kleinrock. 1964. *Communication Nets: Stochastic Message Flow and Delay.* New York: McGraw-Hill.

Vulnerability of the Internet to Attack

There is increasing concern about deliberate attempts to sabotage the operation of the Internet. Recent reports, including the 1999 CSTB report *Trust in Cyberspace*[40] and a National Security Telecommunications Advisory Committee report,[41] identified a number of vulnerabilities of the Internet (as well as of the PSTN). These vulnerabilities are associated with failures of hardware and software as well as the system's susceptibility to malicious attack. Indeed, there are a number of points of potential massive vulnerability in today's Internet, including the integrity of the addresses being routed, the integrity of the routing system, the integrity of the domain name system, and the integrity of the end-to-end application communication (Box 2.3).

Considerable attention has been devoted to the Internet as part of the late-1990s examination of the nation's critical infrastructure. In 1997, the President's Commission for Critical Infrastructure Protection issued a report[42] highlighting concerns about the vulnerability of several infrastructure sectors, including information and communications; it found both a growing dependence on and vulnerability associated with such infrastructures. The next year, 1998, saw the issuance of Presidential Decision Directive 63, which focuses on protecting critical infrastructure against both physical and cyber attack, and the establishment of a National Infrastructure Protection Center, located in the Department of Justice, which is indicative of law enforcement's growing attention to the problem of malicious attacks on infrastructure, including the Internet.

The network also threatens the security of users because it can serve as the conduit for a variety of attacks against their systems. Various forms of attack exploit weaknesses in end-user systems, allowing an unauthorized attacker to read or manipulate information in the systems. Some attacks involve breaking into a system for the purpose of obtaining or modifying its data. Fraudulent entries might be made in accounting files, pictures on Web pages might be replaced with others that the attacker finds humorous, or sensitive information might be accessed. Or, an attack might simply overwrite (destroy) data. A man-in-the-middle

---

[40]Computer Science and Telecommunications Board (CSTB), National Research Council. 1999. *Trust in Cyberspace*. Washington, D.C.: National Academy Press.

[41]National Security Telecommunications Advisory Committee (NSTAC). 1999. *Network Group Internet Report: An Examination of the NS/EP Implications of Internet Technologies*. Washington, D.C.: NSTAC, June.

[42]President's Commission for Critical Infrastructure Protection (PCCIP). 1997. *Critical Foundations: Protecting America's Infrastructures*. Washington, D.C.: PCCIP. Available online at <http://www.pccip.ncr.gov/report_index.html>.

attack does the same thing from the vantage point of some intermediate system that has access at some point between the sender and receiver (e.g., a router or gateway). Other attacks do not target the data but attack the resources for its transport—a denial-of-service attack might be implemented simply by filling a communications link with junk messages, consuming much or all of the available bandwidth, thereby slowing or denying its intended use. Attacks can be launched against the systems or networks of particular ISPs or end users or more broadly against the Internet's infrastructure.[43] The Internet also serves as a conduit for the rapid transmission of viruses—computer code that can alter or destroy data in computer systems—which are readily attached to files and sent by e-mail to users of a network.[44] As new viruses continue to be invented and distributed, techniques for detecting and mitigating their effects must be developed as well.

The threat posed by Internet vulnerabilities is magnified by several coincident developments. Tools to exploit Internet vulnerabilities are readily disseminated. They can be distributed to a large number of technically unsophisticated users, some of whom may not even be aware of the implications of using them. Also, as an increasing number of users access the Internet through broadband services, their machines become platforms for launching attacks, such as denial of service, that are more effective when the attacker has a high-speed connection to the Internet. (This is somewhat compensated for by the even greater speed used by ISPs and large servers, which renders saturation attacks more difficult simply because it is harder to completely congest the target computer's communications link.) At the same time, the always-on systems of broadband users become targets for attackers and may be captured and used, unbeknownst to their owners, as relays for further attacks on the network. In such an environment, ISPs have to take steps to protect their own networks as well as the customers connected to it. The types of attacks discussed here are varied; while those who conduct the attacks may be unsophisticated, those who develop the capabilities are resourceful and creative.

While a number of measures can be implemented within the network

---

[43]For example, the routing infrastructure itself might be attacked by hijacking a TCP connection or inserting incorrect routing information into the system. Or, the name service infrastructure could be attacked on a global basis by launching a denial of service against the Domain Name System's root computers.

[44]In 2000, several viruses disseminated as e-mail attachments spread widely and received a great deal of media attention. Most prominent was the "I Love You" virus, which spread by exploiting a vulnerability in the Microsoft Outlook e-mail software.

BOX 2.3 Internet Vulnerabilities

A recent Computer Science and Telecommunications Board report, *Trust in Cyberspace*,[1] examined vulnerabilities associated with the Internet. These fell into several categories: link failures, congestion, operational errors, software and hardware failures, and malicious attacks. A 1999 report by the National Security Telecommunications Advisory Committee (NSTAC) also examined the vulnerabilities in the context of relying on the Internet for national security/emergency preparedness activities.[2] The following compilation is drawn primarily from the CSTB report, supplemented by the NSTAC report:

• *Link failures.* Link failures, most commonly caused by damage to buried cables by construction crews, have been cited as the biggest cause of public telephone network outages;[3] they also have implications for Internet reliability. The Internet was in fact specifically designed to tolerate this sort of component failure; routing by its very nature seeks out alternative paths. In practice, however, the ability to respond is limited. There simply may not be enough capacity elsewhere in the network to carry the traffic. Also, routing may not adapt quickly enough to prevent packet loss or delays in packet delivery. To prevent instabilities and oscillations that might occur in the event of transient failures, routing algorithms are designed to not respond immediately to reports of communication link failures. In addition, to provide increased stability, particularly in the face of possible attacks or configuration errors by other network operators, ISPs may rely on static configuration of major routes across network boundaries. These require explicit intervention to respond to some link failures.

• *Congestion.* Congestion may be just a result of increased demand or it may be a result of failures elsewhere in a network or service denial attacks such as traffic flooding. The Internet is not able to manage information associated with

---

[1]Computer Science and Telecommunications Board (CSTB), National Research Council (NRC). 1999. *Trust in Cyberspace.* Washington, D.C.: National Academy Press.

[2]National Security Telecommunications Advisory Committee (NSTAC). 1999. *Network Group Internet Report: An Examination of the NS/EP Implications of Internet Technologies.* Washington, D.C.: NSTAC, June.

[3]Network Reliability and Interoperability Council (NRIC). 1997. Final Report of the Network Reliability and Interoperability Council. Washington, D.C.: Federal Communications Commission, July 15.

---

to enhance robustness, the Internet's architecture, in which service definition is pushed to the end systems connected to the network, requires many security issues to be addressed at the edges of the network. Both the performance of individual applications and services and the overall integrity of the network are therefore placed in the hands of these end systems. As more and more end systems with widely varying degrees of trustworthiness are added to the network, the more tenuous the assump-

specific users, connections, and sources/destinations. Routers, which are not designed to capture such information, can only resort to queuing, marking, or discarding packets when their buffers start to fill; the network relies on mechanisms such as TCP by which the sender and receiver adapt on an end-to-end basis to congestion within the network. Thus, applications that do not behave in this fashion, whether for performance or malicious reasons, can create persistent congestion.

• *Operational errors.* Like other complex systems, the Internet is subject to a variety of operational errors. *Trust in Cyberspace* cites a number of examples of operational errors that have occurred in the Internet, including errors in storing information in DNS databases and routing tables.

• *Software and hardware failures.* Data about failures due to router outages do not seem to have been collected. What can be said, according to *Trust in Cyberspace*, is that devices at the edges, which are generally ordinary computers running commercial operating systems, are the most vulnerable. On the hardware side, one major issue is the availability of electrical power. Many parts of the Internet have not been designed to the same standard for robust power supplies; the PSTN, in contrast, has been engineered such that it has redundant power supplies throughout.[4] The PSTN also supplies its own power to end-user devices; a simple telephone will operate even if the local power has failed. In recent years, however, this distinction has been fading as people increasingly make use of telephone devices—cordless phones being the most common example today—that are dependent on local power, just as an Internet-connected computer would be.

• *Malicious attacks.* Malicious attacks on the Internet are facilitated by the general accessibility of the Internet, the widespread availability of both documentation and source code for Internet protocols, and failures to fix known vulnerabilities in systems. *Trust in Cyberspace* pointed to several major avenues of attack on the network infrastructure and measures to address them: name server attacks (development of new countermeasures that work in large-scale, heterogeneous environments) and deployment of cryptography to secure the DNS, attacks on the routing system (research on means to secure routing protocols), and denial-of-service attacks (wider use of updated software, new product development, and better software engineering).

---

[4]Backup power is, of course, not a panacea. Backup systems fail on occasion, and testing them has itself resulted in power failures.

tion of mutual trust becomes.   Thus, absent the adoption of new measures both within the network as well as at its edges, security violations of varying degrees of severity can be expected to continue. In particular, the dependence on end systems means that much of the security burden rests on vendors of applications and operating system software as well as on the users that configure and operate those systems.

Concerns about these issues have led to investment in research aimed at addressing some of these shortcomings. The Internet's vulnerability stems in part from the difficulty, today, of tracing the location from which attacks such as denial of service have been launched, making it difficult to identify an attacker after the fact. One approach under development aims to allow an attack to be traced, without requiring access to ISP logs, if the attack involves a lot of packets. Other research is aimed at tracing attacks without storing large amounts of information, thereby reducing the storage burden and alleviating the privacy concerns that would arise from ISPs logging of detailed information on the traffic passing over their networks.

In many cases, however, the Internet is vulnerable to attack not because there are no technologies to protect it but because they are not used, whether for lack of perceived need or lack of knowledge about such measures. Known vulnerabilities are frequently not addressed despite the promulgation of patches to fix them. Enhanced technologies such as single-use passwords, cryptographic authentication, and message digest authentication technology have been developed and are starting to see deployment. Nonetheless, many network operators do not necessarily use these capabilities to defend their systems; plain text passwords, which are readily guessed or captured, remain the authentication technique in most common use. Likewise, while many data access or modification attacks are made by insiders (people within the organization), the most commonly installed intrusion detection and prevention technology is a firewall, which by nature provides only limited defense and only protects against attacks across the perimeter they defend—the intruder who succeeds in getting inside the defense walls ends up with free run of the interior unless a defense in depth has been put in place.

Responses to these vulnerabilities have been mixed, and continued work will be required. Specifying and deploying the needed upgrades to the protocols and software used in the Internet is a complex problem. They are a result of both group development efforts and marketplace dynamics. These, in combination, determine what is developed and whether and when it is adopted and deployed. An indicator of both today's problems and prospects for future improvements is the relatively recent move by the IETF to prevent those proposing Internet standards from sidestepping analyses of security implications.[45] Within the Internet

---

[45]The September 1998 guidelines and procedures for IETF working groups state as follows: "It should be noted that all IETF working groups are required to examine and understand the security implications of any technology they develop. This analysis must be included in any resulting RFCs in a Security Considerations section. Note that merely noting a significant security hole is no longer sufficient. IETF developed technologies should not add insecurity to the environment in which they are run" (Internet Engineering Task Force (IETF). 1998. *IETF Working Group Guidelines and Procedures*, RFC 2418. IETF, p. 22. Available online from <http://www.ietf.org/rfc/rfc2418.txt>).

marketplace, progress is evident because some ISPs see robustness and service guarantees as an enticement to attract customers.

More Adaptive Routing

Improvements in robustness will become increasingly important as service-level agreements between providers and customers (including other providers) begin to specify high reliability. There is considerable debate among those who design and operate the Internet's networks about the relative priority to be attached to improving the reliability of components and to increasing the adaptive performance of the network. One approach is to make components more reliable, the argument being that this improvement, taken in combination with the Internet's current level of robustness, would yield a network potentially far more reliable than the PSTN. Another approach, which is based on the belief that engineering extremely reliable equipment is extremely expensive, is that the Internet should be able to achieve much better overall reliability with less reliable but less costly components by improving its adaptive performance.

Robustness depends on software as well as hardware, and achieving a high level of robustness, particularly when a strategy of using lower cost, less reliable hardware is adopted, depends on software and deployments that enhance the Internet's adaptability in the face of individual component failures. A principal means of adaptation is the modification of routing paths to reflect information discovered about links and routers that are not operational. Today's routing protocols were developed at a time when major links were significantly slower than they are now. Improved routing algorithms, suggested by Djikstra in 1970 but widely implemented only in the past decade (in the open shortest path first routing protocol), have improved reliability and robustness. Still, the rate at which the network adapts to failures remains fairly sluggish. Routing could, in principle, recover from failures (or incorporate newly available capacity) in tens of milliseconds, but the historically based timer settings that are found in deployed routers permit recovery only on much longer timescales of tens to hundreds of seconds—a timescale long enough to have a noticeable impact on users and to result in the failure of many individual transactions.

Why do the routing protocols have such long time constants? The basic reason is that a local routing change can, in principle, have global consequences. For example, one might have a situation in which the failure of just one link would cause significant traffic flows leaving the United States to shift from an eastward (Atlantic Ocean link) to a westward (Pacific Ocean link) path.   The circumference of the earth is approximately 40,000 kilometers, so for communication at the speed of light it takes a data packet slightly more than 0.1 seconds to go around the earth. That represents a lower bound; in practice, the time it takes a data packet to go around the earth will be substantially longer, owing to delays in the various network elements it must traverse in the Internet. Any routing protocol that takes into account the global consequences of a routing change has to adjust on a timescale longer than this roughly 0.1-second minimum; otherwise, the results of the routing computation will not be globally consistent—for example, there would be no use suddenly sending traffic via the Pacific if routing information describing what the routers located in Asia should do with the traffic has not had time to make it there yet. However, it turns out that most local link failures do not have global consequences. So if there were designs for propagating routing information that could limit the consequences of certain classes of changes, the network could respond much faster. The development of these sorts of bounded schemes would make a good class of research. Faster adaptation—whereby failure of an Internet element triggers a quick rerouting of traffic—also depends on supporting capabilities such as rapid failure detection.

To increase robustness, redundancy is also needed in the major communications links. Optical fibers, for example, are carrying growing amounts of traffic as wave division multiplexing (WDM) increases the capacity of each fiber and, accordingly, the impact if it fails. The sharing (multiplexing) of communications facilities means that it is increasingly difficult to provision physically diverse communications links between two given sites. For example, two nominally different communications links, even when obtained from different providers, may in fact run over the same fiber, in the same fiber bundle, or in the same conduit, meaning that they are both vulnerable to a single physical disruption (e.g., a backhoe inadvertently cutting a buried fiber bundle). Finally, as the next section discusses, the extent to which the Internet is able to adapt to failures depends on how the interconnections between providers are designed and implemented.

Putting It Together

The heterogeneous, multiprovider nature of the public Internet poses additional robustness challenges. The Internet is not a monolithic system, and the several thousand Internet service providers in North America range in size from large international providers to one-room companies serving a single town with dial-up service. The business demand for these operators to provide a high level of redundant facilities, constantly manned operation centers, or highly trained staff—and their ability to do so—varies considerably. Nonetheless, all these different providers, with their different goals for availability, reliability, and so on, interoperate to provide the global Internet service.

The section above described why it can be difficult to provide sufficiently diverse communications paths. Doing so is a necessary but not sufficient condition for increasing the robustness of interprovider links. Traffic cannot be routed to alternative paths if the interprovider connection agreements overly constrain the number of paths the data can follow. For example, interconnection agreements often contain provisions, aimed at preventing traffic dumping (one provider dumping traffic onto segments of another provider's network), that have the effect of permitting traffic between a particular point on one ISP's network and a point on another ISP's network to follow only one specific path. If that specified link fails, there are no alternative paths for the traffic to follow (until the failure is detected and other traffic flow arrangements are put in place).

ISPs devote considerable resources to detecting and responding to failures and attacks. Problems that cross ISP boundaries represent a particular challenge as the reliability of any one part of the Internet (and thus the reliability of the whole Internet) can depend on what happens within other ISP networks. Not all ISPs have the same level of expertise or capabilities, and one may trace a problem only to find that it originates with a provider that lacks the facilities or expertise to address it. There have been instances of failures in one ISP that have caused DNS failures, routing failures, or transmission failures in a neighboring ISP. ISPs depend on expert network operators to maintain the health of their individual networks as well as the Internet as a whole. They continue to track problems and troubleshoot on an ad hoc basis (e.g., through the informal relationships that exist among the expert network operators) and through loose coordination mechanisms (e.g., the North American Network Operators Group) in order to minimize network service outages. And industry groups such as IOPS have been convened to tackle robustness issues.

It is hoped, but is by no means certain, that better tools and methods will result in operations that are more robust. ISPs must be able to resist attacks that originate within other ISPs (e.g., foreign ISPs with perhaps unfriendly intentions) but at the same time must interconnect with other ISPs to preserve the basic transport function of the Internet. However, more structured and effective methods and tools are required for robust operation, especially to protect against intentional malicious attacks that originate in a connected ISP. The design of such protocols and methods is, however, still largely a research issue.[46]

---

[46]Computer Science and Telecommunications Board (CSTB), National Research Council. 1999. *Trust in Cyberspace.* Washington, D.C.: National Academy Press.

Application Reliability and Robustness

Given the Internet's layered architecture, responsibility for ensuring that a given application works properly is diffuse. The Internet's design allows each user to decide what applications to run over it. Because it is the software running on computers attached to the network rather than software in the routers that determines what applications can be run, the Internet service provider does not, in general, see what application the user is running and may not take specific steps to support it. A consequence is that a user who obtains software for a new application such as Internet telephony may be surprised to discover that the part of the Internet to which he or she is attached is not provisioned to satisfactorily support the application.

An application such as telephony thus raises not only the question of how to address reliability and quality across network providers but also the question of who in fact is providing the service. Telephony may be offered by an ISP or by a third party. The third party may simply offer hardware or software, in which case users would be able to set themselves up for Internet telephony on their own, without any Internet service provider being involved (or even having knowledge of how its network is being used). Or, a third party may offer services via the Internet that are related to placing calls, such as a directory service that allows one to determine the Internet device associated with a particular user and thus place a call. In this case, although a service provider can be identified, it need not have established any relationship with the Internet service providers responsible for actually serving the customer and carrying the data associated with a telephone call. In the absence of specific service arrangements made by customers or an Internet telephony provider, an Internet provider that happens to be carrying voice traffic will not in general even know that its facilities are being used for telephony. A user might then place a 911 call and discover that the ISP serving that user has not provided a robust connection to any 911 facility. This separation of Internet service from application means that, with today's Internet, one cannot assume that the robustness of an infrastructure is appropriate for the robustness of the application.

One response to a view that "telephony is telephony" (that is, no matter what technologies are used) would be to impose quality, robustness, and emergency service requirements only on the parties that specifically offer Internet telephony services. These parties would be responsible for negotiating with the Internet providers who carry traffic for them to provide an acceptable quality of service. However, this approach is not easily implemented when an application comes in the form of shrink-wrap or downloadable software that is installed by the consumer and intended to be run over whatever network the consumer subscribes to.

Another response would be to wait for market and technology developments. Mobile phones were deployed despite obvious limitations in quality and availability, and the users simply adapted their expectations. Internet applications may be introduced with similar expectations. They may then be improved over time, either because the quality of the network increases or because the application designers incorporate features to query or test the network's quality and compensate for it—a development that may or may not happen.

Robustness and Auxiliary Servers

Sometimes ISPs do make special provisions to support particular types of content or services. One popular, partial solution to scaling and quality of service issues is to distribute content servers at strategic points in the Internet. Their use raises an interesting reliability trade-off. On the one hand, as evidenced by the substantial investment in deploying caching and proxy services, such capabilities are viewed by many as an essential tool for making usable services that would otherwise be compromised by network congestion. On the other hand, the robustness concerns associated with some of these capabilities can be viewed as a good example of the principle that today's performance enhancements can become tomorrow's problems.

In some cases, the use of the servers is integrated into the application during the publishing process. Web pages are rewritten to point the user toward secondary content servers. In other cases, the caches are introduced in the form of content routers that are deployed by the ISP. The content routers, which operate outside the control of either the end user or the content provider, will typically filter packets that appear to request a Web service by looking at the TCP port numbers, and they will route these packets to the local cache server or content server regardless of the IP destination address.

Because both practices insert a set of auxiliary servers in the infrastructure, they have implications for robustness, as any failure of the servers would affect the end-to-end availability of the service. But their implications for robustness are different. When the usage of auxiliary servers is decided by the content provider at the application level, the responsibility for providing the right content and providing robust servers remains with that content provider. Wrong decisions, poor reliability of auxiliary servers, or implementation mistakes only affect the products of a specific publisher, without compromising the service experienced by other users. In contrast, a network provider that decides to intercept Web requests and to route them to its own content servers may run a greater risk, as there is no way for the content provider or end user to correct the failure of a cache server by requesting the same information from another server; by the same token, there is no way to stop the content server from modifying the information.

Toward Greater Reliability and Robustness: Reporting Outages and Failures

Overloads, failures, operator errors, and other events on occasion disrupt user activities on the Internet. Industry organizations such as NANOG[47] and IOPS[48] provide forums for the exchange of information among ISPs about both problems and solutions. Anecdotal reports (e.g., press reports and e-mail exchanges among network operators and other industry experts) provide additional information. Thus we have some indication of the sources of failure, which include the following:

- Communications links that are severed by construction workers digging near fiber-optic cables;
- Network operators that issue incorrect configuration commands;
- Inadequately tested software upgrades that cause systems to fail; and
- Deliberate attacks that are carried out on Internet systems and services.

But information on Internet failures has not been reported or analyzed on a systematic basis. From the standpoint of both customers and policy makers, more systematic Internet statistics[49] would be helpful in both appraising and improving the Internet's robustness. Also, a requirement to report problems would create pressure to increase the overall reliability of the Internet. It could also help consumers distinguish among providers with different service records and it might help providers detect recurring patterns of failures, so that the root cause could be eliminated.[50]

---

[47]See <www.nanog.org>.

[48]See <www.iops.org>.

[49]Such information was available on the NSFNET, for which Merit, Inc., collected and published statistics.

[50]For example, in the case of PSTN reliability reporting, the Network Reliability Steering Committee used the FCC-mandated data to identify construction activity resulting in damage to fiber-optic cables as the factor responsible for more than 50 percent of facility outages and, further, found that more than one-half of these occurrences were due to the failure of excavators to notify infrastructure owners or provide adequate notice before digging.

There is an important distinction between the needs of customers and the needs of those seeking to understand and eliminate problems. The performance of ISPs can be monitored by independent organizations that publish reports for subscribers or the public. A buying guide of sorts, this type of information helps a customer assess the service of the various ISPs. Independent monitoring may discover and report outages, but it does not necessarily provide access to the causal and diagnostic information that is needed to try to eliminate the root cause of problems. The latter goal requires that detailed information on failures be made available to industry groups and/or researchers.

The government has mandated problem reporting in other circumstances. Where public safety is involved, the government has imposed very strict requirements for reporting and analysis (e.g., crashes of commercial aircraft). The government has also required reporting in cases where the issue is not public safety but where a perceived need exists to help the consumer understand the service being provided. Airlines are, for example, required to track and report how late their flights are, lost baggage statistics, and the like.

The Federal Communications Commission requires outage reporting by operators of some elements of the PSTN.[51] It was motivated by concerns that it did not have the means to systematically monitor significant telephone outages on a timely basis, as well as a more general interest in seeing that information on vulnerabilities is shared. A series of major service outages in interexchange and local exchange carrier networks in the early 1990s underscored the need to obtain information that would improve reliability. Under these rules, outages of more than a specified level of severity (duration, number of subscribers affected, etc.) must be publicly documented.[52] For example, service outages that significantly degrade the ability of more than 30,000 customers to place a call for more than 30 minutes must be reported.[53]

---

[51]See FCC Common Carrier Docket No. 91-273, paragraphs 4 and 32 (February 27, 1992), as cited in Network Reliability and Interoperability Council (NRIC). 1997. *Network Interoperability: The Key to Competition.* Washington, D.C.: NRIC, Federal Communications Commission federal advisory committee, p. 12.

[52]47 C.F.R. Section 63.100 sets mandatory reporting thresholds for wireline telephone companies. The requirements are based on the type of outage, the number of affected subscribers, and the duration of the failure.

[53]See Network Reliability and Interoperability Council (NRIC). 1997. *Network Interoperability: The Key to Competition.* Washington, D.C.: NRIC, Federal Communications Commission federal advisory committee, p. 11. Available online at <http://www.nric.org/pubs/nric3/reportj9.pdf>.

Changes in the telecommunications industry led the FCC, in 1998, to ask the Network Reliability and Interoperability Council (NRIC) IV to explore reliability concerns in the wider set of networks (e.g., telephone, cable, satellite, and data, including the Internet) that the PSTN is part of. The report of the NRIC IV subcommittee looking at needs for data on service outages[54] called for a trial period of outage reporting. NRIC V, chartered in 2000, has initiated a 1-year voluntary trial starting in September 2000 and will monitor the process, analyze the data obtained from the trial, and report on how well the process works.[55]

ISPs are not, at present, mandated to release such information. Indeed, the release of this type of information is frequently subject to the terms of private agreements between providers. This situation is not surprising, given the absence of regulation of the Internet and the high degree of regulation of the telephone industry. As the Internet becomes an increasingly important component of our society, there will probably be calls to require reporting on overall reliability and specific disruptions. It is not now clear what metrics should be used and what events should be reported, what the balance between costs and benefits would be for different types of reporting, or what the least burdensome approach to this matter would be. One response to rising expectations would be for Internet providers to work among themselves to define an industry approach to reporting. Doing so could have two benefits—it might provide information useful to the industry and it might avoid government imposition of an even-less-welcome plan.

As noted above, one important reason for gathering information on disruptions is to provide researchers with the means to discover the root causes of such problems. For this to be effective, outage data must be available to researchers outside the ISPs; ISPs do not generally have research laboratories and are not necessarily well placed to carry out much of the needed analysis of the data much less design new protocols or build new technologies to improve robustness. Also, data should not be anonymized before they are provided to researchers; the anonymity hides information (e.g., on the particular network topology or equipment used)

---

[54]See Network Reliability and Interoperability Council (NRIC). 2000. *Network Reliability Interoperability Council IV, Focus Group 3, Subcommittee 2, Data Analysis and Future Considerations Team.* Washington, D.C.: NRIC, Federal Communications Commission federal advisory committee, p. 4. Available online at <ftp://ftp.atis.org/pub/nrsc/fg3sc2final.PDF>.

[55]See Network Reliability and Interoperability Council (NRIC). 2000. *Revised Network Reliability and Interoperability Council - V Charter.* Washington, DC: NRIC, Office of Engineering and Technology, Federal Communications Commission. Available online at <http://www.nric.org/charter_v/>.

from the researcher. However, in light of proprietary concerns attached to the release of detailed information, researchers must agree not to disclose proprietary information (and must live up to those agreements). Disclosure control in published reports is not simply a matter of anonymizing the results; particular details may be sufficient to permit the reader of a research report, including an ISP's competitors, to identify the ISP in question. Attention must, therefore, also be paid to protecting against inadvertent disclosure of proprietary information.

Looking to the future, the committee can see other reasons why ISPs would benefit from sorting out what types of reliability metrics should be reported. For example, it is not hard to imagine that at some point there would be calls from high-end users for a more reliable service that spans the networks of multiple ISPs and that some of the ISPs would decide to work together to define an "industrial-strength" Internet service to meet this customer demand. When they interconnect their networks, how would they define the service that they offer? Since the performance experienced by an ISP's customer depends on the performance of all the networks between the customer and the application or service the customer is using, each ISP would have an interest in ensuring that the other ISPs live up to reliability standards. Absent a good source of data on failures (and a standardized framework for collecting and reporting on failures), how would the ISPs keep tabs on each other? In the process of defining a higher-grade service, ISPs will want to understand what sort of failure would degrade the service, and it is this sort of failure that they ought to be reporting on. From this perspective, outage reporting shifts from being a mandated burden to an enabler of new business opportunities.

It is unlikely that simple, unidimensional measures that summarize ISP performance would prove adequate. Creating standard reporting or rating models for the robustness and quality of ISPs would tend to limit the range of services offered in the marketplace. What form might such user choices take? Consider, as an example, that an ISP that experiences the failure of a piece of equipment might face a tough trade-off. It could continue to operate its network at reduced performance in this condition or undergo a short outage to fix the problem—a choice between an extended period of uptime at much reduced performance and a short outage that restores performance to normal. Some of the ISP's customers—e.g., those who depend on having a connection rather than on the particular quality of that connection—will prefer the first option, while others will prefer the second. Indeed, some may be willing to pay extra to get a service that aims to provide a particular style of degraded service. (Such a "guaranteed style of degradation" is an interesting variation on QOS and does not impose much overhead.) These considerations suggest that, more generally, there is a need for many different rating scales or, put another way, a need for measuring several different things that might be perceived as "quality" or reliability. Combining them into a single metric does not serve the interests of different groups (user or vendor or both) that are likely to prefer different weighting factors or functions for combining the various measures.

QUALITY OF SERVICE

The Internet's best-effort quality of service (QOS) makes no guarantees about when, or whether, data will be delivered by the network. Together with the use of end-to-end mechanisms such as the Transmission Control Protocol (TCP), which provides capabilities for reassembling information in proper order, retransmitting lost packets, and ensuring complete delivery, best effort been successful in supporting a wide range of applications running over the Internet. However, unlike Web browsing, e-mail transmission, and the like, some applications such as voice and video are very time-sensitive and degrade when the network is congested or when transmission delays (latency) or variations in those delays (jitter) are excessive. Some performance issues, of course, are due to overloaded servers and the like, but others are due to congestion within the Internet. Interest in adding new QOS mechanisms to the Internet that would tailor network performance for different classes of application as well as interest in deploying mechanisms that would allow ISPs to serve different groups of customers in different ways for different prices have led to the continued development of a range of quality-of-service technologies. While QOS is seeing limited use in particular circumstances, it is not widely employed.

The technical community has been grappling with the merits and particulars of QOS for some time; QOS deployment has also been the subject of interest and speculation by outside observers. For example, some ask whether failure to deploy QOS mechanisms represents a missed opportunity to establish network capabilities that would foster new applications and business models. Others ask whether introducing QOS capabilities into the Internet would threaten to undermine the egalitarian quality of the Internet—whereby all content and communications across the network receive the same treatment, regardless of source or destination—that has been the consequence of best-effort service.

Beyond the baseline delay due to the speed of light and other irreducible factors, delays in the Internet are caused by queues, which are an intrinsic part of congestion control and sharing of capacity. Congestion occurs in the Internet whenever the combined traffic that needs to be forwarded onto a particular outgoing link exceeds the capacity of that link, a condition that may be either transient or sustained. When congestion occurs in the Internet, a packet may be delayed, sitting in a router's queue while waiting its turn to be sent on, and will arrive later than a packet not subjected to queuing, resulting in latency. Jitter results from variations in the queue length. If the queue fills up, packets will be dropped.

In today's Internet, which uses TCP for much of its data transport, systems sending data are supposed to slow down when congestion occurs (e.g., the transfer of a Web page will take longer under congested conditions). When the Internet appears to be less congested, transfers speed up and applications complete their transaction more quickly. Because the adaptation mechanisms are based on reactions to packet loss, the congestion level of a given link translates into a sufficiently large packet loss rate to signal the presence of congestion to the applications that share the link. Congestion in many cases only lasts for the transient period during which applications adapt to the available capacity, and it reaches drastic levels only when the capacity available to each application is less than the minimum provided by the adaptation mechanism.

Congestion is generally understood to be rare within the backbone networks of major North American providers, although it was feared otherwise in the mid-1990s, when the Internet was commercialized. Instead, it is more likely to occur at particular network bottlenecks. For example, links between providers are generally more congested than those within a provider's network, some very much so. Persistent congestion is also observed on several international links, where long and variable queuing delays, as well as very high packet loss rates, have been measured.[56] Congestion is also frequent on the links between customers' local area networks (or residences) and their ISPs; sometimes it is feasible to increase the capacity of this connection, while in other cases a higher capacity link may be hard to obtain or too costly. Where wireless links are used, the services available today are limited in capacity, and wireless bandwidths are fundamentally limited by the scarcity of radio spectrum assigned to these services as well as vulnerable to a number of impairments inherent in over-the-air communication.

At least some congestion problems can be eliminated by increasing the capacity of the network by adding bandwidth, especially at known

---

[56]See V. Paxson. 1999. "End-to-End Internet Packet Dynamics," *IEEE/ACM Transactions on Networking* 7(3):277-292, June. Logs of trans-Atlantic traffic available online at <http://bill.ja.net/> show traffic levels that are flat for most of the day at around 300 Mbps on a 310 Mbps (twin OC-3) terminating in New York.

bottlenecks. Adding bandwidth does not, however, guarantee that congestion will be eliminated. First, the TCP rate-adaptation mechanisms described above may mask pent-up demand for transmission, which will manifest itself as soon as new capacity is added. Second, on a slightly longer timescale, both content providers and users will adjust their usage habits if things go faster, adding more images to Web pages or being more casual about following links to see what is there and so on. Third, on a longer timescale (on the order of months but not years), new applications can emerge when there is enough bandwidth to enough of the users to make them popular. This has occurred with streaming audio and is likely to occur with streaming video in the near future.

Also, certain applications—notably, real-time voice and video—require controlled delays and predictable transfer rates to operate acceptably. (Streaming audio and video are much less sensitive to brief periods of congestion because they make use of local buffers.) Broadly speaking, applications may be restricted in their usefulness unless bandwidth is available in sufficient quantity that congestion is experienced very rarely or new mechanisms are added to ensure acceptable performance levels. A straightforward way to reduce jitter is to have short queue lengths, but this comes at the risk of high loss rates when buffers overflow. QOS mechanisms can counteract this by managing the load placed on the queue so that buffers do not overflow However, the situation in the Internet, with many types of traffic competing in multiple queues, is complex. Better characterization of network behavior under load may provide insights into how networks might be engineered to improve performance.

Concerns in the past about being able to support multimedia applications over the Internet led to the development of a variety of explicit mechanisms for providing different qualities of service to different applications—e.g., best effort for Web access and specified real-time service quality for audio and video.[57] Today, two major classes of QOS support different kinds of delay and delivery guarantees (see Box 2.4). They are based on the assumption that applications do not all have the same requirements for network performance (e.g., latency, jitter, or priority) and

---

[57]In essence, these proposed QOS technologies resemble those that have proven effective in ATM and Frame Relay networks, with the exception that they are applied to individual application sessions or to aggregates of traffic connecting sets of systems running sets of applications rather than to individual circuits connecting pairs of systems. The mathematical difference between IP QOS and ATM QOS is that ATM sends variable-length bursts of cells, while IP sends variable-length messages. The biggest operational difference is that ATM QOS is generally used in ATM networks carrying real-time traffic, while QOS is generally not configured in IP networks today.

that the network should provide classes of service that reflect these differences.[58]

There is significant disagreement among experts (including the experts on this committee) as to how effective quality-of-service mechanisms would be and which would be more efficient, investing in additional bandwidth or deploying QOS mechanisms. One school of thought, which sees a rising tide of quality, argues that increasing bandwidth in the Internet will provide adequate performance in many if not most circumstances. As higher capacity links are deployed, the argument goes, Internet delays will tend to approach the theoretical limit imposed by the propagation of light in optical fibers, and the average bandwidth available on any given connection will increase. As the overall quality increases, it will enable more and more applications to run safely over the Internet, without requiring specific treatment, in the same way that a rising tide as it fills a harbor can lift ever-larger boats. Voice transmission, for example, is enabled if the average bandwidth available over a given connection exceeds a few tens of kilobits per second and if the delays are less than one-tenth of a second, conditions that are in fact already true for large business users; interactive video is enabled if the average bandwidth exceeds a few hundred kilobits per second, a performance level that is already obtained on the networks dedicated to connecting universities and research facilities. If these conditions were obtainable on the public Internet (e.g., if the packet loss rate or jitter requirements for telephony were met 99 percent of the time), business incentives to deploy QOS for multimedia applications would disappear and QOS mechanisms might never be deployed.

Proponents of the rising tide view further observe that the causes of jitter within today's Internet are poorly understood, and that investment in better understanding the reasons for this behavior might lead to an understanding of what improvements might be made in the network as well as what QOS mechanisms would best cope with network congestion and jitter if tweaking the network is not a sufficient response.

There are, however, at least some places within the network where there is no tide of rising bandwidth, and capacity is intrinsically scarce. One example is the more expensive and limited links between local area networks (or residences) and the public network. Even here, however,

---

[58]This presumes, of course, that one should meet the full range of requirements in a single infrastructure with a single switching environment. This is not necessarily an optimal outcome; while the Internet has been able to support a growing set of service classes within a single network architecture, it is an open question what network models would best support the broad range of communications service profiles.

BOX 2.4 Quality-of-Service Mechanisms

Differentiated Services (diff-serv)

Diff-serv,[1] a set of proposed IETF standards, would allow ISPs to provide customers with a quality of service that is better than the default best-effort service. The idea is to use part of the packet header as a service class indication. (It does so an ongoing basis; unlike int-serv, described below, it does not provide for on-demand requests for a quality of service for a particular communications session.) Such an enhanced service might give the customer better service up to a particular bandwidth ceiling, perhaps with a cap on the total amount of data transmitted in a given time interval. A premium service might also provide guarantees such as specified maximum packet loss rate or an upper bound on latency. The class definition can be one of strict separation (such as "class X gets at least 10 percent of the total available resource"), one of priority ("class Y gets what class X does not use"), or one of service ("packets in class Z are never queued more than z milliseconds"). There is quite a lot of debate on the actual definition of classes. With diff-serv, customers can select one or more service classes and are able to specify different QOS classes for different applications (e.g., using a high-end service for video conferencing while using best-effort service for file transfer and e-mail exchanges). Access to these service classes would be enforced at the edge of the network through the use of filters by IP addresses, and routers in the network would use the service-class label to determine how packets are queued. Diff-serv depends in large part on ISPs using the additional revenue derived from premium services to adequately provision their networks to support the offered services. While simple diff-serv mechanisms have been demonstrated to provide a high probability of meeting users' QOS expectations for point-to-point communications,[2] the guarantees are probabilistic, meaning that the ISP cannot make absolute service guarantees.

Integrated Services (int-serv)

Int-serv[3] provides quantifiable, end-to-end QOS guarantees for particular data flows. It makes use of a signaling mechanism, the resource reservation pro-

---

[1]S. Blake et al. 1998. *An Architecture for Differentiated Services.* Internet Engineering Task Force, Network Working Group, RFC 2475. December. Available online at <http://www.ietf.org/rfc/rfc2475.txt>.

[2]D. Clark and J. Wroclawski. 1997. *An Approach to Service Allocation in the Internet.* IETF Draft Report, July. Cambridge, Mass.: Massachusetts Institute of Technology. Available online at <http://diffserv.lcs.mit.edu/Drafts/draft-clark-diff-svc-alloc-00.txt>.

[3]R. Braden, S. Shenker, and D. Clark. 1994. *Integrated Services in the Internet Architecture: An Overview.* Network Working Group, Internet Engineering Task Force. RFC 1633, June. Available online at <http://www.ietf.org/rfc/rfc1633.txt>.

tocol (RSVP)[4] that allows applications to specify requirements for bandwidth and end-to-end latency. The int-serv model is somewhat analogous to that of the telephone network, where services are requested on an as-needed basis and where if resources are not available to provide the requested service then the network returns a busy signal rather than providing a degraded service. As currently defined, every application flow (e.g., a single video call) needs its own reservation, and each reservation requires that a moderate amount of information be stored at every router along the path that will carry the application data, which can lead to scaling challenges if int-serv is widely used. Another set of challenges arises when multiple ISPs are needed to connect the end points of a connection; int-serv reservations that cross network boundaries are difficult to administer, and methods are needed to allocate and bill for the costs of reserving capacity in multiple ISPs.

Other Approaches

Shortcomings of diff-serv and int-serv have prompted researchers to explore alternative QOS mechanisms that lie somewhere between the two—providing finer granularity and stronger guarantees than are provided by diff-serv while avoiding the scaling and administrative problems associated with int-serv. One such approach, Integrated Services over Specific Link Layers, would combine the end-to-end service definitions and signaling of int-serv with the scalable queuing and classification techniques of diff-serv.[5] Another approach, referred to as virtual overlay networks (VONs), would add capabilities to routers within the Internet to permit the creation of virtual networks in which traffic within an individual flow would compete with other packets on the same VON but not with traffic from other flows.[6] Multiple VONs could be created to serve different applications; they would be connected to different end points and offer different levels of service. Among the open questions associated with this approach are how to specify properties of an overlay network, how to dynamically administer resources on routers associated with an overlay network, how to avoid scaling issues as the number of overlays becomes large, and how to rapidly classify large numbers of flows.

------

[4]R. Braden, L. Zhang, S. Berson, S. Herzog, and S. Jamin. 1997. *Resource ReSerVation Protocol (RSVP): Version 1 Functional Specification*, RFC 2205. Network Working Group, Internet Engineering Task Force, September. Available online at <http://www.ietf.org/rfc/rfc2205>.

[5]This work is being carried out by the IETF's Integrated Services over Specific Link Layers working group. The group's charter is available online at <http://www.ietf.org/html.charters/issll-charter.htm>.

[6]For an overview, see Kenneth P. Birman. 2000. "The Next Generation Internet: Unsafe at Any Speed?" *Computer* 33(8).

SOURCE: Adapted in part from Computer Science and Telecommunications Board, National Research Council. 2000. *Networking Health: Prescriptions for the Internet*. Washington, D.C.: National Academy Press. Available online at <http://www.nap.edu/catalog/9750.html>.

some will argue that it is better to invest in increased capacity of the gateway link than in mechanisms to allocate scarce bandwidth. As noted above, wireless links are inherently limited in capacity and are therefore candidates for QOS. Prospects for the use of Internet QOS technologies in this context depend in part on whether QOS services are provided at the Internet protocol layer or through specialized mechanisms incorporated into the lower-level wireless link technology. Current plans for third-generation wireless services favor the latter approach, suggesting that this may not be a driver of Internet QOS.

Service quality, like security, is a weak-link phenomenon. Because the quality experienced over a path through the Internet will be at least as bad as the quality of the worst link in that path, quality of service may be most effective when deployed end to end, on all of the links between source and destination, including across the networks of multiple ISPs. It may be the case that localized deployment of QOS, such as on the links between a customer's local area network and its ISP, would be a useful alternative to end-to-end QOS, but the effectiveness of this approach and the circumstances under which it would prove useful are open questions.

The reality of today's Internet is that end-to-end enhancement of QOS is a dim prospect. QOS has not been placed into production for end-to-end service across commercial ISP networks. Providing end-to-end QOS requires ISPs to agree as a group on multiple technical and economic parameters, including on technical standards for signaling, on the semantics of how to classify traffic and what priorities they should be assigned, and on the addition of complex QOS considerations to their interconnection business contracts. Perhaps more significantly, the absence of common definitions complicates the process of negotiating QOS across all of the providers involved end to end. ISP interest in differentiating their service quality from that of their competitors is another potential disincentive to interprovider QOS deployment.

There are also several technical obstacles to deployment of end-to-end QOS across the Internet. One challenge is associated with the routing protocols used between network providers (e.g., Border Gateway Protocol, or BGP). While people have negotiated the use of particular methods for particular interconnects, there are no standardized ways of passing QOS information, which is needed for reliable voice (or other latency-sensitive traffic) transport between provider domains. Also, today's routing technology provides limited control over which peering points interprovider traffic passes through, owing to a lack of symmetric routing and the complexities involved in managing the global routing space. Exchanging latency-sensitive traffic (such as voice) will, at a minimum, require careful attention to interconnect traffic growth and routing configurations.

While the original motivation for developing quality-of-service mechanisms was support of multimedia, another factor has been responsible for a sizable portion of recent interest in quality of service: ISPs that wish to value-stratify their users, that is, to offer those customers who place a higher value on better service a premium-priced service, need mechanisms to allow them to do so. In practice, this may be achieved by mechanisms to allocate relative customer dissatisfaction, degrading the service of some to increase that of others. (Anyone who has flown on a commercial airliner understands the basic principle: lower-fare-paying customers in coach have fewer physical comforts than their fellow travelers in first class, but they all make the same trip.) Value stratification may be of particular interest in situations where there is a scarcity of bandwidth and thus an interest in being able to charge customers more for increased use, but value stratification may also find use under circumstances where ISPs are able to provision sufficient capacity to meet the demands of their customers and customers perceive enough value in a premium service to pay more for it.

There is a central tension in the debate over QOS. If the providers, in order to make their customers happy, add enough capacity to carry the imposed load, why would one need more complex allocation schemes? Put another way, if there is no overall shortage of capacity, all that can be achieved by establishing allocation mechanisms is to allocate relative dissatisfaction. Would providers intentionally underprovision certain classes of users? As indicated above, the answer may be yes under certain marketing and business plans. Such differentiation of service packages and pricing are sustainable inasmuch as customers perceive differences and are willing to pay the prices charged.

One consequence of the development of mechanisms that enable disparate treatment of customer Internet traffic has been concern that they could be used to provide preferential support for both particular customers and certain content providers (e.g., those with business relationships with the ISP).[59]   What, for instance, would better service in delivery of content from preferred providers imply for access to content from providers without such status? What people actually experience will depend not only on capabilities possible from the technology and the design of marketing plans but also on what customers want from their access to the Internet and what capabilities ISPs opt to implement in their networks.

---

[59]See, for example, Center for Media Education. 2000. *What the Market Will Bear: Cisco's Vision for Broadband Internet*. Washington, D.C.: Center for Media Education. Available online at <http://www.cme.org/access/broadband/market_will_bear.html>.

The debate over quality of service has been a long-standing one within the Internet community. Over time, it has shifted from its original focus on mechanisms that would support multimedia applications over the Internet to mechanisms that would support a broader spectrum of potential uses. These uses range from efficiently enhancing the performance of particular classes of applications over constrained links to providing ISPs with mechanisms for value-stratifying their customers. The committee's present understanding of the technology and economics of the Internet does not support its reaching a consensus on whether QOS is, in fact, an important enabling technology. Nor can it be concluded at this time whether QOS will see significant deployment in the Internet, either over local links, within the networks of individual ISPs, or more widely, including across ISPs.

Research aimed at better understanding network performance, the limits to the performance that can be obtained using best-effort service, and the potential benefits that different QOS approaches could provide in particular circumstances is one avenue for obtaining a better indication of the prospects for QOS in the Internet. Another avenue is to accumulate more experience with the effectiveness of QOS in operational settings; here the challenge is that deployment may not occur without demonstrable benefits, while demonstrating those benefits would depend at least in part on testing the effectiveness of QOS under realistic conditions.

3

Keeping the Internet the Internet:
Interconnection, Openness,
and Transparency

What is referred to as "the Internet" is actually a set of independent networks interlinked to provide the appearance of a single, uniform network. Interlinking these independent networks requires interconnection rules, open interfaces, and mechanisms for common naming and addressing. (The issues associated with interlinking the Internet with the Public Switched Telephone Network are considered separately in Chapter 4.) The architecture of the Internet is also designed to be neutral with respect to applications and context, a property referred to here as transparency. This chapter examines the current and expected future state of these interconnections and interfaces.

INTERCONNECTION: MAINTAINING END-TO-END SERVICE THROUGH MULTIPLE PROVIDERS

The Internet is designed to permit any end user ready access to any and all other connected devices and users. In the Internet, this design translates into a minimum requirement that there be a public address space to label all of the devices attached to all of the constituent networks and that data packets originating at devices located at each point throughout the networks can be transmitted to a device located at any other point. Indeed, as viewed by the Internet's technical community in a document that articulates the basic architectural principles of the Internet, the basic goal of the Internet is connectivity.[1] Internet users expect that their Internet service provider will make the arrangements necessary for them to access any desired user or service. And those providing services or content over the Internet expect that their Internet service provider(s) will similarly allow any customer to reach them and allow them reach any potential customer. (Subject, of course, to whatever controls are imposed at the behest of the subscriber for security purposes.)

To support these customer expectations, an Internet service provider must have access to the rest of the Internet. Because these independent networks are organized and administered separately, they have to enter into interconnection agreements with one or more other Internet service providers. The number and type of arrangements are determined by many factors, including the scope and scale of the provider and the value it places on access for its customers. Without suitable interconnection, an Internet service provider cannot claim to be such a provider—being part of the Internet is understood to mean having access to the full global Internet.

In 1995, interconnection relied on public network access points where multiple providers could exchange traffic.[2] Today, there is a much larger set of players and a much greater reliance on private interconnects—that is, direct point-to-point links—between major network providers. Indeed, there are multiple arrangements for interconnecting Internet service providers, encompassing both public and private (bilateral) mechanisms, connections between commercial networks and public network facilities, and even arrangements for connecting networks defined by ownership or policy as "national" to the international Internet complex. Some of these international connections are constrained by concerns raised by national governments about specific kinds of content being carried over the Internet.

Connections among Internet service providers are driven primarily by economics—in essence who may have access to whom with what quality of access and at what price—but all kinds of considerations are translated into policies, frequently privately negotiated, that are implemented in the approaches to interconnection and routing. A significant feature of today's competitive Internet service marketplace is that direct competitors must reach interconnection agreements with each other in order to provide the overall Internet service that their customers desire. These

---

[1]B. Carpenter, ed. 1997. *Architectural Principles of the Internet*, RFC 1958. Network Working Group, Internet Engineering Task Force, June.

[2]Private interconnections existed then as well, but since everyone was also connected via the government-funded NSFNet backbone, they were viewed as backdoor connections to handle instances of high traffic volume.

business agreements cover the technical form of interconnection, the means and methods for compensation for interconnection based on the services provided, the grades and levels of service to be provided, and the processing and support of higher level protocols. Interconnection also requires that parties to an agreement establish safeguards—chiefly in the form of rules and procedures—to ensure that one provider's network is not adversely affected by hostile behavior of customers of the other provider.

While, as evidenced by the Internet's continued growth as an interconnected network of networks, the existing interconnection mechanisms have proven adequate thus far, concerns have been expressed about interconnection. Interprovider, public-private, and international connections all raise questions of public policy, or Internet governance. This section focuses on interprovider connections because it is these connections that drive the shape and structure of the Internet.

Structure of the Internet Service Provider Industry

There are several thousand Internet service providers in the United States.[3] These providers cover a range of sizes, types of services they provide, and types of interconnections they have with other service providers. The Internet service provider business has grown substantially, with entry by many new players, following the phasing out in the mid-1990s of the government-supported NSFNet backbone. Changes in the nature of these players are as significant as changes in the number. As the mix has evolved, so have business strategies. One sees ISPs chasing particular segments of the market (e.g., they specialize in consumers or businesses or they run Web server farms), trends toward consolidation though mergers and acquisitions, and moves to vertically integrate a full range of services, from Internet access to entertainment, news, and e-commerce. The interlinked networks that are the Internet form a complex web with many layers and levels; the discussion that follows should not be taken to suggest simplicity.[4]

---

[3]One source of information on Internet service providers is *Boardwatch* magazine's *Directory of Internet Service Providers*. Golden, Colo.: Penton Media, June 1999. Available online from <http://boardwatch.internet.com/isp/summer99/introduction.html>), it lists 5078 ISPs in North America, a figure that covers a wide range of sizes and business models.

[4]See, for example, the results of Bell Labs' Internet Mapping Project, which provides a visualization of data gathered in mid-1999 indicating the complexity of the Internet. A number of maps are available online at <http://www.cs.bell-labs.com/who/ches/map/gallery/index.html>.

A straightforward and useful way to categorize ISPs is in terms of the interconnection arrangements they have in place with other providers. The backbone service providers, which include commercial companies as well as several government-sponsored networks like DOE's ESNET, use trunk capacities that are measured in gigabits, or billions of bits, per second. Roughly a dozen of the ISP companies provide the backbone services that carry a majority of Internet traffic. These providers, termed "tier 1," are (recursively) defined as those providers that have full peering with at least the other tier 1 backbone providers. Tier 1 backbones by definition must keep track of global routing information that allows them to route data to all possible destinations on the Internet—which packets go to which peers. They also must ensure that their own routing information is distributed such that data from anywhere else in the Internet will properly be routed back to its network. Tier 1 status is a coveted position for any ISP, primarily because there are so few of them and because they enjoy low-cost interconnection agreements with other networks. They do not pay for exchanging traffic with other tier 1 providers; the peering relationship is accompanied by an expectation that traffic flows—and any costs associated with accepting the other provider's traffic between tier 1 networks—are symmetrical. Tier 1 status also means, by definition, that an ISP does not have to pay for transit service.

Much of the Internet's backbone capacity is concentrated in the hands of a small number of tier 1 providers, and there is some question as to whether it is likely to become even more concentrated, in part through mergers and acquisitions. Concerns about market share in this segment have already emerged in the context of the 1998 merger between MCI and WorldCom, at that time the largest and second largest Internet backbone providers. In that instance, European Union regulators expressed concerns about the dominant market share that would have resulted from such a combination. In the end, to get approval for the merger, some of MCI's Internet infrastructure as well as MCI's residential and business customer base was sold off to Cable & Wireless and the merger went forward.[5]

Some of the advantage held by the very large players lies in their ability, owing to their large, global networks, to provide customers willing to pay for it an assured level and quality of service. These very large companies provide customers with solutions intended to allow those customers, in turn, to connect with higher levels of performance to other

---

[5]See, for example, Mike Mills. 1998. "Cable & Wireless, MCI Reach Deal; British Firm to Buy Entire Internet Assets." *Washington Post.* July 14, p. C1.

users in the same network, using such technologies as virtual private networks, and they also offer widely dispersed customers the convenience of one-stop shopping. Such large players also allow customers to inter-connect to the public Internet but generally without making the service guarantees. Part of their dominant position also stems from their tier 1 status, which assures their customers (including tier 2 and tier 3 ISPs) of their ability to provide a high quality of access to the public Internet. In addition, tier 1 providers, by determining how and with whom they inter-connect, affect the position of would-be competitors.

Below tier 1 sit a number of so-called tier 2 and tier 3 service provid-ers, which connect corporate and individual clients (which, in turn, con-nect users) to the Internet backbone and offer them varying types of ser-vice according to the needs of the target marketplaces. This group spans a wide range of sizes and types of providers, including both a small set of very large providers aimed at individual/household customers (e.g., America Online) and a large number of smaller providers. These include providers of national or regional scale as well as many small providers offering dial-up service in only a limited set of area codes.[6] A recent trend has been the emergence of so-called free ISPs, which provide residential Internet service at no charge, typically in exchange for a demographic profile of the customer and an agreement by the customer to view adver-tising material delivered along with the Internet service. This class also includes the networks operated by large organizations, including those of large corporations, educational institutions, and some parts of govern-ment. These ISPs cannot generally rely on peering alone and must enter into transit agreements and pay for delivery of at least some of their traffic. Some of these providers have not invested significantly in build-ing their own facilities; instead they act as resellers of both access facilities (e.g., dial-up modem banks) and connectivity to the Internet backbone.

While industry analysts have long predicted increased consolidation and the demise of the smaller providers, recent trends indicate that the business remains open to a large number of players.[7] However, optimism here is tempered by two considerations. First, many of the very small players are only active in small markets or geographical regions. Second,

---

[6]Matt Richtel. 1999. "Small Internet Providers Survive Among the Giants." *New York Times.* August 16, p. D1.

[7]*Boardwatch* magazine's directory of Internet service providers in North America showed continual growth in the number of ISPs from February 1996 to July 1999. See *Boardwatch* magazine's *Directory of Internet Service Providers.* Golden, Colo.: Penton Media, June 1999. Available online from <http://boardwatch.internet.com/isp/summer99/introduction.html>.

subscriber data show that a single player, America Online, with more than 20 million subscribers, has a significant share of the consumer market.[8] Another area of interest is the emerging broadband market. The recent flap over open access illustrates the concerns that some have about the market share and the behavior of the providers of the communications links themselves (i.e., the facilities' owners), the Internet service providers, and the content providers, with which both facilities and service providers may have business arrangements.

Another recent trend has been the establishment of a new form of ISP, the hosting provider. This type of ISP operates both single-customer (dedicated) and shared-application servers, typically providing Web services on behalf of companies who would rather outsource the management of machine rooms and Internet connectivity. They offer customers a certain level of service (as seen by those throughout the Internet that make use of the customer's service) by arranging for (purchasing) transit services with a sufficient set of backbone connections.

Interconnection Mechanisms and Agreements

Internet interconnection arrangements in some ways echo those of telephony, since the public telephone network is also a collection of distinct networks linked together to provide a uniform service. However, telephony, unlike the Internet, leverages and reflects decades of state, federal, and international regulation and standards-setting that have shaped the terms and conditions of interconnection, including financial settlements. Internet interconnection, by comparison, is relatively new, and the technology, market structure, and arrangements are evolving.

Providing Internet-wide interconnectivity requires that the parties who own and operate the constituent networks reach agreement on how they will interconnect their networks. The discussion in this section looks at interconnection at three levels: the physical means of interconnection, the different patterns of traffic exchanged by providers (transit and peer), and the financial arrangements that underlie and support the physical means and different traffic patterns. The focus here is on teasing out the essential elements of interconnection, but this should not be taken to mean that interconnection is a simple matter. There are many players at many levels, and in each case there is more than one choice of physical interconnection, logical interconnection, and financial arrange-

---

[8]Data from Telecommunications Report's online census, January 2000, reported in David Lake. 2000. "No Deposit, No Return: Hard Numbers on Free ISPs." *The Industry Standard*, March 27.

ment, and implementation of each choice depends on a complex set of negotiated agreements.

Physical Interconnection

Public exchanges are a way of making the interconnections between a number of providers more cost-effective. If n providers were individually to establish pairwise interconnections, they would require $n(n-1)/2$ direct circuits. A public exchange, where all n providers can connect at a common location, permits this to be done much more inexpensively, with n circuits and a single exchange point. A provider interconnects to an exchange point, either physically—by installing his own equipment and circuit into a specific location (e.g., the MAE-West facility at NASA Ames Research Center or the Sprint NAP in Pensauken, New Jersey)—or logically—by using a leased network connection to an interconnect provider through an ATM or Ethernet network (e.g., the MAE-East ATM NAP in northern Virginia or the Ameritech ATM NAP in Chicago). These interconnect networks are usually operated by large access providers, who hope to derive considerable revenue by selling access lines to ISPs wishing to attach to each other through the access provider's facilities.[9]

In recent years, the public interconnects have acquired a relatively poor reputation for quality, in part owing to congested access lines from the exchanges to tier 1 providers, which results in packet loss, and in part owing to exchange point technology that cannot operate at speeds comparable to major backbone trunks. This trend is likely to accelerate as large backbones move to extremely high-speed wavelength division multiplexing (WDM)-based trunking, which exceeds the data rates that can be handled by today's exchange point technology.

Another option is to use a direct, point-to-point connection. One motivation for point-to-point connections is to bypass the bottleneck posed by a public exchange point when traffic volumes are large. Between large providers, connections are usually based on high-performance private interconnects, for example point-to-point links at high speeds (DS-3 or higher). Direct connection can also provide for better management of traffic flows. The very large volume of traffic that would be associated with a major public access point can be disaggregated into smaller, more easily implemented connections (e.g., a provider manages

---

[9]If they provide direct connections to multiple provider networks, public exchanges can also turn out to be very efficient places to locate other services such as caches, DNS servers, and Web hosting services. And because public exchanges bring together connections to various providers, they are also useful places to conduct private bilateral connection through separate facilities.

10 OC-3 connections to 10 different peers in different locations rather than a single OC-48 connection to a single exchange point that then connects to multiple providers). Another reason for entering into private connections is the desire to provide support for the particular service level agreements and quality-of-service provisions that two networks agree to in their peering or transit agreement.

Logical (Routing) Interconnection

When two or more ISPs establish an interconnection, they exchange route advertisements to specify which data packets are to be exchanged between them. Route advertisements describe the destination Internet addresses for which each provider chooses to accept packets from the other. These advertised routes are loaded, generally through automated mechanisms, into each other's routing tables and are used to determine where (including to which providers) packets should be routed based on their destination address.

There are two common options for how providers accept each other's traffic: transit and peer. In the transit model, the transit provider agrees to accept and deliver all traffic destined for any part of the Internet from another provider that is the transit customer. It is possible that two providers in a transit arrangement will exchange explicit routing information, but more typically the transit provider provides the transit customer with a default route to the transit network while the transit customer provides the transit provider with an explicit set of routes to the customer's network. The transit customer then simply delivers to the transit provider all packets destined for IP addresses outside its own network. Each transit provider establishes rules as to how another network will be served and at what cost. The transit provider will then distribute routing information from the transit customer to other backbones and network providers and will guarantee that full connectivity is provided. Address space for the customer provider may come from its transit provider or from its own independent address space should that provider have qualified for such allocation. (The issues surrounding address allocation and assignment are discussed in Chapter 2.) [10]

The preferred way for large providers today to interconnect is through peer arrangements. In contrast to transit arrangements, where one provider agrees to accept from the other traffic destined for any part of the

---

[10]Some providers or customers engage in the practice of multihoming, whereby they establish transit connections with multiple ISPs, generally to provide redundancy. This can introduce both technical and management issues, including how to allocate traffic among the multiple paths, that will not be discussed in detail here.

Internet, in a peering relationship, each provider only accepts traffic destined for the part of the Internet it provides. Peers exchange explicit routing information about all of their own addresses along with all of the addresses of their transit customers. Based on that routing information, each peer only receives traffic destined for itself and its transit clients. This exchange of routing information takes the form of automated exchanges among routers. Because the propagation of incorrect routing information can adversely affect network operations, each provider needs to validate the routing information that is exchanged.

For smaller providers the only option (if any) for physical interconnection is typically at a public exchange point. Location at a peering point implies that the peering relationship may still suffer from poor (or at least uncontrolled) service quality, since the exchange point or the connections to it may be congested; they may, however, be very cost-effective, especially for smaller providers. Once interconnectivity is established through a public exchange, providers may attempt to enter into a bilateral peering agreement with other providers located at the same interconnect. This can be a cost-effective means of bilateral peering, because connectivity to many other providers can be aggregated onto a single connection to the exchange.

Financial Arrangements for Interconnection

The issue of compensation for interconnection is a complex one. The essence of interconnection is the handing over of packets, according to the routing information that has been exchanged, to be routed onward toward their destination. Compensation reflects the costs associated with provisioning and operating sufficient network capacity between and within ISP networks. As a basic unit of interconnection, packets are somewhat akin to call minutes in voice telecommunications. However, architectural differences between the Internet and PSTN make accounting in terms of packets much more complicated than call-minute-based accounting. Even if an infrastructure were to be put in place to count and charge on a packet-by-packet basis, the characteristics of packet routing would make it difficult to know what the cost associated with transmitting a given packet would be.[11] As a result, interconnection schemes that are

---

[11]Several of these characteristics are noted in a paper by Geoff Huston. 1999. *Interconnection, Peering, and Settlements*, Technical Report. Canberra, Australia: Telstra Corporation, Ltd., January. They include the following: packets may be dropped in the course of their transmission across the Internet; the paths that packets follow are not predetermined and can be manipulated by the end user; and complete routing information is not available at all points, so that the undeliverability of a packet may not be known until it approaches its destination.

used in other contexts, such as the bilateral settlements employed in international telephony, are not used in the Internet, and interconnection has generally been established on the basis of more aggregated information about the traffic exchanged between providers. Some of these issues have to do with the cost of the interconnection, traffic imbalances (e.g., one provider originates more traffic than it terminates), and relative size (one provider offers greater access to users, services, and locations than the other). Two financial models predominate; one is linked to the transit model and the other to the peer provider model discussed above.

In the transit model, a transit customer buys transit service from a transit provider and pays for an access line to that larger provider's network. These arrangements take the form of bilateral agreements that specify compensation (if any) and the terms of interconnection, including service guarantees (level and quality of service) that each party makes. In the early days of the commercial Internet, providers did not pay for transit services. Before ISPs insisted on payment for transit, nonbackbone ISPs could become free riders in the so-called hot potato scenario, whereby a network would dump traffic for destinations beyond those advertised by a particular provider, thereby forcing the backbone ISP to carry traffic it had not agreed to carry. Private interconnects help prevent free riding, because it is more straightforward to identify this condition given a direct mapping between the link and a single provider.

In the peer model, two ISPs agree to a peer relationship based on a perception of comparable value. These agreements are generally barter agreements between peers that assume an exchange of a roughly comparable level of traffic or, on some other basis, that the costs and benefits of a peer relationship will be mutually beneficial. Peer barter arrangements echo what is called in telephony "sender keeps all" or "bill and keep"— the network to which a customer connects keeps the fees paid by that customer for traffic carried on both its and another provider's network. Peering among the tier 1 providers is perhaps the most visible, but peering is also conducted among smaller players and at the regional or local level. Logical peering and financial peer relationships generally coincide, but there are exceptions. In some instances a customer will pay for a nontransit service that, logically though not financially, looks like peering. For example, ISP A may pay ISP B for access to B's customers but not B's peers.

The value attached to either transit or peer relationships is not based only on the number of bits exchanged nor is it based solely on the origin, destination, or distance—it also reflects the value attached to particular content. Consider, for example, a large, consumer-focused ISP ("ISP A") and a major, popular content provider that is connected to the Internet through another provider ("ISP B"). ISP A will be judged by its customers based on the quality of service that it provides. To the extent that A's customers value content directly available from ISP B, customer judgment of ISP A will depend on the quality of the interconnect established between A and B. Thus ISP A may be willing to pay extra for higher capacity links to ISP B in order to ensure better performance for customers accessing the content provider. The complementary argument may also hold true: the content provider may well derive revenue from advertising that in turn depends on the return rate of viewers, so it (and, consequently, its ISP) will be willing to pay extra for interconnection relationships that ensure that customers of ISP A receive a good quality of service. (This is a major business consideration for the Internet hosting providers described below.) Accordingly, the performance that a consumer experiences with a particular piece of content depends in part on the capacity of the interconnects between the consumer's and content provider's computers, which in turn depends in part on the willingness and ability of the consumer and content provider (and their ISPs) to pay for those interconnections.

Chapter 2 discusses a number of issues surrounding quality of service (QOS) mechanisms, including the dim prospects for deployment of interprovider QOS; here we discuss some issues related to interconnection. If the stresses associated with the development and evolution of today's peering and transit agreements, which have generally only addressed much broader service level agreements, are any guide, establishing agreements that enable interprovider quality of service would prove difficult. Providing guarantees of better service to a subset of users means that resources are set aside that become unavailable for other users. This can only develop if higher grades of quality of service are sold at a premium price and if there are mechanisms to adequately compensate ISPs. If the necessary business agreements would take years to develop, then interprovider QOS would take years to deploy. Also, congested interconnections exacerbate quality-of-service differences between connections across a given provider's network, as compared with connections across multiple provider networks. They often result in companies connecting all their sites through a single provider's network rather than through a variety of providers and depending on this interprovider connectivity. They also result in large content-hosting providers almost always attaching to each of the major backbone networks (usually as a transit customer rather than a peer) to bypass interprovider interconnects and improve overall robustness of access for their customers.

Specific mechanisms for quality of service are starting to show up in parts of the Internet, but not as generally deployed, end-to-end services that any application can take advantage of to reach users Internet-wide. They are being offered only inside specific ISPs as product differentiators or being bundled with specific applications (such as Internet telephony). Thus there is pressure for alternatives to the baseline Internet. What content or service providers do today is enter into an agreement with a company that delivers specialized content services located throughout the Internet so as to improve the quality of the connection seen by end users. For example, RealAudio or Akamai will load streaming media content onto their servers. The Internet is being overlaid by these application-specific delivery networks. These overlay networks do not provide end-to-end connectivity between the original content or service provider and the end user and are open only to those providers who are willing and able to pay for specialized services.

Considerations Affecting Decisions to Enter into Peering Agreements

As noted above, peer status is advantageous to ISPs because it means that they will not have to pay other providers for transit and because for its customers it is taken as evidence of a high service quality. In making financial arrangements to support its interconnection with the rest of the Internet, each provider is strongly motivated to maximize its revenue streams from its customers and minimize its expenses, including charges paid to other providers. There are, therefore, natural pressures for each provider to want to become a peer and for a peer to resist one of its customers asserting a peer relationship and for it to resist one of its peers asserting that it should, in fact, be a customer rather than a peer.

The issue of who could attain peer status first received considerable publicity in 1997 as a result of announcements by UUNET and Sprint that they would no longer peer freely with any and all networks (along with an announcement by PSINet that it explicitly would agree to peer with smaller players), raising concerns in some circles about the implications for smaller networks. These concerns have lingered; reflecting the significant barrier to entry for an Internet provider that peering represents, smaller ISPs and new entrants have resorted to litigation to attempt to attain peering.

Part of the difficulty of assessing peering issues is the fact that the terms of peering agreements are private. There are some generally understood criteria used by backbone providers to determine whether or not another network qualifies for peering or is viewed as a potential customer for that ISP's transit services. These criteria generally include (1) having a national network with a dedicated transcontinental backbone of at least a certain speed, (2) exchanging a minimum amount of traffic with that ISP (usually with comparable amounts of traffic travelling in both directions), (3) providing around-the-clock operational support, and (4) agreeing to abide by certain rules and policies in how routing traffic is

processed and/or filtered. However, these are only general considerations, and the terms of peering agreements are private. As the standards
and requirements are usually covered by nondisclosure agreements, their
contents and components are not widely known. This private approach
reflects in part the multidimensional, subjective determination of who is
and who is not a peer.

ISPs are motivated to be conservative in this process. If an ISP pub-
lishes explicit rules, these are an invitation to lawsuits in the event that it
either declines to peer with an entity that arguably meets the published
rules or agrees to peer with an entity that arguably does not. By contrast,
companies that really are peers, and thus clearly stand to benefit from
peering, will usually realize this and conclude appropriate agreements if
discussions can be carried out in a relatively private context. If an objective framework for deciding who are peers were to be developed, it would
entail either the industry itself agreeing on one or a governmental (or,
given the Internet's global reach, an intergovernmental) entity developing one, both of which are problematical and may lead to fewer peering
arrangements, not more. Absent such a framework, peering will be based
on the premise that two parties try to prove to each other that they are
peers.

The economics of a proposed peering relationship is the dominant,
but not the only, consideration that goes into a decision to peer or not.
Fundamentally, agreements between tier 1 providers and smaller providers pose additional challenges because the asymmetrical traffic carried by
the two classes raises questions about compensation for the costs associated with the connection and the termination of the smaller network's
traffic. The absolute volume of traffic also matters. Because the expense
associated with setting up dedicated links makes sense only when lots of
traffic is being exchanged, it is not cost-effective to establish a private
interconnect unless a significant amount of traffic is being exchanged.
Few small providers are in a position to use the private peering approach,
and large providers are unlikely to view private interconnects with small
providers as attractive. The costs of establishing these links are also usually much less for a facilities-based provider; non-facilities-based providers are at a cost disadvantage in implementing such interconnects. There
are also concerns on the part of tier 1 providers about the potential for
free-riding in peering. For this reason, many large tier 1 backbone providers are reluctant to peer with smaller networks because doing so would
open them up to this vulnerability.[12]

---

[12]Interconnect technologies that provide more point-to-point control over traffic flows,
such as ATM, offer some advantages in dealing with this problem but do not completely
eliminate it.

Peers need not be the same size, and there are cases where the major backbones will peer with smaller providers despite the asymmetry in traffic capacity. For instance, even if swapping traffic on a barter basis would not be supported based solely on the amount and balance of traffic exchange, it may prove attractive to the backbone provider if the smaller provider has a network, albeit modest in size, that is national or world-wide in scope. It is possible in such circumstances to fashion a peering agreement in which the smaller provider interconnects with the backbone at enough places such that all the smaller provider's traffic stays within the smaller provider's own network most of the time, thus minimizing the cost to the larger peer.

Competitive positioning also enters into the equation. In general, there is an interest in retaining a competitive advantage over new en-trants. The type of interconnections that a provider has in place is an important business consideration because it establishes the service qual-ity that customers experience when transferring data across the provider's boundary. Indeed, many would-be ISP customers rely on the type of peering being used as an indicator of quality. Because private intercon-nects can provide a better service quality owing to their greater capacity, dedicated nature, and ability to more carefully manage the traffic across them, the existence of such interconnects is often seen by customers as a sign that a provider offers generally higher quality Internet service.[13] Peer status is used at least in part because there are no agreed-on quantitative metrics and processes for evaluating the quality of Internet interconnec-tions, particularly public metrics that detail the status of connectivity. The question of measuring quality is exacerbated by the dynamic growth in the volume of traffic throughout the Internet as well as by changes in the types of traffic being carried.

In addition, to alleviate concerns that a customer of today may be-come a competitor tomorrow, most tier 1 providers have rules in place disqualifying existing customers from becoming peers. Thus, a smaller provider just entering the market may find that it must by definition purchase transit in order to provide Internet access service, but that its status as a customer will prohibit it from attaining peer status in the future. These trends of course reinforce the position of the established larger players. Indeed, it has been asserted that in the past several years no ISP has been able to attain tier 1 status without doing so by purchasing

---

[13]Large customers often specify tier 1 status as an element in requests for proposals for Internet service (at least in part because there are no well-agreed-to quantitative metrics and processes for evaluating the quality of Internet interconnection; this problem is exacer-bated by the dynamic growth of traffic in backbones, such that connectivity that might have been considered good at one point in time may be wholly inadequate 6 months later).

an ISP that already had full peering status.[14] As a result, in order to grow its traffic with a tier 1 provider so that it can attain peer status, a new entrant may have to discount its product substantially to entice new customers who will put up with a lower quality of service in the meantime. Alternatively, it could pay a substantial amount to a backbone provider in order to achieve high quality interconnection or purchase a provider that already has peering agreements.

Robustness considerations also come into play when providers consider entering into a peering relationship. Limits in the protocols used to exchange critical routing information as well as in the hardware and software used in the core of the Internet mean that full peering can lead to a breakdown of the routing system. Provider A may peer with provider B in such a way that provider B is only supposed to provide routing information for provider B's directly attached customers and those providers it is providing transit for. But a very simple error in a routing configuration may flood provider A's router with bad routing data such that a large amount of provider A's traffic would be inadvertently sent through provider B, which may not have the capacity to properly deliver that data, resulting in a service outage for provider A's users.[15] Also, while routing information is exchanged and processed automatically, configuring the routing requires judgment, as does troubleshooting when problems arise. Problem resolution depends in part on informal interactions among network operators. ISPs must acquire the necessary skills, some of which are best obtained from prior employment at a provider that already has a network of the size, scope, and complexity of a tier 1 provider. As a consequence, an ISP may avoid entering into a peer relationship with another provider if it feels the other provider does not have the proper personnel or processes in place to prevent routing disturbances.

Evolution of Interconnection Models

The discussion above reflects the interconnection arrangements that have historically prevailed in the Internet industry. Recently there have

---

[14]*The Cook Report on Internet*, November 1999, p. 10. Available online at <http://www.cookreport.com/08.08.shtml>.

[15]One example of this was reported in "Risks List." *Risks Digest* 19(12), May 2, 1997. "On 23 Apr[il] 1997 at 11:14 am EDT, Internet service providers lost contact with nearly all of the U.S. Internet backbone providers. As a result, much of the Internet was disconnected, some parts for 20 minutes, some for up to 3 hours. The problem was attributed to MAI Network Services . . . which provided Sprint and other backbone providers with incorrect routing tables, the result of which was that MAI was flooded with traffic." Available online at <http://www.infowar.com/iwftp/risks/risks-19/19_12.txt>.

been innovations in interconnection that provide alternatives to the conventional binary choice between attaining peer status or becoming a transit customer. Similar innovations have been tried before on a not-for-profit basis, such as in some of the public exchanges. What is new today are moves by both existing players and new entrants to use new business models for interconnection. The committee is aware of a number of instances where tier 1 providers have entered into arrangements that are somewhere between the pure peer interconnection and the pay-for-transit interconnection. As with conventional peering agreements, the terms are subject to nondisclosure, so it is difficult to characterize or examine them in detail. But their existence is one indication that the Internet industry is responding to market forces by providing such alternatives.

One prominent example of an entrant following a new business model is InterNAP, which has built a business around providing an alternative to conventional peering or transit. InterNAP establishes high-performance interconnection points in key locations and then connects these points to top ISPs, including a number of the tier 1 providers. The connection arrangement lies halfway between peering and transit. The business relationship resembles a transit model inasmuch as InterNAP pays for the connection/service and thus has a predictable-service-level agreement. But the routing relationship is peering—it only forwards traffic into an ISP if it will be terminated there. It does have to pay for transit services in some cases but claims that a majority of the routes in the default free zones are available to it through peer routing. InterNAP is able to pay a reasonable price for its connections because it is mostly delivering traffic into each ISP that would eventually get there anyway by some other route. With these interconnection relationships established, it then sells Internet access to smaller ISPs, who—it claims—receive a better quality service than if they had purchased transit service from just one ISP or made use of a public exchange and experience less hassle than if they had tried to negotiate a number of peering relationships on their own. InterNAP also provides service to major Web hosts, who then can connect to most large ISPs without having to manage individual relationships with them.

Because it was historically seen as too cumbersome to charge on an individual basis for the transfer of data packets, the Internet has traditionally been based on the establishment of revenue-neutral boundaries at its center, where the major tier 1 ISPs connect, and on the selling of transit service to downstream providers on the basis of rough measures such as link capacity or average data rates. This simple model has worked reasonably well but does not give content providers or ISPs any way to make additional payments to support a desired service level. Nor are there processes in place that allow a content producer to transfer money through its ISP to the ISPs of its target consumers to reduce the costs that either ISP incurs in carrying its content to the target consumers.

In response to these perceived shortcomings in the Internet's inter-connection arrangements, content cache providers are introducing new financial models. Akamai provides a good example. It places servers within the networks of ISPs, as near the consumer as possible. Content producers who want to ensure access by their customers pay Akamai to host their content, and Akamai (in some cases) pays the ISP to host the Akamai server. This new financial mechanism allows the content producer to pay the ISPs that serve end users. The arrangement has both advantages and disadvantages. One advantage is that it provides a nonconsumer source of revenue for ISPs. On the other hand, as discussed in more detail below, this sort of infrastructure is an application-specific delivery overlay network that a producer can only use by paying for it, so it is somewhat of a departure from the Internet's traditional architecture.

Monitoring Internet Interconnection

In contrast to telephony, which has been the subject for many years of economic oversight and regulation, the Internet is by and large unregulated, with the Federal Communications Commission having, thus far, demonstrated no interest in intervening in it. Another avenue for intervention is the application of antitrust law in particular instances; in the Internet context, this has taken the form of reviews of proposed mergers. It is the view of this committee that current policy should continue, as should monitoring.

The Internet interconnection market model has risks. It assumes a reasonably competitive environment, where competition among ISPs keeps transit agreement charges reasonable, where there is no one ISP so dominant that it can refuse to peer with any other and thus force all the other ISPs to pay for access to the dominant ISP's customers, and where there is not pervasive vertical integration of backbone ISP and content and service businesses. The small number of tier 1 providers and the difficulties of attaining this status have, however, raised concern about the competitiveness of the ISP marketplace, in particular about the barriers to market entry. As discussed above, for a provider to attain tier 1 status, it must by definition reach peering agreements with all (or at least most) other tier 1 providers; a provider's inability to reach agreements with all or most of them is sufficient to prevent the provider from becoming a tier 1 provider. Additionally, providers offering transit service frequently incorporate into their interconnection agreements restrictions on transit customers becoming peers. Thus, where a provider starts with some or all of its relationships being of the transit sort, it may be unable to attain tier 1 status. The emergence of alternatives to the pure peer or transit interconnection models suggests, however, that the marketplace may be finding ways to reduce these pressures by introducing interconnection models that better suit the business needs of parties that seek to establish an interconnection agreement.

The existence of public exchanges means that some form of connection to the Internet is generally available to all providers; this, in turn, means that concerns can focus on the nature, terms, and quality of interconnection rather than on participation. While these considerations are also key to interconnection in the PSTN, they are significantly more complex and dynamic in the Internet. At any given point in time there is a wide range of applications and services in use across the Internet, each with different implications for interconnection. And all indications are that new types of applications and services will continue to emerge on a regular basis. Related to this is the variability in the value attached to Internet data packets—in other words, the price that a party would, in principle, be willing to pay for transmission of an individual packet depends on a number of factors, including the application the packet is associated with, its content, and its points of origination and termination.

OPENNESS AND INNOVATION

The Internet was developed first as a joint research effort and then as a joint engineering effort by the research community. The standards development process, which came to be formalized through the Internet Engineering Task Force (made up of technical experts from academia and industry), emphasized standardization because it grew out of a highly diffuse but collaborative development environment. In that environment, new concepts would be experimented with and then a project would be launched that included parallel development of implementations and standards. Eventually, several companies would offer compatible products. These attributes were responsible for a healthy competition among designs for applications and the protocols they use and frequently for the development and availability of multiple implementations of products that would be available from multiple vendors. Crucially, these multiple implementations have been consistent with the development and adoption of a single standard for key functions.

It should be noted that the term "standard" refers to several different types of specifications, including the following:

1. An application programming interface (API) published by a software provider. A developer may need to enter into a contract to make use

of the API, and the specification is subject to change at any time at the discretion of the software provider;

2. A complete specification published by a corporation (e.g., Sun's Java language, the Microsoft Windows APIs, and the Microsoft/Intel-driven PC architecture). In such cases, the companies or organizations that develop the specification have at least some degree of control over what changes are made to the specification.

3. An open specification published by a neutral institution, such as the World Wide Web Consortium (W3C) or the IETF. Developed under appropriate procedures, this approach permits multiple actors to develop and control a standard without running afoul of antitrust laws.

4. A standard that is enforced by some regulatory authority, such as the National Television Systems Committee (NTSC). These are standards that have, until the development of the HDTV standard, been mandated for all U.S. television broadcasters. Many of them are developed in industry (by individual companies or industry consortiums) and are then adopted as official standards.

The core standards employed in the Internet tend to fall into the third category, although some fall into the second.[16]

The terms "standard" and "open standard" are not synonymous. The Internet model for development is characterized by openness, which refers to the ability of multiple vendors to independently construct products that work with one another. Openness means that customers can mix products from one vendor with products from another (e.g., use one vendor's client software with another vendor's server) and that applications from one vendor operate over infrastructure provided by another. Openness relies crucially on the development and adoption of standards. An interface designed with only one vendor's products in mind can be readily implemented only in that single vendor's environment. From this perspective, privately designed interfaces that are publicly published are not open interfaces. Standardization processes enable multiple vendors to cooperate on the development of new elements that will allow them to

---

[16]Closely allied with open standards is the practice of open source, best known as the mechanism through which the Linux operating system is distributed and developed. Open source practices resemble the third type (open specification published by a neutral institution) but in a somewhat different fashion. All parties are free to implement their own modifications to the open source (with the use of the resulting code subject to whatever use agreement was attached to the original code base), but an individual or organization generally decides which modifications are incorporated into what is considered the standard code base.

develop new markets—markets that are much larger than would be the case if each developed its own competing technology. Then the vendors compete by providing competitive products that build on the standardized elements. When this process works well, it results in greater benefits for both vendors and customers.

Critical Open Standards in the Internet—The Hourglass Architecture

The existence of an abstract bit-level network service as a separate layer in a multilayer suite of protocols provides a critical separation between the actual network technology and the higher-level services through which users actually interact with the Internet. *Realizing the Information Future*[17] depicted this layered modularity as an hourglass, with an "open bearer service" at the narrow waist (Figure 3.1). In the Internet, this abstract, bit-level transport service is provided by the Internet Protocol (IP). At this level, bits are bits and nothing more. Above the waist, the glass broadens out to include a range of options for data transport and applications. Right above the IP layer is the transport layer, which is made up of the enhancements that transform the basic IP bit transport service into the range of end-to-end delivery services needed by the applications—reliable, sequenced delivery; flow control; and endpoint connection establishment. The Transport Control Protocol (TCP), the most commonly used transport mechanism, is often lumped together with IP as TCP/IP. There is, however, an important distinction: IP defines those features that must be implemented inside the network, in the switches and routers, while the transport layer defines services that are the responsibility of the end node. The upper layers, above IP and transport, are where the applications recognized by typical users reside, such as e-mail, streaming audio and video, and the Web. The technologies below the waist make up the bit-carrying infrastructure and include both the communication links (copper wire, optical fiber, wireless links, and so on) and the communication switches (packet routers, circuit switches, and the like). Figure 3.2 shows where some familiar Internet technologies, protocols, and applications fit within the hourglass construct.

Imposing a narrow point in the protocol stack removes from the application builder the need to worry about details and evolution of the underlying network facilities and removes from the network provider the

---

[17]Computer Science and Telecommunications Board (CSTB), National Research Council. 1994. *Realizing the Information Future: The Internet and Beyond.* Washington, D.C.: National Academy Press.

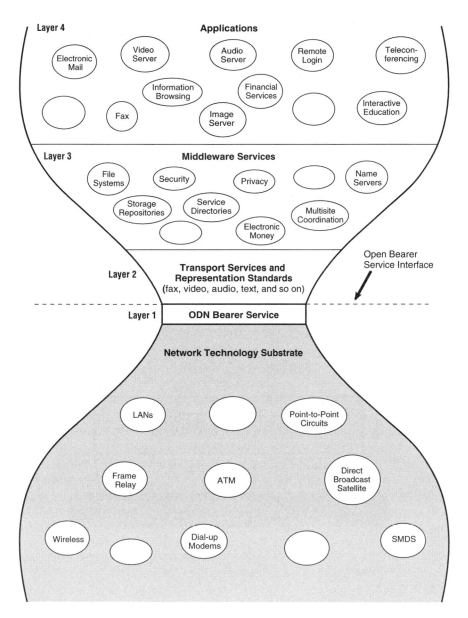

FIGURE 3.1 The hourglass model of Internet architecture. SOURCE: Computer Science and Telecommunications Board (CSTB), National Research Council. 1994. *Realizing the Information Future: The Internet and Beyond.* Washington, D.C.: National Academy Press.

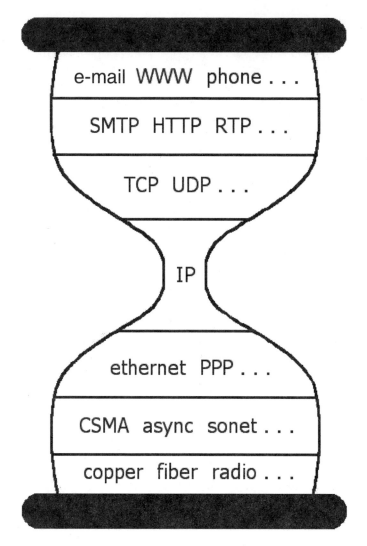

FIGURE 3.2 How some Internet-related technologies, protocols, and applications fit into the hourglass model. SOURCE: Adapted from a figure by Steve Deering, Cisco Systems.

need to make changes in response to whatever standards are in use at the higher levels. This separation of IP from the higher-level conventions is one of the tools that ensure an open network; it hinders, for example, a network provider from insisting that only a controlled set of higher-level standards should be used on the network, a requirement that would inhibit the development and use of new services and might be used to limit competition. The core functions—those that lie at or near the waist of the hourglass—are the most critical functions where openness must be guaranteed to enable innovation. When these core interfaces to the network are not open, multivendor application innovation is more difficult. Possible consequences include constrained user choice and deterioration in the quality of products that vendors offer.

Just which functions should be considered to lie in the waist of the hourglass—that is, implemented according to a single, Internet-wide standard and available throughout the Internet—is open to interpretation and debate, and there is no consensus among those who design, operate, or use the Internet. The core standards are understood by many to include more than just IP, but opinions differ as to what else should be included. Indeed, in the hourglass metaphor, the curved side walls of the glass do not draw a sharp distinction between what is in the waist and what lies above it. What other than IP is needed in practice?

- *Domain Name System.* The DNS, which provides a common set of names for hosts connected to the Internet, is generally viewed as an essential core function of the Internet. Some would also include additional network directory services in the category of core functionality. (While a single directory service has not been universally adopted, this is one of the solutions offered to deal with conflicts between the DNS name space and trademarked names; see Box 2.1 in Chapter 2.)
- *Routing protocols.* Providers must typically exchange routing information at interconnect points. Have the routing structure and routing protocols become critical enough for interoperability that they should be considered to lie at the core? This issue is especially important in the light of increasing doubts that today's routing architectures will continue to be adequate as the network continues to expand.
- *Dynamic Host Configuration Protocol (DHCP).* This network protocol enables a DHCP server to automatically assign an IP address to an individual device attached to a network. It might be the case that many applications that do not even require TCP functionality will still depend on DHCP to obtain an Internet address when they are started up.

Some also believe that significant benefits would result if standard mechanisms for authentication were widely available. This and other middleware functions are ones where application builders and users can both realize substantial benefits when standard solutions are deployed.

In recent years, the same processes that enabled growth and innovation in the network layers have started to have an even more dramatic effect on higher-level protocols and, accordingly, on user-visible applications. For instance, a protocol like HTTP also provides a type of core functionality, albeit in the narrower space of the World Wide Web rather than the Internet as a whole. The flap over instant messaging openness (e.g., AOL's Instant Messenger and Microsoft's MSN Messenger) illustrates the tensions that arise between those who argue for openness (through standardized interfaces that are open to all application developers) and those who seek to retain or increase their market share (through closed, proprietary protocols). In each of these instances, there are tensions between creativity and openness, typical of any standardization effort. In each, the affected parties—application developers, service providers, and consumers—must decide when and where one or the other should be emphasized.

While most of this discussion has examined the upper half of the hourglass, the innovation that the Internet's architecture enables at the "transmission" level is another crucial element of the Internet's success. Keeping IP service independent of the technology below it has several benefits. First, competition at the technology level—which can be expected to reduce cost and increase function—will be greater the less the service definition constrains innovation in communications technologies. The abstract interface means that users are free to select among competitive service providers. Underlying hardware (and the software required to enable it) can be changed without changing the application software. The consumer who uses a particular Web browser with his dial-up Internet service can use the same browser if he switches to a DSL or cable modem service and is able to shop around for better performance or price without incurring a switching cost for the applications he runs (although investments may have to be made in new hardware or software associated with the Internet service itself). Second, the technology independence also provides significant stability over time. IP can outlive any particular technology over which it is implemented and IP can be implemented on top of new communications technologies as they emerge—as has happened already with Ethernet, ATM, frame relay, and cellular digital packet data (CDPD), to name a few.[18]

---

[18]However, the emergence of new communications technologies has led to efforts to modify TCP in order to improve performance. For example, the throughput with standard TCP is reduced below the apparent capacity of the communications link when traffic flows over a satellite link because the standard TCP algorithm uses a probing algorithm that requires the sender to wait for old data to be acknowledged before increasing the data rate. Because the distance over which signals must travel is considerably greater for geostationary orbit satellites than for terrestrial links, one must wait correspondingly longer for the radio signals carrying the acknowledgment to be transmitted from receiver to sender. The

The Internet As a Platform for Application Innovation

The Internet is widely acknowledged to be a key platform for creative and innovative applications across the communications, information, commerce, and entertainment businesses. Much of this innovation rests on the hourglass architecture, discussed above, which encourages independent evolution of the network, services, and applications, enabling incremental support for new media (e.g., sound, animation, video) without changing the infrastructure visible to the application. This architecture allows applications to take advantage of network bandwidth innovations and permits users to run applications regardless of who their network provider is.

While some of these applications that run on top of IP are vendor-specific and proprietary, many others are themselves based on open standards. The processes established by the Internet Engineering Task Force for creating new protocols that rely on the core protocols are open to anybody and designed to be vendor-neutral. The open process by which protocols are developed also means that the protocols are very well documented, facilitating the development of applications and creating a large base of expertise.

These simple, standard interfaces also allow applications to aggregate other applications very simply. For example, an e-mail application (e.g., Hotmail) can be combined with an advertising application (e.g., DoubleClick) and a news service (e.g., Reuters) with relatively little work. This ease of aggregation also permits secondary opportunities to build services that Internet applications can reuse, such as news feeds; advertising; middleware services such as authentication and name registration; and infrastructure services such as online data storage and application hosting.

The rosy expectations for electronic commerce rest on the standardized, open Internet protocols and the ease with which applications can be developed and aggregated. E-commerce, particularly where the sale of

---

same problem occurs, to a lesser extent, with any long-latency Internet link, and the satellite issue is recognized as one instance of a broader class of long-latency link performance problems. Another communications technology development driving efforts to revise TCP is the use of wireless data links for Internet traffic. In this case, the higher errors rate and consequent packet loss associated with wireless transmission reduce throughput because the TCP algorithm interprets packet loss as an indication of network congestion and attempts to adapt to this apparent congestion by reducing the transmission rate. Efforts are under way in the IETF and other venues to develop modifications to TCP that accommodate these new technologies while remaining backward-compatible with existing TCP implementations.

physical goods is involved, also depends on successful implementation of the back-office functions of inventory management, order fulfillment, and shipping. It has also leveraged other key business innovations such as just-in-time inventory and rapid package delivery services.[19]

These characteristics of the Internet have been instrumental in attracting the thousands of companies developing applications and services that rely on the Internet, leading to billions of investment dollars. The net result is a competitive industry that rapidly channels new ideas into products of value to end users and that has been rapidly creating a fountain of technology and customer assets. Also, by providing what appears to the user to be a single network, the Internet allows an application to reach nearly every customer and business, creating an enormous market opportunity through the network effect, which says that the value in connecting people and services is proportional to the square of the number of connected people and services.

In a reflection of its successes, the term "Internet" has attained a status akin to a valued brand name for both businesses and end users. Indeed, no other platform for computing and communications applications today shares all of these attributes. Investors, developers, and users alike have viewed the Internet as a place of enormous opportunity and a community rich in information and applications. The amount of private and corporate investment dollars poured into developing new Internet applications has been stunning. This climate set the stage for tension between, on the one hand, the potential for seemingly unbounded innovation in applications and services and, on the other, the potential for Internet-based businesses to foster market consolidation, to raise barriers to open access, and to drive other outcomes in their effort to make and maximize profits.

Evolution of Internet Standards Setting

Several trends have emerged that run counter to the openness paradigm that has characterized the Internet's development. Companies develop products and technologies in the hope of capturing a market. One trend is that technical issues are becoming complicated by the desire to achieve or exploit a competitive or proprietary advantage as well as quality. This may well be an inevitable consequence of the market forces in-

---

[19]Because it depends on shipment of goods to individuals, which tends to be more expensive than bulk shipments to retail outlets, business-to-consumer commerce may also have benefited from the ability to offset the perceived costs by not collecting sales tax for out-of-state shipments. (See the section on taxation of Internet-based commerce in Chapter 5 for a discussion of these tax issues.)

volved, but given the benefits afforded by standards, maintaining a balance between standards and proprietary trends is important. Companies will push for standards when they need them for business but will keep many key aspects of the technology, such as specific data structures or algorithms, proprietary, often protecting them as patents or trade secrets. Another important factor is marketplace demands for speed of innovation; it costs time as well as other resources to develop a product that involves proposing a new standard, which means that a standards process can work against innovation and responsiveness to customer demand.

The growing stakes in the standards process itself threaten to overwhelm the traditional open standards mechanisms along the lines of those provided by the IETF (Box 3.1). They mean that the interests reflected by participation in the IETF are increasingly not only technical but also commercial, and participants are more political in what they do and do not say to influence standards setting. Companies also may seek to protect their ideas through patent protection. These factors make it more difficult for standards bodies to address and fill gaps in what the market has provided. The larger market and more widespread interest also mean that the number of participants has grown; it is very difficult for a working group of 100 or 200 people to do design work. As was the case in the past, much of the standards development work is done in smaller design teams within the working group and then vetted by the larger group. Nonetheless, the participation of many more individuals increases the likelihood that compromises will be made that degrade the quality and crispness of a standard.

Institutions have reacted to these challenges in many different ways. The IETF standard process underwent several revisions, all of which tended toward more formality in order to cope with the increased attendance. The International Telecommunication Union (ITU) has tried to streamline its already formal processes in order to shorten the standard-setting cycles. And various new forums have arisen that focus on specific subjects; they have adopted policies that expedite the development of standards. In fact, the IETF does not hold the monopoly on Internet standards development. When developing Internet standards, companies and industry groups are likely to select whichever standards body they believe will be the most effective avenue for their business plan, and they may pursue simultaneous standardization efforts in multiple forums. In addition to the IETF, several more traditional standards bodies, including the ITU, International Organization for Standardization (ISO), the European Telecommunications Standards Institute (ETSI), the American National Standards Institute (ANSI), and the Institute of Electrical and Electronics Engineers (IEEE), are developing and adopting standards re-

BOX 3.1 IETF Standards Process

The Internet Engineering Task Force (IETF) is generally acknowledged as the body with primary responsibility for reviewing and establishing key standards that allow computers connected to the Internet to interact and communicate with each other, including the prevailing standards for routing, network management, e-mail delivery, and so forth. The IETF's standards process is designed to be a "fair, open, and objective basis for developing, evaluating, and adopting Internet Standards." The stated goals for this process are (1) technical excellence, (2) prior implementation and testing, (3) clear, concise, and easily understood documentation, (4) openness and fairness, and (5) timeliness. The IETF differs from more traditional international standards-making organizations such as the ISO or ITU in that it charges no dues, has no formal membership, and uses a less formal and more open standards-making process.

The IETF holds three meetings each year, which anyone may attend, but the bulk of its work is accomplished through public electronic mailing lists. The IETF is divided into eight functional areas: applications, Internet, next-generation Internet Protocol, network management, operational requirements, routing, security, and transport and user services. These areas are divided further, as the need arises, into working groups chartered to achieve particular goals. Working groups generally disband after they complete their assigned tasks. Involvement in IETF activities is open to all individuals who are interested in its work, and membership is determined largely by which electronic mailing lists one subscribes to or what working group within the IETF one participates in. Community involvement is considered an important element of the Internet standards process. The standards process is designed to provide all interested parties with an opportunity for participation and comment. At each stage of standards development, specifications are repeatedly discussed and their merits are debated in open meetings or through public electronic mailing lists. Before a particular standards action is taken up by the IETF's management body, for example, a last call for comments is issued using the IETF's public announcement e-mail list.

Internet standards are developed, disseminated, and published formally by the IETF in the *Request for Comments* (RFC) series, which started in 1969 as descriptions of design work for the ARPANET. Each Internet standard has a corresponding RFC label (for example, the file transfer protocol, FTP, is described in RFC 959). Specifications generally arise from the efforts of a working group, although some are developed by individuals and some are specifications developed by other standards groups (for example, HTTP, developed by the World Wide Web Consortium (W3C), was adopted as an IETF standard). Some RFCs are standards, with varying levels of maturity ("proposed", "draft", or "full" protocol standards) and a separate class for policies ("best current practice"). However, unlike traditional standards bodies, which publish standards, the concept behind the RFC series is "community memory." As a result, the vast majority of RFCs are either historical—that is, they describe experiments in progress or carried out at one time—or simply informational. The informational category includes proprietary product specifications, white papers on various subjects, poetry, and annual April Fools' Day jokes.

The IETF works in close cooperation with three other bodies. The Internet Society (ISOC) is a professional society concerned with the growth and evolution of the Internet; the ISOC board of trustees is responsible for approving appointments to the Internet Architecture Board (IAB) from among the nominees submitted by the IETF nominating committee. The Internet Architecture Board (IAB) is a technical advisory group of the ISOC that is chartered by the ISOC trustees to provide oversight of the architecture of the Internet and its protocols and to serve in the context of the Internet standards process as a body to which the decisions of the Internet Engineering Steering Group (IESG) may be appealed. The IAB is responsible for approving appointments to the IESG from among the nominees submitted by the IETF nominating committee. The IESG, composed of the IETF area directors and the chairperson of the IETF, is responsible for the technical management of IETF activities; it administers the Internet standards process according to rules and procedures that have been accepted and ratified by the ISOC trustees and is directly responsible for the actions associated with the development and approval of Internet standards. Together, these bodies provide a structure in which the IETF operates, with the ISOC and IAB bodies providing ultimate oversight of IETF standards making.

An RFC that is intended by its authors to develop into an Internet standard must work its way through the three IETF maturity levels mentioned above: proposed standard, draft standard, and Internet (full) standard. Standards actions—entering a specification into, advancing it within, or removing it from the standards track—must be submitted for approval by the IESG. The first level, proposed standard, is accorded to specifications that have undergone extensive community review and are generally stable, well understood, and considered useful.

The next level in the standards track is that of the draft standard, which refers to specifications that are sufficiently stable and unambiguous to provide the basis for developing the software that implements them. Draft standards are considered to be near-final specifications, and any changes are likely to be changes to solve specific problems that arise when the standards are placed in large-scale use in production environments.

The final step in the standards track is the Internet (full) standard, reached when technologies are mature and generally believed to be of significant benefit to the Internet community. While they are by and large stable, specifications adopted as Internet standards may continue to be refined based on experience with their use or the emergence of new requirements.

SOURCES: S. Bradner. 1996. *The Internet Standards Process – Revision 3*, RFC 2026. Network Working Group, Internet Engineering Task Force. Available online at <http://www.ietf.org/rfc/rfc2026.txt>; Internet Architecture Board (IAB), Internet Engineering Steering Group (IESG). 1994. *The Internet Standards Process – Revision 2*, RFC 1602. Available online at <http://www.ietf.org/rfc/rfc1602.txt>; G. Malkin and the IETF Secretariat. 1994. *The Tao of the IETF – A Guide for New Attendees of the Internet Engineering Task Force*, RFC 1718. Available online at <http://www.ietf.org/rfc/rfc1718.txt>; and D. Crocker. 1993. "Making Standards the IETF Way." *StandardView* 1(1). Available online at <http://www.isoc.org/internet/standards/papers/crocker-on-standards.shtml>.

lated to the Internet. Also, there are a number of instances where more narrowly focused interests and a desire for faster standards development have led to the use of consortium-based alternatives to either the IETF or more traditional standards bodies. These groups, such as the World Wide Web Consortium or the Wireless Access Protocol Forum, tend to be narrower in scope, less open, and more industry-centered. Internet standards are being developed in an active, diverse, and dynamic market space—a model that parallels the freewheeling creativity of the Internet.

There are two basic, conflicting views on Internet standards. One is that there should be exactly one standard for any function, and that this standard should be debated in an environment that guarantees fair representation of all parties and fair processing of all contributions. The second view is that there may well be many competing standards for the same function, and that market competition will select which standards best serve a given function. The telecommunications world embodied by the ITU traditionally adopted the first view. The reality of the Internet market, on the other hand, fosters the second view. Today it can be argued that the market impact of standards from treaty bodies such as ITU is essentially indistinguishable from the impact of those from other bodies. The acceptance and use of a standard has more to do with its applicability to marketplace demand or the ability of a dominant vendor to deploy code that becomes a de facto standard than with what standards body approved it. Examples such as Java, developed by Sun, or the initial Web protocols, which were developed by an informal group of research institutions, show that the market can also widely adopt more open solutions before they are blessed by any standards group.

Given incompatible options for protocols, the Internet market, as a tippy market, will pick one when the need arises. This does not mean that only one protocol will necessarily be adopted for a particular purpose: POP and IMAP are a compatible set of protocols for Internet mail both of which can be employed locally without affecting the standard interface used by senders and recipients of e-mail. However, between incompatible suites, the market picks a solution: the very strong force of what economists call network externality means that the benefits of being able to communicate widely are so strong that they drive the widespread adoption of one of the alternatives. The force here is much stronger than it is in, say, operating systems, where consumers continue to sustain both Macintosh and Unix platforms despite the dominant share held by Windows. In networking, the need to communicate is the dominant factor, and losers are prone to fall by the wayside. For example, despite the fact that some believed that it was less capable, the Simple Network Management Protocol (SNMP), which was more widely used, won out over an arguably better, competing protocol for network management, the Common Management Information Protocol (CMIP).

The choices made by the market vary. Sometimes it chooses a vendor's proprietary solution and in other cases it chooses an open standard over the vendor-controlled solution. A key example of the open standard winning was the choice of basic network transport protocol, in which the Internet's open standard, TCP/IP, beat out the proprietary Xerox Network Systems (XNS) standard despite the fact that Xerox and other vendors supported the latter. In the absence of an open standard, the market will also generally pick a winner. For example, when Sun developed the Network File System (NFS) and Remote Procedure Call (RPC) protocols (used to access files across networked computers and control the execution of programs on other computers), there was no open standard (e.g., IETF) alternative in development. After the fact, there were some weak calls for the development of an open alternative, but these never resulted in the development of an alternative standard.[20]

If a competent open standard is made available, it would be attractive in the market and could win out over proprietary standards. But if there is no competent standard, the market still will pick an alternative (the tipping phenomenon). Why are open standards less frequently developed than proprietary ones? Several factors contribute. Today, industrial development is so rapid that pressures to focus on products limit the amount of time technical staff in industry can spend on efforts aimed at the broader Internet community. Moreover, there is a fundamental tension between, on the one hand, having a freedom of choice that enables individual players to reap the benefits of innovation and, on the other, picking standards that benefit all. In essence, this is a prisoners' dilemma game. A common standard maximizes social welfare because the larger market engenders network externalities. But each player is tempted to diverge from the common standard if it believes it might be able to capture the entire market (or a large portion of it) for itself. At the same time as industry is less likely to support the development of open standards, government is investing less to support the work of an academic, noncommercial core of people who care about developing open standards. And, finally, incentives are drawing people from the research community into industry.

A situation where standards are more likely to be proprietary (or at least vendor-controlled) is not an obviously bad thing. Vendor-controlled standards can, like patents, be pro-innovation. If vendors are unable to

---

[20]A working group in the IETF is developing an improved version of NFS in cooperation with Sun.

reap the benefit of investment, investment would be stifled. However, vendor interests in proprietary standards sometimes reflect less an interest in turning a vendor standard into a revenue stream through licensing than a desire to use vendor control of a standard to hold onto market share. However, this is not a case where one situation is clearly bad and the other clearly good (e.g., open versus proprietary or licensing versus control); rather, an appropriate balance must be struck.

One contributor to continued vitality in the development of open standards is support for the networking research community. Government has supported open standards for the Internet not by directly setting or influencing standards but by providing funding for the networking research community. Such research leads both to innovative networking ideas and to specific technologies that can be translated into new open standards, which in turn can offer a richer set of alternatives in the marketplace.

END-TO-END TRANSPARENCY

Closely associated with the concept of openness, which speaks to the use of common standards for communications across the Internet, is the notion of end-to-end transparency. A product of two fundamental properties of the Internet—the hourglass, end-to-end architecture and the unique addressability of devices attached to the Internet—transparency is a defining characteristic of the Internet. The hourglass-like architecture, in which the Internet protocol provides the fundamental means of sending data across the Internet, allows any type of communication, application, or service to ride on top of the Internet. With suitable software running at each end and no knowledge other than each other's Internet address, any two devices connected to the Internet are able, in principle, to enter into any desired type of communication, provided there is enough network capacity and sufficiently low or predictable latency (delay) to support the application.

Crucially, this communication takes place as a result of actions by users at the edges of the network; new applications can be brought to the Internet without the need for any changes to the underlying network or any action whatsoever by Internet service providers. Indeed, over the life of this report, many new applications and associated communication protocols have emerged. A noteworthy example is the rapid emergence and ensuing widespread use of a group of new protocols (e.g., Napster and Gnutella) that are designed to allow distributed sharing of files among Internet users, frequently for the purpose of exchanging music encoded in the mp3 format. (The challenges to intellectual property protection prescnted by these protocols have, of course, given rise to controversy about the implications of their use and led some to attempt to block their use.)

As has been noted by a number of observers of the Internet, transparency often falls short of the ideal described above.[21] Pragmatic measures taken in response to operational considerations (e.g., making address management more tractable or coping with a shortage of available addresses) are one factor that clouds transparency. Another factor is technical measures taken by both users and ISPs aimed at protecting networked computers from attack or enhancing the performance of a network by controlling the use of applications that place particular demands on network resources. And the business and marketing strategies of some Internet players involve offering services that are not fully transparent. In examining transparency issues, it is important to distinguish between transparency violations that users choose to adopt and those violations that are imposed on them.

Addressing Issues

One transparency challenge concerns the means by which computers are assigned Internet addresses. It is common practice today to assign Internet addresses in a dynamic rather than static fashion. Dynamic assignment provides an address on request from a networked computer, generally via the Dynamic Host Configuration Protocol (DHCP), from a pool of globally unique Internet addresses. This makes configuration and management easier and also reduces the number of IP addresses required to support a group of computers. When a device is turned on or reset (in the case of a permanently connected computer) or makes a connection to a network (in the case of a dial-up connection), it uses the DHCP protocol to send a message to a DHCP server to have an address assigned to it. The server responds with a message containing an IP address, and the software running on the device configures the device to adopt that address. When addresses are assigned in this fashion, the relationship between device and address is not constant over time; the address is fixed

---

[21]For example, transparency has been a topic of interest to the Internet Architecture Board (IAB). A recent draft report issued through the IETF echoes a number of these issues (Brian Carpenter. 1999. *Internet Transparency*. Internet Engineering Task Force Internet Draft (work in progress), December. Available online from <http://www.ietf.org/internet-drafts/draft-carpenter-transparency-05.txt>). The IAB also held a workshop on the subject (M. Kaat. 1999. *Overview of 1999 IAB Network Layer Workshop*. IAB Internet Draft (work in progress), October. Available online from <http://search.ietf.org/internet-drafts/draft-iab-ntwlyrws-over-02.txt >).

only until the device is disconnected from the network, reset, or powered down.

As a result, an application cannot rely on the IP address to reach a device directly to complete a call—a dynamically assigned IP address does not uniquely identify a particular device over time. This situation is quite unlike that of other sorts of addresses such as phone numbers, where a person's phone number is statically mapped to a telephone or a location (though there are calling features, such as call forwarding, that allow a limited form of dynamic rerouting to occur by making use of databases within the telephone network). Thus if one were to implement an IP-based telephony service, one could not use a dynamically assigned address directly. Dynamic assignment is not an insurmountable problem, however. Solutions must make use of indirection, in which a directory service is established to provide a mapping between some sort of identifying name and the current IP address that should be associated with that name. Keeping the directory up to date requires that each device send a message to the server on start-up notifying it of the current IP address that should be associated with its name. Maintaining an up-to-date directory with accurate data and operating the directory with sufficient integrity that its information can be trusted is a difficult technical and social problem. Work on a protocol that provides such a capability is now a proposed standard from the IETF. Provided that a suitably robust service can be implemented, dynamic addresses are as suitable as static addresses for any sort of application, and dynamic address assignment can be thought as a situation that requires additional technology development and deployment rather than a fundamental obstacle to transparency.

Another addressing-related challenge to transparency is posed by network address translation (NAT), a technology introduced in Chapter 2 in connection with addressing and routing issues. NAT provides a workaround that permits multiple computers attached to a network to share a smaller number of globally assigned Internet addresses. NATs and firewalls including NAT functions are employed by users and ISPs for a variety of reasons. These include providing a larger number of computers with Internet access using a limited pool of Internet addresses, providing local control over the addresses assigned to individual computers, and providing the limited degree of security that is obtained by hiding internal addresses from the Internet.

Network address translation involves the mapping of a set of local addresses, which are not visible to the outside world (i.e., not visible on the Internet), to a global address (i.e., visible on the Internet). A crucial distinction between NAT and dynamic addressing is that the mapping takes place without any explicit communication between the device and the NAT about the address assignment that has been made. The device continues to use its local address without regard to the action of the NAT; the NAT takes care of translating the addresses on packets flowing in and out of the network between the two sets of addresses.

A transparency problem arises because this translation is performed only on the portion of the packet that labels the destination addresses (analogous to the address on an envelope) not on any addresses that are contained within the packet (analogous to the addresses contained in the text of a letter inside the envelope). The reason that translation cannot in general be done on the addresses within the packet lies at the heart of the transparency question: because the Internet architecture permits any application to run over the Internet, the NAT cannot in general know where and in what form the addresses are placed within the packets.

To make such an application work, one of two things must happen. One option is for the NAT to include an application layer gateway that has knowledge of the application's protocol, thereby allowing it to identify and translate the address as it is transmitted. Many NATs provide this gateway function for commonly used applications such as File Transfer Protocol (FTP). This need for NATs to be application-aware violates a basic attribute provided by the hourglass architecture—that one is free to employ new applications running over the network without having to make any changes whatsoever within the network. There are also costs associated with deploying computers with sufficient computing power to carry out the application-level translations. The other option would be for the application to discover that the network is making use of NAT and then make the necessary translations itself; requiring an application to learn about the details of the network is an undesirable violation of the basic Internet architecture.[22]

Significant problems arise if one wishes to initiate communications between two computers, each of which is sitting behind a NAT, since neither has a way of knowing the internal address of the other. Consider an application like IP telephony. With NAT, one must resort to using a third computer outside either network to act as a telephony server that bridges between the other two. A particular problem is that the only way for a computer behind the NAT to discover that it is receiving an incoming call is for it to repeatedly ask, or poll, the telephony server if there is a

---

[22]One other option is to avoid passing addresses. This solution works in some cases where a protocol does not inherently require the exchange of global identifiers but was implemented that way prior to the advent of NAT. However, the applicability of this solution is limited because some types of applications require that globally unique identifiers be transmitted from one computer to another.

call. Such a work-around places increased demands on both network capacity and the telephony server.

Another set of situations where NAT raises difficulties are ones where simultaneous communications among devices that sit behind a NAT (i.e., local) and devices that sit outside a NAT (i.e., remote) are desired. Examples of such situations include multiparty conferencing (telephony or video) and games; both are situations where there can be a mix of local and remote participants. Signaling becomes more complicated because an application cannot provide the same address information to applications running on local and remote machines. It is not impossible to handle these situations, but they make the software more complicated to implement correctly and more difficult for users to configure properly. Similar problems arise if people start installing appliances, such as security devices, that need to be accessed from both the inside and the outside of the house (i.e., behind the home gateway or outside of it).

NAT also interferes with security protocols such as IPSec,[23] though not with higher-layer security protocols such as SSL or S/MIME. The basic problem is that if the packet payload is encrypted, addresses within it cannot be translated by a NAT. Because IPSec is a more broadly applicable protocol, used notably for standard Internet-layer virtual private networks, the incompatibility is a significant concern for some users.

Nonuniform Treatment of Bits

Internet transparency also implies the uniform treatment of all traffic—in terms of the application, protocol, and format and in terms of the content of the communications being carried across the Internet. In its idealized form, the hourglass architecture treats all bits uniformly, with their transmission through the network a function of one thing only—available capacity (and whatever controls the end points place on the communications, such as the TCP pacing algorithms). The situation is slightly different when quality-of-service technologies are built into the network (discussed in detail in the section on quality of service in Chapter 2) in order to provide for special treatment of particular classes of traffic, in accordance with a customer's contract with an ISP; in this context, "uniform" means uniform within a particular class.

Transparency is limited by the blocking of particular types of Internet communications, pursuant to choices reflecting ISP policy, the preferences of individual customers, or, in the case of larger organizations that

---

[23]S. Kent and R. Atkinson. 1998. *Security Architecture for the Internet Protocol*, RFC 2401. Available online at <http://www.ietf.org/rfc/rfc2401.txt>.

operate their own network infrastructure, organizational policy. These restrictions fall into two broad categories: restrictions placed at the edges in order to meet the objectives of end users and restrictions placed within the network by Internet service providers.

The classic example of a restriction placed on transparency at the edge of the network is the firewall, which is a blocking device placed at the entry point to a subnetwork and operated by either the customer or the ISP on behalf of the customer. It can be configured to exclude those types of communications that are not desired or, more stringently, to block all content not explicitly designated as acceptable. Typically, these restrictions are used to block traffic that could be used to exploit vulnerabilities of the computers within the network. Communications may also be blocked on the basis of the application being run (e.g., when a business seeks to enforce a prohibition on the use of streaming media applications by its employees to reduce bandwidth use or increase worker productivity) or content (e.g., filters that block objectionable content).

How is undesired traffic filtered? Internet applications are generally associated with particular "ports," which are a set of numerical identifiers each of which is associated with a particular type of service or application. These are somewhat standardized; for instance, an HTTP server is frequently associated with port 80. To protect computers against certain types of attack, a firewall can block packets associated with particular ports (and thus applications) that are known to pose a risk. Firewalls will frequently block packets associated with unknown ports as well, in order to keep rogue applications from carrying on unauthorized communications. An application not identified to the firewall as permissible can attempt to circumvent the firewall by making use of another port, perhaps one that is dynamically adjusted (so-called port-agile applications). For example, Real Networks software is both port- and protocol-agile, able to switch from the default UDP protocol to TCP or even HTTP running over a standard port for HTTP traffic when firewalls block the preferred protocol. From the perspective of the application developer, this is done for legitimate (i.e., nonmalicious) reasons, to increase access to end users. From the perspective of the operator of a particular network, however, it may be viewed as subverting a policy decision that may have also been made for legitimate reasons (e.g., to reduce the traffic on a network or prevent those connected to that network from running applications that an organization has decided to prohibit). Port numbers are perhaps the easiest method of filtering, but filtering can also be performed using other information contained in packet headers or the contents of the data packets themselves.

In a response to the difficulties of providing large quantities of data or a high quality of service to end users, the Internet is being overlaid by application-specific delivery networks and caching services. Content or service providers may, for example, enter into an agreement with a company that delivers specialized content services located throughout the Internet so as to improve the quality of the connection seen by their end users. Local caching or overlay distribution networks do not provide end-to-end connectivity between the original content or service provider and the end user. Also, depending on the particular technical and business model, such networks may only be available to those providers who are willing and able to pay for specialized services.

Such service elements in the Internet provide optimizations that make the network more usable for particular applications. If they work properly, they maintain the illusion of end-to-end behavior. But if they fail to work properly, the illusion of transparency can be broken (see the section "Robustness and Auxiliary Servers" in Chapter 2). Importantly (from a transparency perspective), these are not inherent services that end systems can depend upon. This has several implications. First, where these service elements are not implemented in the network, the end user can still employ the full range of services and applications, though the performance may be degraded relative to what would be possible if the enhancements offered by network service elements were available. Second, applications cannot depend on these enhancements being present in all networks. Third, a new application can be deployed without necessitating changes within the network, although its performance may not be optimal in the absence of supporting elements within the network. In short, the introduction of supporting elements does not necessarily violate the end-to-end architecture but at some point makes it effectively impossible to use a nonsupported service.

A related issue has to do with ISP interpositioning, in which an ISP adds facilities to the network to intercept particular requests for Web pages or elements of Web pages, such as graphics, and replace them with ISP-selected content. For example, an ISP might select information or advertisements that are locally relevant, in much the same way as local advertisements are inserted into network programming by local broadcast stations or cable system operators, to rewrite Web pages or some portions of Web pages. Such a practice may, of course, be seen as a value-added service, but it diverges from the end-to-end content delivery model that has characterized the Internet thus far. It has the potential to deprive both end users and publishers of full control over how content is delivered, particularly where it occurs without control by the end user.

The port-agile tactic described above illustrates the broader point that there are limits to the extent to which the content or applications can be blocked. Since the Internet's architecture allows application writers to layer traffic of their choosing over the basic Internet protocols, it is, in general, difficult to recognize all instances of an application. Application writers can also modify their application protocols to stay one step ahead of attempts to block them. A likely result of persistent attempts at blocking would be an escalating battle in which firewall software authors and ISPs attempt to identify and block applications while application developers work to find ways to slip past these filters. The long-term result of such a struggle might well be a situation where much of the traffic is hard to identify, making it difficult to implement blocking policies. Another technical development could also fundamentally limit the ability of ISPs to filter traffic: widespread adoption of encryption at the IP layer (e.g., deployment of IPSec) would preclude ISPs from examining the information being transmitted or deducing the application being run using information contained in packet headers above the IP layer. If it wished to continue to impose controls under such conditions, an ISP might be forced to adopt a policy that blocks everything that is not identifiable and expressly permitted.

Market and Business Influences on Openness

Economic pressures as well as technical developments are having an impact on transparency and the end-to-end principle. In the consumer ISP market, there are many consumers who are more than willing to subscribe to networks that do not follow the classic Internet provider model in all respects, selecting from among a small number of ISPs that provide a somewhat sheltered environment or at least preferential offering of selected services and content. For example, if one looks at mass-market consumer behavior today, with thousands of ISPs to pick from, most consumers select AOL, an offering that emphasizes access to its custom content over access to the full Internet. (Of course, AOL ended up responding to consumer pressure by adding access to the full range of Internet content.) The 2000 AOL-Time Warner merger is another sign that Internet players believe there is a business case for combining access and content offerings. Such vertical integration, where a network provider attempts to provide a partial or complete solution, from the transmission cable to the applications and contents, could, if successful, cause a change in the Internet market, with innovation and creativity becoming more the province of vertically integrated corporations. Microsoft's "everyday Internet" MSN offering further supports the notion that businesses see a market for controlled, preferred content offerings as a complement to the free-for-all of the public Internet.

Vertical integration has several obvious economic motivations. Open interfaces can make it harder either to coordinate changes at more than one level, which might be needed for some forms of innovation, or to capture as much of the benefits of innovation as integration might allow. On the other hand, the telecommunications industry, once highly integrated vertically, provides evidence that there are limits to vertical integration. Today, pressures are confronting the makers of telecommunications equipment as multiple vendors whose products are organized horizontally collectively challenge the vertically integrated circuit switch. An important enabler of this trend has been the transparency and openness of IP technologies. IP-capable hardware and software can be purchased from many vendors. And it is no longer necessary to own the facilities of a network to offer voice services over it.

Many businesses are customers of a fairly small number of very large networks, which have substantial incentives to hold on to their customers. To do so, they can use such means as leveraging the billing relationship with the customer or their ability to deliver service to the customer premises. Also, providers that have a large market share have incentives to try to own or co-own the most popular services for their customers so as to keep them inside their network.

These economic and business forces can act as disincentives to the continued free sharing of the best infrastructure ideas. Large scale creates additional incentives to providers to build their network with internal proprietary protocols that optimize the performance of both applications and the network in such areas as reliability, security, or control over bandwidth and latency. A leading example of where such optimizations might be deployed is telephony, but other possibilities include e-mail and chat, caching, video, and routing. Hotmail's valuation as an e-mail service or ICQ's as a service for instant messaging reflects the number of customers they are able to serve. For example, Hotmail does not use the Internet-standard mail protocols internally nor does it use standard POP or IMAP for external access by users.[24] Such internal deployments start to have implications for applications running at the edges of the Internet. Today Hotmail is at sufficient scale that special code to support its proprietary protocol is written into e-mail clients; the result is that a frequently used Internet service is no longer running the standard Internet protocols. Equipment suppliers are similarly willing to accommodate such customer demands; their routers are more programmable than ever to support custom protocols. There is a tension here between immediate improvements and long-term benefits: today's optimization may be tomorrow's roadblock, and design choices made to optimize a particular application may or may not turn out to be benefi-

---

[24]The proprietary protocols are intended to allow it to scale better. Hotmail does, however, allow users to read standard POP e-mail accounts through Hotmail.

cial when a new application emerges. Also, the extent to which optimization will occur in a decentralized network such as the Internet is limited by difficulties in reaching agreement to deploy optimizations networkwide. Another pressure for nonstandard protocols, illustrated by the recent flap over instant messaging protocols, is the desire to differentiate oneself from competitors and capture value above the basic IP bit-transport service.

Thus, market pressures, combined with technical pressures relating to optimization, raise the prospect that we might end up with several "separate" Internets differentiated by the use of proprietary protocols or customized content. One scenario would be that some dozen or half-dozen tier 1 service providers would operate somewhat separately, although still using IP and other standard Internet protocols to enable some degree of interoperability among them. If a situation develops where several large providers start using proprietary protocols inside their networks, the incentives for new content and application development could shift. Content and application developers will target the networks of these large companies rather than an abstract Internet, and at the same time the large providers will have a huge incentive to make it difficult for customers to switch to another provider. As a result, tying applications to their proprietary protocols becomes good business—early on they might even pay application developers to do this. A base of, say, many millions of customers might justify the cost of the extra coding and maintenance that supporting multiple protocols would require. Some of this can be seen today, for example, in AOL's system, where providers of content and services, most of whom also do business on the Internet, register AOL keywords and develop AOL-specific content to allow AOL users to access their content and services. The potential viability of applications being developed for environments that are less inclusive than the Internet is also illustrated by the content being developed for the wireless access protocol (WAP, a standard aimed at mobile phones and similar wireless platforms) and Palm's Web clippings.

However, there are forces arrayed against the possibility of this more closed model supplanting the more open Internet model. One is that anonymous rendezvous and the ability to support transitory relationships appear to be important capabilities. E-commerce, which is an important Internet application, depends on the ability to establish connections between two previously noncorresponding companies; multivendor value chains have become critically important in today's networked economy. In fact, many customers explicitly need to work across multiple organizational overlays without having to agree to use a particular network. This point was demonstrated by past attempts to develop standards for electronic data interchange (EDI): interoperable protocols are mandatory and balkanization appears to be useful only in the short term. Providers offering noninteroperable EDI solutions were profitable for a while, but the lack of interoperability among systems ultimately stifled the growth of EDI. On the Internet today, there is a good deal of investment in a new data description standard from the World Wide Web Consortium, XML, to be used for business-to-business e-commerce, and many industry groups are working to define standards for describing data in specific domains so as to enable interoperability on a large scale.

Suppose three ISPs develop different protocols to deliver a particular application over the Internet. To reach customers within closed networks, they would need to make their protocol work over each of the closed network's proprietary protocols and might also need the closed networks to configure their networks to enable the applications to work. From the perspective of the would-be application provider, the ISPs become a roadblock to innovation. If, on the other hand, we assume that there are proprietary ISP protocols, but ISPs also support IP end-to-end in some fashion, application providers can choose to make their protocol run over IP and bypass the constraints of the closed network provider (at least until the provider notices a large fraction of its IP traffic in this new protocol). It is this sort of marketplace dynamic that is valuable.

Another drawback of the closed solution is that it may end up imposing undesirable costs on all parties. For example, for both consumers and application developers, closed solutions represent a lock-in to a single solution (where the lock-in reflects the cost of switching). For the customer, it may mean investing in new hardware and software; for the developer, it may mean retooling a product. From the perspective of a provider, there is the risk that deviation from standards means that they will miss out on some new "killer app" developed elsewhere that offers them dramatic new business opportunities (e.g., an increased customer base or demand for enhanced services).

There have been examples of proprietary solutions that found it difficult to gain widespread acceptance on the Internet. For instance, the past decade saw a debate on whether to adopt the ISO X.400 standard, the Internet standard SMTP, or one of a number of proprietary systems for e-mail. The market settled on SMTP, and the other proposals have become largely moot. More generally, there are obstacles to proprietary approaches being adopted Internet-wide. All of the users on the Internet will not sign up with a single provider all at once, and few users only need to be able to interact with other users connected to the same single provider. For example, in an e-mail exchange, neither the sender nor the receiver is likely to know (or care) which ISP the other is using or which e-mail standard their respective ISPs are using. They simply want to exchange an e-mail message. The success of a proprietary solution depends on the Internet provider developing and offering working gateways to all the other services, which will entail additional cost to the provider. From the perspective of customers, open standards help maximize the benefits they realize from the sheer quantity of people and services they can interact with. If all belong to a single Internet, the benefits of adding a new user to it accrue to everyone located anywhere on the Internet, whereas in a partitioned Internet, the benefits of an additional user would be limited to the customers of that user's ISP. The recent past has also seen pressures placed on online providers that relied on proprietary technologies. Non-Internet-based online providers have had to respond to the Internet phenomenon by supplementing their more closed content and services with access to the full Internet or by reinventing themselves as Internet-based services.

Today, both fully open and sheltered models are being pursued with vigor in the Internet marketplace, reflecting different business models and different assumptions about the desires of consumers. Consumer ISPs cover a broad spectrum, with more closed services at one end that emphasize their custom content and services and more open services at the other end that emphasize Internet connectivity but may also provide some preferred content or services. To date, the more closed providers have also continued to offer some degree of access to the wider Internet through the connectivity afforded by the basic Internet protocol (with a few having adding this support in response to market demands). Which path the Internet market takes from here will affect the shape of future innovation.

Keeping the Internet Open

Provision of open IP service ensures that whichever service provider a consumer or business picks, the consumer or business can reach all the parties it wishes to communicate with. Much as the PSTN dial tone offers customers the ability to connect to everyone else connected to the global PSTN network, open IP service offers access to all the services and content available on the public Internet. In the absence of an open IP service, who you can communicate with is a function of the service provider you pick. (Note that the *quality* of service is still a function of the service provider you pick.) Open IP service is also an enabler of continued innovation and competition. Anyone who creates a better service that runs over IP can distribute software supporting it to thousands or millions of users, who can then use it regardless of who their service provider is.

Open IP service requires support of the Internet Protocol (IP), globally unique Internet addresses, and full interconnection with the rest of the networks that make up the Internet. (Some additional capabilities may be required; some perspectives on what else should be included as a core service were presented above.) Open IP service is content independent—that is, the service provider does not filter the customer's traffic based on content, except with the consent and knowledge of the customer. However, because the Internet's default service is best effort, this definition can make no promises about the quality of the access. The quality of connectivity will depend on the agreement a customer has with its service provider and the agreements that this provider has with other Internet service providers.   Indeed, in a free market, it is reasonable to have differentiation of services to satisfy customers who want to pay more for a service they deem better. It is important to point out that one possible outcome of the tension between open service and ISP service differentiation is that the current best-effort service will continue to be provided as a transparent, end-to-end service but that end-to-end transparency across multiple providers will not be provided for the more demanding (and potentially more interesting from a commercial standpoint) applications such as telephony and audio and video streaming that may depend on QOS mechanisms.

Because IP connectivity affords users the potential to misbehave or pose unacceptable demands on the network, this definition of open IP service is not intended to preclude service providers that want to ensure safe, effective operation or meet the desire of customers to block certain types of IP traffic from restricting how their network is used. An ISP may, for example, block particular traffic to prevent its customers from launching attacks on other customers of the ISP (or users elsewhere on the Internet). It may also filter particular types of traffic to protect its customer computers from attacks. And an ISP may restrict traffic volumes where bandwidth resources are limited to ensure that all users have fair access. Of course, ISPs and their customers may differ over whether a particular filter enhances the operation of the ISP's network or unnecessarily restricts the behavior of a customer; full disclosure of filtering practices provides consumers with the means to make informed choices when selecting an ISP.

4

Collisions Between Existing Industries and Emerging Internet Industries: Telephony As a Case Study

INTRODUCTION

The general-purpose nature of the Internet and its basic technology makes it possible to provide services at least comparable to those provided by other communication systems. Perhaps the clearest such trend today is the growing use of Internet technology by providers of telephone service and the emergence of a variety of voice communications services over the Internet. For reasons that range from reducing the costs of conventional telephony by using less expensive technology, to bypassing the tariff structure of the existing public switched telephone network (PSTN), to innovating new forms of telephony services and applications, many efforts are under way to use the Internet and its technology components to provide voice services. These services do not merely duplicate those provided by the PSTN; the ease with which new applications can be introduced over the Internet opens up the possibility of a wide range of applications involving voice and the introduction of many different enhancements to what we think of as telephony today.

Telephony over the public Internet is in its infancy, but telephony over IP networks that provide appropriate provisioning or quality-of-service technology is already viable today. Where Internet voice is deployed on existing data backbones lacking supporting quality of service and/or provisioning, such service today is generally a second-best alternative. However, in other cases, where IP telephony is used either with separately provisioned bandwidth or with supporting quality-of-service

151

technologies, it has proven to be competitive with circuit-switched technologies. There are numerous small-scale examples of such deployments
for long-haul telephony as well as several instances of large-scale systems, including two Chinese telephone networks (China Telecom and
Uninet).[1] Telephony over IP networks is also being deployed within
enterprises (generally replacing PBX functionality), with the goal of
achieving lower costs by operating a single network carrying both data
and voice.[2]

These developments are emblematic of a broader trend toward
Internet services that overlap and potentially exceed or even supersede
communications services that have long existed as distinct industries with
distinct policies and regulations governing them. Another emerging service is Internet distribution models for audio and video, which overlap
the capabilities of traditional radio and television broadcasting and music
and video publishing and distribution. In both cases there are conflicts
between the new technologies, systems, and players made possible by the
Internet and the policies, regulations, and practices that have shaped the
extant industry. This chapter focuses on telephony, where the conflicts
have now become quite visible, but many of the issues explored here are
also relevant to these other sectors.[3]

WHAT IS IP TELEPHONY?

The terms "IP telephony" and "voice over IP" are used synonymously
in this report to describe the broad range of options for using Internet-
Protocol-based, packet-switched networks in support of telecommunications services of various sorts, typically for voice communications. (The
committee is careful in its use of the term "Internet telephony," because
the term implies that the public Internet is used to carry telephone calls,
which not all IP-based telephony does.) IP may be used for some or all of
the transmission and interconnectivity path as well as to provide switching, control, and services facilitation (e.g., call setup). IP telephony
encompasses services that provide connectivity among normal telephone

---

[1]See Leslie Chang. 1999. "Internet Phone Service Catches on with Millions in China—
Rivals Challenge China Telecom with Cheap Rates." *Wall Street Journal.* December 21,
p. A14.

[2]The committee does not provide data on the extent of IP telephony deployment because
assembling such information is complicated by the diverse offerings, definitional questions,
and the highly dynamic nature of the business.

[3]This chapter is not intended as a thorough examination of technical issues underlying
Internet telephony. Discussion of some key underlying technical dimensions, such as network robustness, scaling, and quality of service, is located elsewhere in this report.

sets, computers, or other computer appliances, and combinations of these types of devices. IP telephony may be used over a privately owned network, a network owned by the telephony service provider or some other third party, or over the public Internet.

To carry voice over IP, the analog signals are digitized, (usually) compressed to reduce bandwidth requirements, and then broken up into fragments or packets with accompanying routing information for transport over a packet network such as the Internet. They are transported across one or more IP networks, making use of algorithms running on the devices at each end of the call to deal with late or lost packets and possibly also making use of quality-of-service mechanisms in the networks the call traverses. Call quality is determined by the algorithm used to digitize and compress the signals, the capacity of the network, and the effectiveness of any explicit quality-of-service mechanisms that are employed.

IP telephony comes in many flavors; these may or may not involve the public Internet and may or may not involve the PSTN. Some IP telephony applications make use of only an IP network, whereas others make use of both IP networks and segments of the PSTN. If the PSTN is involved in any segment of the call, a gateway is required to translate the data and signaling (e.g., call setup or termination instructions) associated with the call. Another function that is generally provided in any telephony application is a directory lookup service that associates a phone number or other identifier with a particular telephone line or IP device.[4]

Some designs amount to little more than a substitution of IP technology for transport within the network. For instance, IP may be substituted for other means of transporting communications within the networks of telephony providers; this internal substitution of IP technology for transport within the network raises few policy issues that are distinguishable from those raised by the introduction of other new technologies or the entry of new players into the "traditional" PSTN business. Another flavor is the use of IP within the private network of an enterprise, where it replaces the elements of a traditional PBX system or other corporate voice network. Other designs make sole use of IP for transport and Internet application servers for control and directory services, while still others employ hybrids that combine elements of both the Internet and the PSTN. The set of possible sorts of services that might be labeled "IP telephony" is highly diverse and encompasses the following:

- *Network operators and transport media.* For example, backbone trans-

---

[4]The PSTN provides several such mappings, including between subscriber name and phone number (what the telephone directory contains) and between phone number and telephone line.

port within a carrier network, telephony over the public Internet, enterprise networks, virtual private networks, PSTN, and combinations of these;

• *End-user equipment*. For example, conventional telephones, IP-based special-purpose devices (appliances), and general-purpose computers;

• *Local access technology*. For example, PSTN analog lines, IP data networks, and IP over DSL;

• *Interfaces and gateways between IP and PSTN elements*. For example, analog phone lines, ISDN primary rate interfaces, Switching System 7 (SS7)—or none in the case of pure IP telephony; and

• *Architectures*. For example, telephony services may be provided by a single vendor in a centrally managed way (perhaps over a dedicated network) or provided as a distributed service with individual users placing calls end-to-end over the Internet, perhaps making use of services such as directory lookup provided by a third party.

NEW AND EVOLVING ARCHITECTURES FOR TELEPHONY

To understand the technical, operational, economic, and policy issues related to IP telephony, it is useful to understand the role of architectures and examine some specific examples. The concept of an architecture has been a cornerstone in the development of telecommunications systems. An architecture first requires that the underlying system be treated in terms of a set of commonly understood elements and that these elements have a clearly demarcated set of functions and interfaces that allow for combining the elements.[5] An architecture is driven by two factors in addition to the identification and selection of elements and interfaces: technology and world view. The state of the technology places bounds on what is achievable. The world view is the way an individual, entity, or organization views the world, its relationship to that world, and how that world and that relationship will evolve over time. The PSTN, for example, with its more centralized architecture, reflects a world view different from that of the Internet, with its more distributed design. The limits imposed by technology are typically less confining than the limits that are self-imposed by the designers or architects; in practice, therefore, world view is often the more powerful driver of architecture.

---

[5]Terrence McGarty. 1990. "Alternative Networking Architectures: Pricing, Policy, and Competition, Information Infrastructures for the 1990s." John F. Kennedy School of Government, Harvard University, November.

IP Telephony Architectures

A multitude of network architectures and implementations are encompassed by the label "IP telephony." One way to portray this diversity is to portray it in terms of architectural classes. A four-class taxonomy, with illustrations of each class, is presented in Figure 4.1.

Even a single class of architecture has many possible configurations. As shown in Figure 4.2, the telco-to-telco (class 1) architecture encompasses two quite different ways of employing voice over IP, even though each way makes use of a basic PSTN-IP gateway to convert telephony signals into IP packets. The first (Figure 4.2a) consists of a dedicated network or channel configuration that uses a private network. The operation of this design can be explained as follows. A telephone user in, for example, New York desires to call a telephone user in Moscow. The local telephone user in both cases will access the system by means of a standard telephone. The user places the call to a local exchange carrier, which then sends the call to another switch. This switch places the call through an IP gateway node (IGN) that connects locally to a router and the call proceeds over a private network. The process is reversed on the terminating side. The gateway provides translation from the telephony world to the IP domain by performing three conversions—between telephone signaling and IP signaling, between the conventional voice signal and data packets, and between telepone numbers and IP addresses (if required). The second class 1 approach (Figure 4.2b) is the public Internet approach adopted by a number of IP telephony start-up companies. It uses the same generic form of entry—a gateway between the PSTN and an IP data network—but replaces packet transport over dedicated IP links with transport over the public Internet. It reflects both a different architecture and a different world view of IP telephony. For example, in contrast to the architecture using a private IP network, there is no PSTN switch or function (such as a billing system) provided by a switch.

Increasingly, one sees new applications based on a comingling of the Internet and PSTN telephony architectures. These emerging offerings include "click-to-speak" voice conversations launched from Web pages and unified messaging services (which combine voice mail, e-mail, and fax). Another application, Internet call waiting, is aimed at customers who use a single phone line for both normal phone service and their dial-up connection to the Internet. While the service, which uses the Internet to inform a customer when a call is being made to the customer's phone line, appears on the surface to be quite similar to conventional call waiting, it has very different requirements behind the scenes. Implementation of conventional call waiting is internal to the telephone switches in

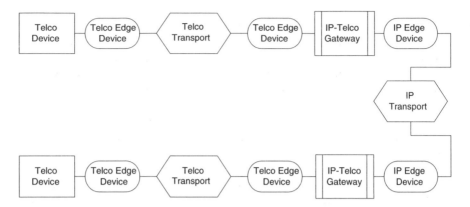

Class 1: Telco to telco. The end users employ existing telephony equipment through a conventional PSTN connection while IP (either private network or Internet) is used for a portion of the connection through interconnects with the PSTN (e.g., IP used over long-distance segments).

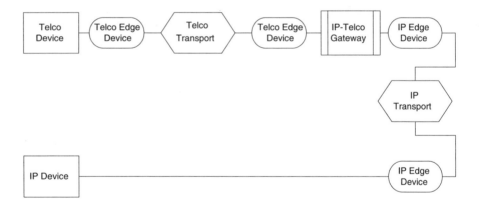

Class 2: Telco to IP. Conventional telephone devices are interconnected with IP telephony devices (a computer or other IP-enabled device).

FIGURE 4.1 Four classes of IP telephony architectures. SOURCE: Taxonomy adapted (with extensions) from David D. Clark. 1997. *A Taxonomy of Internet Telephony Applications.* Proceedings of the Telecommunications Policy Research Conference (TPRC).

Class 3: IP to IP. Computer telephony devices are used at both ends and the connection is made solely through IP networks or the Internet. While gateways to the PSTN would be added to provide interconnection with PSTN customers, this architecture does not make use of any PSTN elements and thus depends on the development of a full range of signaling services using IP only.

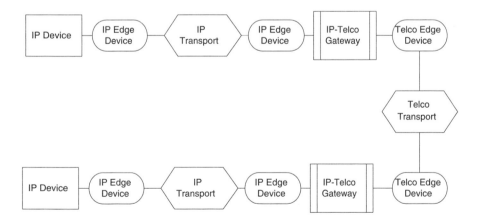

Class 4: IP to telco to IP. Other combinations of PSTN and public and private IP network links. The figure illustrates the use of the PSTN to provide a connection between two Internet "subclouds." This architecture might be used to enable IP telephony across Internet providers in the absence of adequate quality of service or other capabilities over an IP connection.

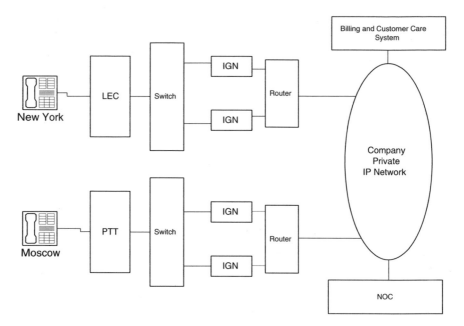

(a) Using a dedicated private network

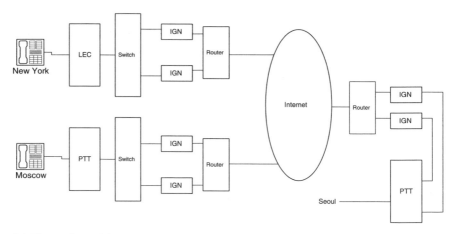

(b) Using the public Internet

FIGURE 4.2 Two examples of class 1 IP telephony configurations. LEC, local exchange carrier; IGN, IP gateway node; and PTT, Post, Telegraphs, and Telephones.

the PSTN; in a hybrid PSTN-Internet application, switches have to communicate with IP routers.

Although the commercial viability of various forms of IP telephony remains untested, the prospect of future developments makes it possible to think in terms of a revolutionary—as opposed to an evolutionary—use of IP technology, in which phone calls become just one application on the public Internet. Not everyone agrees on how compelling the technical and business cases are for offering voice services over the public Internet or what the time frame for such a transition might be, but there is little doubt that both new and existing players will enter this market. The timing and viability of such developments depend in part on being able to provide the transmission resources needed to obtain sufficient voice quality (either by deploying QOS mechanisms across ISP boundaries or by taking advantage of a rising tide of capacity that makes the average quality sufficient to meet voice requirements; see Chapter 2). The motivation for such a shift would not be just the cost reductions associated with using IP-based components and systems but would also be the ability to offer new features, particularly at the human interface, made possible by a shift to more intelligence in end-user devices.

The Evolving Architecture of the PSTN

Over the past several decades, the PSTN has also been changing, from a network with only basic circuit-switching functionality to a circuit-switched network architecture known as the advanced intelligent network (AIN). This architecture makes use of centralized, closed-application databases and a PSTN-specific software development environment (known in PSTN lingo as the service creation environment) to enable a range of capabilities such as toll-free number dialing (including routing a call to the appropriate point), credit card calling, and flexible call forwarding.

As the architecture evolves, the intelligence of the PSTN is becoming increasingly distributed and open. The PSTN's architecture is evolving from the AIN model, which uses centralized switching system databases and interoffice signaling, into a model that uses direct signaling to more distributed databases. There have also been efforts to further separate the applications from the operating system (i.e., the basic switching software) and the underlying infrastructure so as to make the PSTN a more open service creation environment.

The opening up of the PSTN service creation architecture is aimed at increasing the flexibility of the infrastructure and enabling a greater number of parties to create useful services. In the AIN, the service creation environment and the applications are provided by the service provider and generally closed to third parties. Open AIN was proposed by PSTN operators in the mid-1990s as a way of enabling a set of entities beyond the service provider to create services. Today, by virtue of the PSTN's connectivity to the Internet, service creation is being enabled at the edges of the network. These moves toward a more open environment increase flexibility but pose challenges related to maintaining the stable operation of the network; some of these are discussed below.

While the intelligent network is becoming more distributed and open, there is another fundamental change under way in the PSTN: it is becoming more datacentric, with high-speed data access, transport, and switching—an architecture that many believe will ultimately replace the present intelligent, circuit-switched architecture. At the same time, the transport backbone is evolving, with greater deployment of optical transport, such as wave division multiplexing (WDM), to accommodate the voracious demand for bandwidth. IP over ATM over WDM or IP directly over WDM are emerging to replace other optical communications technologies, such as SONET or SDH, as capabilities are introduced into the optical layer. Also, local access is evolving to support higher data speeds as datacentric communications are introduced in the local loop in the form of DSL and digital optical fiber deployments closer to end users in telephone networks and in the form of hybrid fiber coax deployments in cable networks.

PSTN's evolution from a predominantly circuit-switched to a packet-switched architecture is producing a significant change in architecture construct and concomitant operations. New packet-based data (ATM and IP) capabilities are being introduced in combination with the existing SS7.[6] This transformation has included the adoption of new, packet network telecommunications protocols. Along with new protocols to establish connections between IP and PSTN systems, these packet-based capabilities allow voice telephony to continue to be provided even as the network architecture moves away from the circuit-switched model. The new architecture, protocols, and intelligence capabilities together enable a richer set of prospective applications and services, such as Internet call-waiting. While there is surely room for the market to experiment with various price/quality trade-offs, customers will expect the emerging datacentric architecture and technologies to provide the quality they associate with today's PSTN—a challenge being addressed at this time.

------

[6]In the long term, a possible direction is that the introduction of MPLS with core ATM switching could provide the necessary infrastructure and control capabilities.

Architectural Contrasts Between IP Telephony and Today's PSTN

Although the PSTN architecture is changing in significant ways, there remain considerable differences of approach between it and the various architectural alternatives emerging for IP and Internet telephony. These differences, which stem in large part from the fundamental contrast between the PSTN's centralized design and the Internet's open, distributed architecture, include the following:

- *Unlike in the PSTN, in IP telephony the function of transporting the packets carrying voice can be carried out by an entity different from the one providing application services* (e.g., call agents and directory services). This means that voice telephony service can exist as an overlay to IP networks—indeed, voice traffic can be carried over networks unbeknownst to the IP network operators. Application support servers are not even constrained to be located within the same network as the customer—or even the same country. It also means that Internet telephony quality depends not only on the quality of the functions (e.g., a call agent) offered by the telephony provider itself but also on the quality (including reliability and freedom from congestion) of all of the underlying networks over which communications pass.

- *Like other packet data, traffic associated with a phone call over the Internet will transit one, two, or many providers depending on which networks the calling parties are attached to and how the networks are interconnected.* The route taken by a packet is a function of numerous routing decisions made within the network; it may change dynamically, and it is outside the control of the end user.

- *IP telephony application servers do not necessarily provide the same functionality as the PSTN.* For instance, an application server established by a voice telephony overlay service might be concerned only with providing directory and call setup services. Once a call is established, data packets will only flow between the callers, and the voice telephony provider's server will have no access to the content of voice calls. It would, for example, be impossible in this architecture for the telephony provider itself to carry out a wiretap order to provide the content of a call to law enforcement. Nor would the provider itself be able to offer priority routing for emergency calls, as might be desired to provide functionality analogous to 911 telephone calls.

- *The general-purpose nature of the Internet means that it can offer voice communication in novel ways that do not parallel classic telephony.* Telephony is understood to refer to communication between devices attached to the public switched telephone network (e.g., telephony regulations do not apply to two-way radios or in-building intercom systems). The line between telephony and other applications could start to blur. For example, today's popular text-based chat applications may well turn into voice chat. Are the latter to be considered telephony? There are, in fact, a variety of voice-communications-based applications running over the Internet today. Internet-based video games that allow players to exchange voice comments along with the game play do not, owing to their specialized purpose, look like telephony, but the line is not sharp. Edge-driven innovation of voice applications means that such questions are likely to emerge frequently and rapidly.

SCENARIOS FOR FUTURE EVOLUTION

The extent, pace, and nature of a transition to IP- or Internet-based telephony services is unclear. The views of those in the two industries—the Internet and the PSTN—as well as outside observers are based on their perceptions of how fast the Internet and its underlying technologies are evolving as well as on their world views. Many industry analysts predict that the rapid growth of data networks, particularly the Internet, will lead to the melding of voice and data networks, and that voice traffic will increasingly be carried using IP technology.

There are a number of practical reasons why IP telephony could over time supplant traditional PSTN voice services. Carrying data and voice services over a common enterprise network promises reduced infrastructure cost and ease of management. This would be especially true when the volume of data traffic is steadily growing, making the case for investment in a datacentric architecture more compelling. Bypassing the PSTN by using a private data network for voice would also allow an enterprise to avoid long-distance charges.

Others argue that for technical and economic reasons IP may not always be the best or most efficient choice for telephony, particularly in the short run. For instance, voice over IP is sometimes less efficient in its use of communications link capacity than existing PSTN technologies such as time division multiplexing (TDM) or ATM. Another challenge is that putting time-sensitive voice traffic on a corporate data network places substantial new demands (e.g., properly engineering the IP fabric and the underlying network) on network managers unaccustomed to managing a network for voice traffic.

Several technical trends are promoting the integration of voice and IP service and the shift to IP. Efforts are under way to move the full range of voice services to IP technology, which would one day allow IP-based service to supplant circuit-switched network service. As a consequence of this shift, there is likely to be a far richer set of voice services available, raising the prospect of IP-based telephony offering a richer and more powerful suite of services while the traditional PSTN remains in place. At the same time, considerable attention is being paid to the development of IP-PSTN interoperability capabilities in the form of gateways between IP and circuit-switching technologies, enabling the creation of hybrid services.

The course of IP and Internet telephony will be determined in part by the organizational and cultural factors at work in the two historically separate technical communities: those responsible for the PSTN and the Internet. From the PSTN community perspective, given the extensive investment made in deploying SS7 and the capabilities and features required for telephony services, it would be easier to develop new services by leveraging the capabilities of SS7 than by building voice services from scratch.

Efforts to bridge the gap between the communities are evident in the efforts of several IETF working groups, including their collaboration with more traditional telephony groups such as the International Telecommunication Union. Constructing robust gateways between the two infrastructures and building de novo IP-based implementations of all of the required functionality of the PSTN are both formidable challenges. The nature of the challenge as well as the inevitability of a long period of coexistence and interoperation between the technologies argues that success in building a seamless network for the future will benefit from greater cooperation between the two communities.

From the Internet community perspective, the more centralized PSTN architecture runs counter to the distributed, edge-controlled Internet model. Motivated by a belief that open standards will permit more rapid innovation and development of a whole range of new services and applications related to telephony, some advocate IETF-like processes to develop standards that can stand apart from the PSTN. Their advocacy stems in part from an expectation that the PSTN world will not open up PSTN network elements enough to permit the kind and pace of innovation characteristic of the Internet.

Telephony is very much in flux, with many decisions being made in the marketplace today by customers, equipment vendors, and service providers whose landscape is changing rapidly. The PSTN is not monolithic; it has always been composed of multiple networks, and those networks are managed according to diverse philosophies about deployment, upgrading technology, and so forth. The latest trend is the significant increase in the number of players as new competitors emerge in the local telephone market (the competitive local exchange carriers, or CLECs), with entrants such as Qwest and Level 3 challenging the incumbent long-distance telecommunications carriers. Cable operators are providing telephony and Internet access as well as content, and traditional entertainment and media firms are moving to distribute voice, data and video services—the AOL-Time Warner merger accentuates that trend. At the same time, the traditional PSTN service providers are offering cable, Internet, and content services.

The landscape of equipment suppliers is also changing rapidly. Telephone switch suppliers realize that they need to stay competitive and are responding accordingly, although it will be a challenge for them to evolve their business models fast enough to respond to the competition. Traditional suppliers to telecommunications companies for the PSTN in the United States, for example, consisted of a few major switching suppliers such as Lucent (formerly AT&T), Nortel, and Siemens and—since divestiture of AT&T—a plethora of transport and access product suppliers. Their competition now includes manufacturers of other kinds of products, and mergers and acquisitions further blur the lines between previously distinct market segments. In the past few years, traditional router suppliers acquired ATM equipment manufacturers (e.g., Cisco acquired Stratacom), while traditional ATM/frame relay equipment manufacturers (one such was Ascend—previously Cascade) were acquired by Lucent, and the router/hub manufacturer Bay Networks was acquired by Nortel. Now, the traditional telecommunications circuit-switching equipment suppliers, and others as well, are paying greater attention and devoting more resources to packet switching and data networking products, whereas companies such as Cisco are working or combining with other suppliers to meet PSTN and other service provider needs. At the same time, quality-of-service capabilities are being added to cable modems, improvements reflected, for example, in the new DOCSIS 1.1 standard, which supports IP telephony.

Will IP telephony be largely confined to those places where it has proved viable on a large scale today, such as backbone transport within carrier networks or within private IP networks? Or will it ultimately be deployed much more widely on the public Internet? One possibility is that IP telephony networks will be melded together using IP, so that calls are carried end-to-end over IP. It is also possible that there will be many IP telephony networks built by a variety of players (both traditional local and interexchange carriers) that form growing clouds of end users employing only IP telephony inside but relying on the PSTN to carry traffic between them. A factor that argues for this scenario is the difficulty of providing adequate quality of service for calls that flow across multiple IP providers. Because of the larger number of players involved, this difficulty is greatest in the case of telephony over the public Internet. Disincentives to using the public Internet appear likely to decline to the extent that the quality-of-service and reliability issues are resolved, for with these barriers removed, the public Internet allows leveraging of both common technology and common infrastructure.

How will the Internet and the PSTN relate to each other in the future? One possible outcome is that IP telephony and PSTN telephony services continue to coevolve, with considerable effort going into dealing with addressing and signaling issues between the two networks. Another is that the two will develop in parallel but that ultimately the PSTN as it is known today will disappear. A third outcome is that the two will increasingly interoperate and, over time, will converge in terms of the network architecture and the technology employed. In this case, the PSTN will move to a more datacentric architecture, with the Internet and PSTN underlying architectures becoming increasingly similar. Circuit-switching technology would not disappear immediately but would phase out for voice services over the next decade. Underlying this range of possible outcomes is a basic issue: Will IP telephony be driven primarily by the needs of interoperating with the PSTN or by a desire to have new, IP-only features?

INTEROPERATION BETWEEN IP TELEPHONY AND THE PSTN

Whatever the course of change for the Internet and the PSTN, it is clear that for the foreseeable future, dedicated IP networks, the public Internet, the PSTN, and hybrids of these will all play a role in delivering telephony services. From a customer perspective, a smooth transition will depend on the extent to which telephony networks remain interconnected (anyone can continue to place a call to anyone else) and the extent to which it appears seamless to the end user, who will not have to act in very different ways when calling different parties. Achieving this goal will require the development of standards for telephony functions within IP networks and at gateways between IP and PSTN networks. These include the algorithms used to digitize and compress the voice signal (codecs), gateway functions, addressing, directory services, call control, and the like. As with other standardization efforts, this effort will have to balance standardization with flexibility that permits ongoing innovation in telephony services.

A number of groups, with origins in both the telecommunications and Internet sectors, are working to address these issues. Among them are the following:

• *IETF.* A number of IETF groups are working on telephony issues, including the IP Telephony working group, which is developing protocols for call processing and distributing information about gateway capabilities;[7] the IETF Media Gateway Control working group, which is developing an architecture for controlling gateways between the IP networks;[8] and the Telephone Number Mapping group, which is working on protocols for mapping telephone numbers to other attributes (e.g., URLs) that can be used to contact a resource associated with the numbers.[9]

• *International Telecommunication Union Standardization Sector (ITU-T)*. ITU-T activities include ITU-T Study Group 13,[10] which is studying IP-based network issues such as interoperability with other networks, signaling requirements, numbering, and security, and Study Group 16, which is working on protocols and standards for multimedia services.

• *European Telecommunications Standards Institute*. ETSI, the developer of the GSM standard for cellular telephones, has a project, Telecommunications and Internet Protocol Harmonization Over Networks (TIPHON), that is developing an architecture and requirements for interoperability and exploring technical aspects of billing; call control; naming, numbering, and addressing; and quality of service.[11]

• *Softswitch Consortium*. This industry group provides interoperability testing facilities, testing events, specifications, reference implementations, and development resources for a number of voice and multimedia communications standards.[12]

As this list suggests, there are areas of overlap and conflict among the activities of these groups. These have been diminishing, however, and there are instances of collaboration between groups. For example, the IETF Media Gateway Control working group is collaborating with ITU-T Study Group 13.

Central to a successful coevolution is the resolution of interoperability issues in numbering and addressing; signaling and control and service creation capabilities; and robustness concerns. Each area is treated in turn below.

---

[7]See IETF IP Telephony working group charter, available online at <http://www.ietf.org/html.charters/iptel-charter.html>.

[8]See IETF Media Gateway Control working group charter, available online at <http://www.ietf.org/html.charters/megaco-charter.html>.

[9]See Telephone Number Mapping group working charter, available online at <http://www.ietf.org/html.charters/enum-charter.html>.

[10]See ITU-T Study Group 13 home page, available online at <http://www.itu.int/ITU-T/com13/index.html>.

[11]See the TIPHON home page, available online at <http://webapp.etsi.org/tbhomepage/TBDetails.asp?TB_ID=291>.

[12]See Softswitch Consortium Frequently Asked Questions, available online at <http://www.softswitch.org/FAQs/index.html>.

Addressing and Number Portability

No matter what the ultimate end point, telephone number assignment will be more complicated as IP telephony services emerge. Number portability across the public switched telephone network[13] and IP telephony services is an important consideration, at least over the short term. Today, local phone number portability in the PSTN is provided by the local exchange carriers, permitting customers to switch local carriers without changing their standard PSTN phone number.[14] In the future, there may be no conventional telephone number associated with customers using IP telephony; in fact, depending on how their IP address is assigned, they may or may not have a fixed IP address. How will number portability be handled? Several requirements for a smooth evolution stand out. First, customers should be able to in some fashion transfer ("port") their existing telephone number to the Internet-based service, just as customers can today retain, at the same location, the same telephone number when they switch from one local exchange carrier to another, allowing them to continue to receive calls directed to the phone number provided by their original local exchange carrier. Second, there is the question of how someone on the PSTN calls an IP telephony subscriber. This suggests that Internet service providers and other Internet-based telephony providers should be able to issue new telephone numbers to their customers, even to those who do not have conventional telephone service, so as to provide compatibility across calls originated or terminated on conventional and IP-based telephones.

Additional issues arise when a given household uses both PSTN and Internet services. For example, what address or number should be used when a standard PSTN (E.164) number is assigned to a household that uses an IP address (perhaps from an IP telephony directory server that maps a name or other identifier to an address) for an IP telephony appliance? Portability needs to address both aspects for subscribers who wish to port their service as well as for subscribers using IP who wish to change their Internet service providers.

---

[13]E.164 is the ITU standard ("Recommendation") for the international public telecommunications numbering plan, which specifies a geographically hierarchical numbering plan in which numbers are assigned to customers by carriers.

[14]Local number portability was mandated by the Telecommunications Act of 1996. In its rules implementing the act, the FCC allowed local telephone companies to assess charges to recover the costs of implementing and providing portability—both a charge to be paid by other carriers in exchange for the use of number portability facilities and a monthly charge for all telephone customers.

Beyond these more immediate interoperability considerations lie broader questions of addressing. For example, telephone services today already allow using abstractions of the phone numbers. Voice-activated dialing allows a caller to substitute a phrase (e.g., "call Mom") for a phone number. Other services offer a single number that then follows the customer to whatever phone is in use at the time a call is put through. Such abstractions—somewhat like the level of indirection provided by today's Domain Name System, which allows access to Internet devices via a name rather than a numerical address—could also be applied to the IP telephony domain.[15] In the long term, phone numbers could be replaced by other identifiers. How to provide suitable directory services is currently being explored in the forums listed at the start of this section; agreement on a standard will be crucial to building hybrid Internet-PSTN or Internet-only telephony networks that appear seamless to the end user.

While this report does not explore these issues in depth, the issues that arise when one starts to explore solutions for all of these name/ number portability requirements closely resemble those that arise for the Domain Name System (see "Scaling of the Internet's Naming Systems" in Chapter 2). For example, there are similar issues of ensuring scalability, supporting dynamic updating, ensuring that the name/number infrastructure is robust and secure, and authenticating updates to directory entries.

Signaling and Control and Service Creation

As architectures for IP telephony emerge, there are unresolved questions of how they will interface with the existing SS7-based global PSTN, including how signaling and control, the functions that allow calls to be set up and the network to be managed, will be provided for a hybrid PSTN/Internet infrastructure. Solutions must be sufficiently standardized to allow interoperation and yet flexible enough to encourage innovation in new applications. Open questions include the following: What signaling capabilities need to be established to provide messaging across all media (wireless and wireline) and different types of devices? What is required to meet the needs of telephony that runs over the public Internet in contrast with telephony that runs over private networks using IP technology, and what are the implications for the signaling and control infra-

---

[15]Unlike the old naming schemes for telephone exchanges (e.g., "Jacksonville 6-500"), in which there was a fixed mapping between name and exchange, a naming scheme that provides indirection allows the number with which a name is associated to be easily changed, perhaps at the direction of the telephone user.

structure to support these changes? How is quality of service assured across the multiple providers for data services? These are some of the important questions that the working groups described above are addressing.

The control capabilities must be able to handle both the pure IP telephony and the interdomain calls between Internet telephony and PSTN elements. The committee foresees some interesting complications. For instance, a household of the future might well employ both conventional PSTN telephone and IP telephony equipment, with the latter making use of one or more local access technologies (e.g., IP over DSL or IP over a cable modem). Telephones of the future might use a variety of local access technologies, such as IP over ATM or over DSL. It will need to be possible to manage each of these capabilities with the appropriate protocols. Another example of these complications is the click-to-speak service mentioned earlier, which may involve a voice connection between the customer and the service representative or the downloading of streaming video from a server to the prospective customer. A suite of open standard protocols will be needed to enable these interoperable sets of PSTN/Internet services.

Robustness

The robustness of the PSTN benefited in the past from agreement among a relatively small number of players to follow a tightly defined architecture and set of operating practices. As the PSTN market has grown, the number of players has grown, too, potentially affecting robustness. However, the opening up of the PSTN architecture and interoperation with other IP networks give rise to robustness concerns that go beyond those that would be posed by conventional new entrants to the PSTN. These concerns fall into two categories. First, there are concerns about how to ensure the reliability of a more open architecture in which there are fewer controls over the inputs, e.g., signaling and control messages, received by PSTN networks and in which these inputs may interact. Second, there are concerns about how to ensure overload controls and network availability in this more open environment.

As a network is opened up, additional attention must be paid to authentication (Is the originator of the message authorized to perform the function?) and validation (Is a request a reasonable one that can be executed without harm to the network of signaling and control messages?). Another issue is how to localize the impact of problems. How can a more open service creation environment be designed to create new applications without adversely affecting the applications of others? What mediation capabilities and other new service-creation or application programming interfaces should be developed? Can there be service creation at the edges without having to worry about multiple-creator application interactions and adverse consequences? If so, how does this manifest itself in an Internet/PSTN environment—a hybrid of centralized or partially distributed service creation in the PSTN plus the fully distributed service creation of the Internet? How can the combination of SCEs flourish in this evolution? How do the provider-proprietary applications for specific customers affect the service creation environments?

If networks carrying voice networks are to continue to meet stringent performance requirements in the face of opening them to a diverse set of providers, the ability to control against overload and provide enhanced robustness will need to be included. These mechanisms will need to be designed not only into the systems comprising the PSTN/Internet combination but also into the basic signaling and control architecture, to prevent serious congestion, service degradation, and severe outages.

IMPLICATIONS OF IP TELEPHONY
FOR TELEPHONY REGULATION

The emergence of IP telephony heralds conflicts between, on the one hand, IP telephony's practices and assumptions and, on the other hand, the practices and assumptions of the existing regulatory regime. These conflicts stem in large part from the contrast between the dynamic, rapid change that Internet-based innovation enables and the historically relatively stable nature of PSTN technologies and businesses. As IP telephony gains market share, it is likely to have a dramatic impact on the traditional, regulated voice service providers. Such developments have provoked and will continue to provoke calls for voice over IP to be subject to regulation akin to that in place for circuit-switched voice services or for the regulatory regime to be modified in other ways to cover this new form of telephony. As new IP- and Internet-based services emerge that in some way resemble PSTN services that are currently regulated, there will be a number of questions about whether these new services should be treated in the same fashion. At the same time, in the face of competition, PSTN operators may develop and offer new services in order to attract customers, raising questions about how those services will be accommodated within the existing regulatory framework.

The position of the Federal Communications Commission has been to keep the Internet free from unnecessary application of the existing regulations on telecommunications, and many have argued that this hands-off approach has been a significant factor in the Internet's explosive growth.[16]

---

[16]See, for example, Jason Oxman. 1999. *The FCC and the Unregulation of the Internet.* Office of Plans and Policy (OPP) Working Paper No. 31. Washington D.C.: OPP, Federal

Nonetheless, to the extent that IP telephony applications increase their market share, it is reasonable to anticipate that pressure will come from the other players (e.g., other telephony carriers and consumers) to increase regulatory attention to Internet telephony.

The potential inconsistency between the assumptions underlying existing regulations and those that would be applicable to new forms of telephony is well illustrated by one concern raised by local exchange carriers that has been the subject of FCC regulatory attention: Would local termination tariffs be applied to phone calls carried on the Internet? Internet telephony services (or the ISPs that carry the data associated with the phone call) do not, for example, have to pay local exchange carriers for terminating calls when one of the callers is connecting to the Internet via a modem running over a PSTN telephone line (as a conventional long-distance provider is required to do when it hands off a call to a local exchange carrier). Some of the advantages of using the Internet for voice are thus amplified or in some instances even driven by tariff and regulatory artifacts that treat IP and public switched telephone networks rather differently. Such advantages can be seen either as unfair to incumbents or as appropriately reflecting the emerging, evolving nature of telephony.

A key question is whether IP telephony should be subject to common carrier provisions. The implication of such status could be positive (e.g., no liability for the content it carries) or negative (e.g., the need to meet certain standards of operational integrity that go beyond what is required of an Internet, cable, or other noncommon carrier provider) for the IP telephony provider. The Telecommunications Act of 1996 defines telecommunications as the "transmission, between or among points specified by the user, of information of the user's choosing, without change in the form or content of the information as sent and received." A telecommunications carrier is defined as "any provider of telecommunications services, except that such term does not include aggregators of telecommunications services (as defined in section 226)." The act goes on to say that "a telecommunications carrier shall be treated as a common carrier under this Act only to the extent that it is engaged in providing telecommunications services, except that the Commission shall determine whether the provision of fixed and mobile satellite service shall be treated as common carriage."[17] Finally, telecommunications is defined as "the offering of telecommunications for a fee directly to the public, or to such classes of users as to be effectively available directly to the public, regardless of the facilities used."

Communications Commission, July.   Available online at <http://www.fcc.gov/opp/workingp.html>.

[17]A subsequent FCC ruling in fact specifically exempted mobile satellite carriers.

These definitions immediately give rise to the question of whether IP telephony providers or ISPs could fall under common carrier provisions. Resolution of this sort of question will depend on how existing definitions are applied to new technologies and services and, more fundamentally, on whether it is deemed appropriate to apply existing definitions and rules to these newly emerging services. For example, the act's definition of telecommunications could be read to say that if the input is voice and the output is intended to be the same voice, then regardless of the details of how the voice signal is processed internally, voice communications carried over IP would also be considered telecommunications.

One answer to the common carrier question was provided by the FCC in its August 31, 1999, ruling[18] on the Communications Assistance for Law Enforcement Act (CALEA) requirements (see Box 4.1).[19] CALEA required telecommunications carriers to provide assistance for law enforcement in carrying out wiretaps. In its ruling, the FCC mandated that cable television and IP services—inasmuch as they provide telecommunications services and are a telecommunications carrier and thus a common carrier, at least for the purpose of CALEA—are subject to CALEA. The FCC has given IP carriers until September 30, 2001, to comply.[20] This ruling opens the door for a broader interpretation and acceptance of IP telephony as common carriage.

In addition to suggesting future directions with respect to the common carriage status of IP telephony, the effort to apply CALEA in this area also suggests the sorts of societal expectations that surround telephony. The advent of IP telephony raises the questions of whether and how these expectations will be extended to the new technologies and networks. One such expectation is the use of telephony for public safety. Conventional wireline telephones provide enhanced 911 service, which automatically provides public safety organizations with the address of a 911 caller. Cellular telephone service providers are being required to provide analogous information for 911 calls—that is, precise information on the location of the caller.

---

[18]Federal Communications Commission (FCC). 1999. *Second Report and Order in the Matter of Communications Assistance for Law Enforcement Act.* CC Docket No. 97-213, FCC 99-229. Washington, D.C.: FCC, August 31. Available online at <http://www.fcc.gov/Bureaus/Common_Carrier/Orders/1999/fcc99229.txt>.

[19]CALEA, 47 USC 1001, PL 103-414.

[20]The question of whether the IETF should participate in the design or modification of Internet protocols to accommodate requests for law enforcement access to Internet traffic was discussed with much fanfare in the November 1999 plenary meeting of the IETF. Predictably, there were public statements critical of the notion. There were also statements supporting the proposition, citing, for example, vendor anticipation of demand for such capabilities in at least some segments of their worldwide markets.

BOX 4.1 FCC Ruling on CALEA and Common Carrier Status

The view that IP telephony is a common carrier for the purpose of CALEA is supported in paragraph 17 of the FCC's August 31, 1999, order:

17. Common Carriers and Utilities. We adopt our tentative conclusion, with which most commenters agree, that all entities previously classified as "common carriers" should be considered telecommunications carriers for the purposes of CALEA, as should cable operators and electric and other utilities to the extent they offer telecommunications services for hire to the public. Such entities offer services (some subject to CALEA, some not) that use copper-wire, cable, fiber-optic, and wireless facilities to provide traditional telephone service, data service, Internet access, cable television, and other services. The Act's legislative history identifies such entities as subject to CALEA to the extent that their service offerings satisfy CALEA's description of covered services. Entities are not subject to CALEA, however, with respect to services and facilities leased for private networks, pursuant to the statute. In addition, cable television is an example of a service not covered by CALEA because it is not a "telecommunications" service, even if delivered via the same transmission facility as other, covered services.

Paragraph 27 of the order has the following to say about information services such as the Internet or similar IP-based services:

Where facilities are used solely to provide an information service, whether offered by an exclusively-IS provider or by a common carrier that has established a dedicated IS system apart from its telecommunications system, we find that such facilities are not subject to CALEA. Where facilities are used to provide both telecommunications and information services, however, such joint-use facilities are subject to CALEA in order to ensure the ability to surveil the telecommunications services. For example, digital subscriber line (DSL) services are generally offered as tariffed telecommunications services, and therefore subject to CALEA, even though the DSL offering often would be used in the provision of information services. On the other hand, where an entity used its own wireless or satellite facilities to distribute an information service only, the mere use of transmission facilities would not make the offering subject to CALEA as a telecommunications service.

Robustness and quality are also expected of telephony services, manifested in state and federal regulatory attention to carrier performance. The relative ease with which the Internet can offer voice services means that many businesses will be in a position to offer voice services, probably over a broad spectrum of service quality and reliability, from robust and high quality to fragile, unreliable, and low quality. In addition, the ability to overlay telephony on top of existing IP networks and the emergence of mixed PSTN and IP network environments can be expected to raise new questions about which parties are responsible for service quality. Business imperatives and customer demands can be expected to address many of these concerns, but consumers will still need to be clear about the differences between service offerings (e.g., from a consumer protection standpoint) and their acceptability from a performance standpoint (e.g., to meet public safety requirements).

There are also particular economic arrangements in the form of universal service charges and fees attached to telephony aimed at increasing access to telephone service. Today, these are imposed only on conventional telephony service. There are two views on this matter: Some would like to see a level playing field across technologies and providers and others are concerned about the potential for declining revenue from these fees. (A related question is what form universal service takes with respect to Internet service; see Chapter 5 for a discussion of the options.)

Another set of issues arises from inconsistencies between the new technologies and architectures and the assumptions about architecture that are embodied in the existing regulatory regime. Three such issues are as follows:

- *In Internet telephony, there are no meaningful distinctions between local and interexchange carriers.* The existing regulatory regime, in which local and long-distance services are separated and in which customers select a particular long-distance carrier to carry calls outside their local area, does not map onto Internet telephony because the architectures of the two networks are so different. In the PSTN, it is possible—and indeed necessary—to specify the long-distance carrier over which a call is to be switched. In contrast, the Internet architecture and protocols were not designed to provide carrier selection capabilities like those in the PSTN.[21] Today, the only way in which the long-distance segment of a call could be separated from the local segment would be a hand-off to voice services over a PSN interexchange carrier. An insistence that local and long-distance carriers be distinct entities could only be complied with by establishing requirements that run counter to the Internet's basic architecture.

- *Owing to the separability of data transport and application service functions, meeting some regulatory requirements that have been established for telephony will be difficult or require different implementations.* For example, it is possible to construct a telephony service where the application servers concern themselves only with providing directory services and call setup

---

[21]However, under current regulations incumbent local exchanges that provide Internet service must offer their subscribers a choice of long-distance IP network providers.

while the communications associated with the call depend only on the public Internet. If a wiretap is ordered for a customer of an ISP, the application service provider will have no means of allowing law enforcement to access the content of the calls (although it could provide information on the identity of the calling parties). The wiretap might require a different technical approach, such as one that relies on accessing data packets at their entry point to the Internet at the customer's ISP.

• *Attempts to force the Internet to fit the existing regulatory model could inhibit innovation by forcing modifications to the Internet's architecture.* The current regulatory apparatus is, for example, not set up to respond to a world in which new telephony applications can be deployed simply by having a third party distribute some new software and set up a few servers. Already, a number of telephony providers exist as overlays to the public Internet, and it is reasonable to suppose that these will grow in number and market share. One question these providers raise is whom to hold responsible for meeting such mandates as provision of 911 service or compliance with CALEA. There are two general ways in which this could be done. The parties offering themselves as telephony providers could be designated as the ones responsible for meeting the requirements. Or, the requirements could be imposed on the Internet service providers. The second alternative, while it might prove attractive because it makes the ISPs responsible for determining who is and who is not providing voice telephony, could have profound implications for the Internet. If ISPs were required to ensure that voice traffic carried over their networks falls under a particular set of rules, it would become necessary for them to examine all the traffic over their network to screen out "unacceptable" voice communications. Because telephony providers are free, in keeping with the Internet's edge-based innovation model, to design their own protocols for telephony, it can be impossible to reliably identify which traffic is associated with telephony applications. Compliance with screening requirements might, in the end, make it necessary for ISPs to only allow traffic of known, acceptable types to be transmitted, an outcome that runs counter to the hourglass transparency of the Internet. This line of reasoning is discussed in greater detail in Chapter 3.

LOOKING FORWARD:
THE INTERNET AND OTHER INDUSTRY SECTORS

The preceding sections illuminate, in the context of telephony, issues of regulatory inconsistency, protection of incumbent companies, and restructuring of the service as perceived by the consumer. Technological developments and deployment of the first generations of new services make it apparent that the next decade or so will see similar collisions between Internet-based businesses and other large industry sectors.

Looking beyond telephony, some of the easiest collisions to foresee today are Internet-based distribution of music, which is exemplified by the collision between the mp3 encoding protocol and traditional channels of music distribution; the more general transmission of radio-like audio content over the Internet; and, eventually, Internet-based television-like services, which would collide with broadcasting. These applications are not visions of the distant future. Internet-based music distribution is a rapidly growing service, and while little entertainment video is transmitted over the Internet, specialized applications such as continuing education and training video are run over the Internet today. Many radio stations are sending their content over the Internet simultaneously with their over-the-airwaves broadcasts. As industry groups such as traditional network broadcasters, retail CD distribution chains, advertising marketers, and large content-creation organizations find their markets being nibbled at by Internet alternatives, they can be expected to react. The result may be large transformations and dislocations in existing markets; the result may also be stressful for the Internet, its design principles, and its service providers.

One predictable trend is the use of existing regulation by incumbents to protect a legacy industry position. For example, in radio and television, there are rules (about, for example, public access or political access) that presume that space on the broadcast spectrum is scarce. Since capacity on the Internet is not scarce and transmission does not require a federal license, anyone can, in principle, generate and distribute content, and it is not clear that there is a rationale for applying these rules to the Internet. However, much as one comes across similar arguments with respect to telephony, one can easily imagine calls for these rules to be imposed on some forms of Internet content providers. (The argument would be that it is unfair to impose different burdens on producers of similar sorts of content that happen only to use different forms of distribution.) Another area where existing practices and the capabilities afforded by the Internet collide is copyright, where the assumptions underlying the current copyright regime are being stressed by the ability to make perfect copies of digital works as well as by the ease with which they can be distributed over the Internet. The technological, legal, economic, and social factors surrounding copyright are too complex to analyze here; for more discussion, see a recent CSTB study of these issues.[22]

---

[22]Computer Science and Telecommunications Board, National Research Council. 2000. *The Digital Dilemma*. Washington, D.C.: National Academy Press.

5

Implications for Broad Public Policy

INTRODUCTION

So far, the bulk of this report has focused on the Internet from the inside out—how its essential technologies are evolving and how the parties that build and operate it are evolving. In this chapter, the committee looks at the Internet from the outside in, examining some of the broader influences on the Internet that stem from the interests of the individuals and organizations that use it and the special concerns of governments, which have their own objectives and which can help balance and protect the interests of individuals and other parties that use the Internet.

The Internet has become the basis for a widening set of social, political, and economic functions and is becoming ever more pervasive throughout society and its institutions. The benefits resulting from the Internet's intrinsic qualities have an accompanying cost: disruption of the social, political, legal, and economic conventions on which a wide variety of useful understandings have been based. While these consequences have been recognized for a number of years, they have grown in importance as the Internet has become a key societal infrastructure. Reflecting the Internet's increased prominence, a diverse set of stakeholders—both the existing players and new, Internet-focused ones—are paying attention to its impacts.

The scope of the discussion here is limited, consistent with the scope and resources of the project: a small but important and interconnected set of policy issues is outlined. The discussion is intended to illuminate the interplay of technical, economic/business, and public policy factors, drawing on the committee's experience in all three areas. Because the interplay is dynamic—today's observations differ from yesterday's and will be overtaken by events tomorrow—it can be hard to devise practical responses to perceived problems. Nevertheless, responses are being devised, and a variety of technical, business, and public policy actions are already being proposed or attempted. Understanding and monitoring the kinds of issues discussed here is important for making judgments about how individuals, organizations, and governments could or should act in using or shaping the Internet. The question is not just what the Internet does to policy but also what policy can do to the Internet. The second part of the question—how policy affects the Internet—asks how policy decisions that seek to impose particular technological solutions could adversely affect the Internet's architecture and growth as well as how policy decisions in areas such as privacy could affect user acceptance of the Internet and the services that run over it. How these issues are resolved is important to realizing (or limiting) the potential of the Internet. While they are not solely technological issues, their emergence as policy questions and the capacity to address them are shaped by technological developments. This chapter addresses how the architecture of the Internet creates new issues and challenges and requires new approaches from policy makers if policy goals are to be met consistent with the strengths of the design and architecture that underlie the Internet.

The first set of issues—privacy, autonomy, and identity, along with authentication—arises from the sheer size of the Internet and from growth in the number of people and organizations that it interconnects—increasingly, people communicate over the Internet with strangers and others of whom they have limited knowledge or control. This set of issues centers on how the Internet's design, which provides limited information about the identity or location of users, affects how we control our identity or evaluate the identities others present to us[1] and what that means for our understanding of privacy and the uses of anonymity. The Internet provides weak clues about location or identity. Its essential indifference to geography is, of course, valuable when it allows us to check our e-mail from New York one day and from Los Angeles the next, readily retrieve materials stored on a distant computer, or engage in a commercial transaction with someone a continent away. Yet it also raises challenges to laws and practices that are premised on knowing the location of parties to a transaction. An IP address is only loosely related to the geographical location or identity of a user or networked computing resource—this in-

---

[1]See, for example, Sherry Turkle. 1995. *Life on the Screen: Identity in the Age of the Internet.* New York: Simon & Schuster.

formation can sometimes be inferred, perhaps after an exhaustive investigation, but it is not readily available.[2] That some ISPs believe their network topology and the location of their facilities is sensitive proprietary information contributes to the lack of information about location. Nor do many of the applications that run over IP provide authoritative information on either identity or location. The absence of identifying information provides benefits in terms of free expression but raises serious issues about how we manage, recognize, or negotiate identifying information about people and things in the electronic world. The discussion in this chapter examines these competing directions and explores whether relevant design enhancements/changes should be left to competitive forces in the marketplace or require some focused attention by industry and/or government.

The second set of issues—taxation and universal service—is related to government missions. Government is empowered to collect taxes to fund its operations, and it has an interest in both preserving its revenues while also fairly allocating the associated burdens, issues captured in debates about taxation of transactions conducted over the Internet. As the principal actor when it comes to social policy, governments have moved to promote equitable access to the Internet because of its growing value as a medium for economic, educational, civic, and other kinds of opportunities, much as they have done for other infrastructure, such as

---

[2]Interestingly, the Internet did not always have such a loose coupling between IP address and location. This quality stems less from the basic Internet design than from subsequent decisions related to address space management and security. In the early days of the ARPANET, interface message processors (IMPs) required a direct correlation of IP address to port number on the IMP, so one was more likely to be able to tell where a computer was located. There were, however, various ways in which hosts could be connected that would have made it harder to tell where they were located. Moreover, users generally interacted with the network via terminal devices attached to host computers, and these could be located far from the host computers. Also, before CIDR and address aggregation (described in Chapter 2), users did not receive their addresses from providers. Pre-CIDR, addresses were more likely to be globally routed, down to a much finer level of aggregation, which again made it easier to know where devices associated with particular IP addresses were located. Address allocation policies coupled with service issues, such as maintaining security and increasing the ease of getting an Internet connection, did induce large organizations to route all traffic in and out of their entire enterprise, which could span many different locations, through one connection. But with the advent of CIDR and a crackdown on inefficient address space utilization, providers and users were forced into denser and more obscure addressing relationships. Motivated by address shortages and security issues, enterprises are using NAT and firewall technology, in which globally unique addresses are not used within corporate networks, further obscuring location information.

BOX 5.1 Privacy, Anonymity, and Identity

• *Privacy* is the right of individuals to control how information about them is shared, distributed, and used by other parties.
• *Anonymity* is the ability of individuals to interact with others without letting those other parties have any knowledge of their identity. As such, anonymity is a sufficient but not a necessary condition for achieving privacy.
• *Identity* is any distinguishing attribute that is uniquely linked to an individual or object.

---

telecommunications. To the degree that the Internet can credibly claim to be an essential infrastructure for transactions in commerce, political participation, basic education, and many other areas, it will become ripe for consideration for universal service arrangements, which are interventions premised on arguments that market mechanisms will not support widespread access affordable by all. The tradition of universal service was eventually attached to all important information infrastructures in the past—post, telephone, broadcasting, and, less obviously, basic education.

PRIVACY, ANONYMITY, AND IDENTITY

Driven in part by the ease with which information about individuals can be gathered, the Internet has amplified concerns about an interdependent set of issues—privacy, anonymity, and identity (Box 5.1). The closely associated subject of authentication is discussed in the following section. Also discussed here are the trade-offs that all of these might impose on privacy and individual rights. The section outlines important interactions among the Internet's technology, the Internet service providers and related industry actors, Internet users, and policy development and identifies some avenues where progress might be expected. These issues are not new, but Internet growth and penetration have heightened attention to them and are influencing the context within which the Internet is evolving.

Privacy

Concerns about privacy have accompanied and been shaped by the development of technology for over a century.[3] They have grown in

---

[3]See, for example, Samuel Warren and Louis Brandeis. 1890. "The Right to Privacy." *Harvard Law Review* 4(193), which laid out some of the fundamental arguments in favor of

recent years with the introduction and widespread practice of such innovations as sophisticated customer profiling and telephone soliciting. The Internet has aggravated the situation. In surveys, people express concern about the amount of personal information available on the Internet, who controls that information, and how it may be used. For example, a 1998 *Business Week* survey[4] found privacy to be the number one consumer issue facing the Internet, surpassing cost, ease of use, security, or spam. This survey found that 78 percent of online users would increase their use of the Internet if privacy practices were disclosed and that 61 percent of nonusers would be more likely to begin using the Internet if privacy practices were disclosed. (Survey answers notwithstanding, many people do provide personal information; most notably, some have chosen to provide a good deal of personal information in exchange for free Internet access.) The absence of generally accepted, workable solutions is likely to continue to lead to calls for regulation, at least in the most troubling areas. For instance, concern about the online privacy of children—in particular, information they might be induced to reveal about themselves or their families—resulted in the passage of special legislation, the Children's Online Privacy Protection Act of 1998. Although there are pressures for broader change today,[5] the outcome is uncertain. Historically, privacy advocates have been in the minority, people's actions belie the results of opinion surveys, and political pressure in the United States has been insufficient to invoke significant action. Mid-2000 debates over Federal Trade Commission interest in legislation related to online privacy are emblematic. In the United States, people continue to argue about privacy as a legal, protected right, while government-based inquiries into privacy policy have articulated principles for public policy and private action, notably so-called fair information practices. The essential elements of fair information practices are generally described as awareness, choice, data

---

privacy in modern society. The article was occasioned in part by privacy issues created by developments in photography and photojournalism. See also Alan Westin. 1967. *Privacy and Freedom.* New York: Atheneum; Spiros Simitis. 1987; "Reviewing Privacy in an Information Society." *University of Pennsylvania Law Review* 135:707-746; and James Katz and Annette Tessone. 1990. "Public Opinion Trends: Privacy and Information Technology." *Public Opinion Quarterly* 54:125-143.

[4]As reported by TRUSTe at <http://www.truste.org/webpublishers/pub_bottom.html>.

[5]A survey in 2000 by Odyssey, a market research firm, found that 82 percent of online households in the United States agreed that the government needed to play a role in how companies use personal information and 92 percent expressed some distrust of companies when it comes to protecting the confidentiality of personal information. See Steve Lohr. 2000. "Survey Finds Few Trust Promises on Online Privacy." *New York Times*, May 17, p. C4.

security, and customer access.[6] First advanced in the 1970s by a congressionally chartered commission on information privacy,[7] these practices were also discussed in the context of 1990s policy making on the national/global information infrastructure and electronic commerce.[8]

Privacy relates to the use, release, and availability of personal information,[9] that is, any information that is linked to an individual's identity or to attributes closely associated with that individual's identity. Personal information is collected or revealed both directly, as happens when a user enters information into a Web form and submits it, and indirectly, as happens when information is gathered from publicly available information such as an e-mail directory. Whether in physical space or cyberspace, individuals are motivated to provide information about themselves for a variety of reasons, including the following: to obtain a desired product, service, or end result (e.g., a loan commitment or a health claim benefit); to obtain better, more customized/personalized products and services (e.g., personalized news); to obtain specific information of value (e.g., stock quotes) or in anticipation of gaining some unspecified benefit (e.g., current bargains or offers); or to be rewarded with rebates and discounts, loyalty points, or frequent flyer miles. At the same time, people worry, sometimes with justification, that their personal information may fall into the wrong hands or be misused. These concerns include such undesirable results as receipt of annoying and unwanted information or sales pitches; denial of a desired product, service, or end result (e.g., health coverage, an auto loan, or a job); personal embarrassment; damage to one's reputation; loss of trade secrets; or becoming a victim of some criminal activity such as stalking, theft, fraud, or identity takeover.

---

[6]See Department of Commerce. 1998. "Elements of Effective Self-Regulation for Protection of Privacy." Available online from <http://www.ntia.doc.gov/reports/privacydraft/198DFTPRIN.htm>. While all seem to agree on basic principles, there are variations in the privacy frameworks that are used. For example, the Federal Trade Commission added another element, enforcement/redress, in a recent report to Congress. This is not surprising, given the FTC's nature as an agency that makes and enforces rules. See Federal Trade Commission. 1999. "Self-regulation and Privacy Online: A Report to Congress." Washington, D.C.: Federal Trade Commission, July.

[7]Privacy Protection Study Commission. 1977. *Personal Privacy in an Information Society.*

[8]Similar principles are contained in the "Electronic Bill of Rights" presented in the First Annual Report of the U.S. Government Working Group on Electronic Commerce . See U.S. Government Working Group on Electronic Commerce. 1998. *First Annual Report*, November, p. 17. Available online at <http://www.doc.gov/ecommerce/E-comm.pdf>.

[9]"Privacy" is distinct from confidentiality, which refers to the protection of all types of sensitive information and is not necessarily approached from the perspective of protection of personal information per se.

One area of particular concern is that information provided with the user's knowledge can also be used for purposes other than that for which it was originally provided. Web servers can store personal information given by the user while visiting the site; Web site operators can subsequently use that information for other purposes, such as marketing, or provide or sell it to third parties. Users do not necessarily understand or appreciate the value of the information they provide, especially when different bits of information can be combined and used for new purposes. An individual data item by itself might not appear to pose a privacy concern. But when information is combined or associated with other, seemingly harmless bits of information often collected under different circumstances to build a dossier on a user, it may provide insights the user would consider detrimental. For instance, behind-the-scenes tracking of users by means of cookies[10] could permit address information entered at one Web site to be linked with tracking data indicating that a user had browsed several adult content Web sites. The result might be the unwanted, unexpected arrival in the mail of advertisements for adult films. In other cases, combining personal data from different sources can add value for customers. For example, an online bookseller that knows a customer enjoys Danielle Steel novels may send the customer a review of a new book by a different author that has been purchased by other customers with similar tastes.[11] The customer never requested this information but may be glad to receive it. As another illustration, an airline Web site may refer a registered user who wants information about inexpensive vacations to a travel packager, who then e-mails the airline customer about bargain travel opportunities. In both examples a firm uses personal information to offer services and products that some customers perceive as valuable and others as a waste of time, offensive spam, or gratuitous invasions of privacy.

A second area of concern with respect to the Internet is that some personal information can be collected online without the user's direct

---

[10]A cookie is a small piece of information that a Web site stores on your Web browser on your PC and can later retrieve. The cookie cannot be read by a Web site other than the one that set the cookie. Cookies can be used for a number of administrative purposes—for example, to store your preferences for certain kinds of information or to store a password so that you do not have to input it every time you visit a Web site. Most cookies last only through a single visit to a Web site. Users can set up their Web browser to inform them when cookies are set or to prevent cookies from being set.

[11]This type of service relies on collaborative filtering technology, which guides people's choices of what to read, view, purchase, etc. based on information gathered from other people, such as other customers with similar preferences or purchasing patterns.

knowledge or consent (either implied or by opt-out or opt-in decisions[12]). For example, a Web site can store personal information on the user's computer as cookies or as hidden fields in URLs and forms that are accessible by that or other Web sites.

Not only can personal information be collected by all of the organizations and businesses that people interact with on the Internet, but it can also be collected by the Internet service providers themselves. One such example is that ISPs can and do record information on user actions (for internal purposes or to comply with a court order). Such information could include which DNS names are looked up by a particular customer, which Web sites are visited by a customer at what times, and how much information is transferred. Though the technical capability exists, ISPs may or may not regularly gather such information. Considerations include the potential for alienating their customers and the performance degradation that could result from extensive monitoring. Although it is becoming more widely known that service providers can collect personal information, many users are still unaware of this possibility and its implications.

Another privacy concern relates to Internet infrastructure databases. Information can be captured from user e-mail addresses or directories made public by Internet service providers. For example, records of domain name registrations and address allocations have traditionally been available to the public to permit users in other domains to track down problems and get assistance in resolving them. Now, however, these databases are being captured and used for targeted marketing purposes, which has led to calls for not making the data public. This echoes recent litigation over whether the customer proprietary network information (CPNI) collected by telephone companies, which includes the duration, frequency, and location of calls, may be given or sold to telemarketers without the explicit permission of customers.[13] Similarly, when government information that is in principle public but in practice hard to ac-

---

[12]In recognition of both the positive and negative aspects of collecting personal information, privacy experts distinguish between opt-in and opt-out approaches to managing the use of personal information. The first requires that the individual specifically authorize the use to which the information is put, while the second requires only that individuals have the option to state that they do not wish the information to be used in a particular manner.

[13]In August 1999, the U.S. Tenth Circuit Court of Appeals issued a ruling vacating the FCC's CPNI rules. (U S WEST, Inc. v. FCC, 10th Circuit No. 98-9518, filed August 18, 1999), holding that the FCC's CPNI rules "must fall under the First Amendment." The Tenth Circuit Court's mandate has not yet been issued. According to the FCC, further litigation is possible. (See FCC. 1999. Common Carrier Bureau's Homepage for the CNPI Proceeding. Common Carrier Bureau, FCC, September 9. Available online at <http://www.fcc.gov/ccb/ppp/Cpni/welcome.html>).

cess—such as property tax or motor vehicle records—is made readily available over the Internet, this may be viewed as a violation of privacy.[14]

"Online privacy" is generally understood to refer to information collected via e-mail, chat applications, user interactions with Web sites, and the like. The likely proliferation of networked appliances, sensors, and other embedded systems, which was discussed in Chapter 2, introduces new modes of information collection and new issues with respect to individual privacy on the Internet. Networked embedded devices are expected to become a pervasive technology because of the powerful instrumentation that can be achieved by placing sophisticated but low-cost sensor/actuators within physical environments.[15] Much as other networked resources have been used in novel and unexpected ways, it is also reasonable to foresee that networked devices will be used in ways that surpass the original intended uses of the collected data. Some of these will raise new privacy concerns and trigger debates similar to those surrounding online privacy. The same technologies that allow tracking people for legitimate purposes can also be used to monitor their activities invasively. This sort of debate has already arisen in the context of the recent Federal Communications Commission mandate that cellular telephone operators provide the means to determine much more precisely the position of callers when they place 911 (emergency) calls.

These concerns are sure to grow in importance and attention as these devices are more and more widely deployed, as they almost surely will be. As a starting point, it appears reasonable to apply the same basic principles that have been applied to personal information to information that is passively collected by networked devices. That is, individuals should be informed that information about them is being collected and for what purpose, and they should be given the opportunity to view that information and make corrections. There are also issues of whether explicit consent must be obtained (both for initial use and any subsequent uses). For consent to be meaningful and informed, it must be solicited in a carefully stipulated manner, and the individual must be given recourse.

It is unclear, thus far, to what extent voluntary actions are addressing these privacy concerns. The most visible indicator may be statements of privacy policies—verbal disclosures about what information is collected and how it is used. On the positive side, a study by Mary Culnan of the McDonough School of Business at Georgetown University found that

---

[14]A complementary situation where government seeks to capitalize on the broad reach of the Internet is the posting of information about individuals who have violated certain laws.

[15]A separate report from CSTB on these technologies is anticipated in 2001.

nearly two-thirds (65.9 percent) of commercial Web sites that collect personal information post some sort of privacy disclosure.[16] However, the same survey also indicates that only about 14 percent (and fewer than 10 percent of sites that collected personal information) provided privacy disclosure statements that addressed all four basic privacy elements (i.e., awareness, choice, data security, and customer access; for definitions see later in this chapter) and offered contact information to consumers with questions about the firm's privacy policies. A contemporaneous Forrester Research Brief[17] echoes this point, stating that "90 percent of sites fail to comply with the basic four privacy principles," and regular assessments by the Federal Trade Commission and privacy advocates raise questions about the willingness and ability of organizations to undertake this comparatively simple measure.

Technical Approaches to Protecting Privacy

Just as Internet technology can accelerate and complicate the loss of privacy on the Internet, it can also protect that same privacy. For instance, as a countermeasure to the hidden gathering of information via cookies, Web browsers now can be set to deny loading of this personal information or to let users approve them on a case-by-case basis, and other software tools are available to help users manage these cookies. Web users are likely to find this a complex and tedious process, however, and some sites may not function with cookies disabled. As a consequence, new technologies are being developed to automate negotiations over privacy between users and the Web sites they wish to reach and to control the gathering of information based on these negotiations. All of the privacy-enhancement mechanisms are controversial; each embodies a particular set of features and trade-offs. Some have attracted many supporters, but there is thus far no consensus on the best mechanism. This is not surprising, because the technology is still evolving (through experimentation), as are privacy policies and procedures and attitudes about the mix of technical and nontechnical approaches.

One new technological approach is the Platform for Privacy Preferences (P3P), which is being developed by the World Wide Web Consor-

---

[16]Mary J. Culnan. 1999. *Georgetown Internet Privacy Policy Survey: Report to the Federal Trade Commission.* Washington, D.C.: McDonough School of Business, Georgetown University, June. Available online at <http://www.msb.edu/faculty/culnanm/GIPPS/mmrpt.PDF>.

[17]Paul R. Hagen. 1999. *Privacy Wakeup Call.* Cambridge, Mass.: Forrester Research Inc., September 1. Available online at <http://www.forrester.com/ER/Research/Brief/Excerpt/0,1317,7803,FF.html>.

tium.[18] P3P helps the user screen information requests and gives the user control over the delivery of requested information, including negotiation of privacy terms between the user and the service provider. It operates as a kind of digital analog to caller ID and caller ID blocking, whereby an answering party wishes to know who is phoning but may be denied this information if the calling party blocks the request. P3P increases the explicitness with which privacy policies are expressed, allowing the user and the service provider to specify the terms of use for each data item— i.e., how and for what purpose the information will be used and with whom it will be shared. P3P has the appeal of automation—it can diminish the need for ongoing monitoring and intervention by Internet users— but it requires significant setup effort. To specify privacy preferences down to each data element, a user may have to set 100 or more parameters; alternatively, he or she can rely on a program that maps/infers these parameters from a smaller set of higher level preferences (or through learning user preferences by observing behavior). The system can also simply work with default settings that can be overridden by the user. Further complicating use of this technology is that user preferences may change frequently, making it hard to track what was agreed to for each data exchange. It is also an approach that requires multilateral actions— the installation and use of appropriate software—by both providers and user. P3P has already been valuable for its contribution to the debate about online policy. As a sophisticated technical mechanism, it shows how the technology needs to be meshed with practice and procedure by individuals and organizations and illuminates some of the trade-offs involved in protecting on-line privacy.

Policy and Regulatory Approaches to Privacy Protection

The legal and regulatory environment surrounding privacy protection on the Internet remains quite mixed and uncertain. The United States has generally dealt with privacy sector by sector, and policy has generally favored industry self-regulation or other nongovernmental solutions such as the technical approaches described above, although the government has articulated the fair information practices described above. Many firms participate in industry self-regulatory efforts, and many provide custom-

---

[18]World Wide Web Consortium (W3C). 2000. *The Platform for Privacy Preferences 1.0 (P3P1.0) Specification,* W3C Working Draft 10 May 2000. Cambridge, Mass.: W3C. Available online at <http://www.w3.org/TR/P3P/>. See also Joseph Reagle and Lorrie Faith Cranor. 1999. "The Platform for Privacy Preferences." *Communications of the ACM* 42(2): 48-55.

ers with privacy guarantees that go beyond legislative or regulatory requirements, such as opt-in policies, which require explicit customer consent before sharing information. Under the opt-in approach, it is left to
individuals to make their own judgments about which commercial firms
(and other individuals) can be trusted to use their personal information
wisely. In the case of commercial service providers, trust can be engen-
dered and cultivated through a number of factors, including the firm's
brand and reputation; the customer's experience and relationship with
the service provider; referrals and testimony by third parties; the service
provider's stated policies and guarantees, backed by appropriate recourse;
third-party seals of approval that the service provider's policies are acceptable; industry self-regulation; and enforceable contracts, laws, and
regulations. There have been a number of exceptions to the prevailing
self-regulation approach. Federal and state legislation has been passed to
increase the privacy of individual records in certain sectors such as health
care, credit reporting,[19] cable television, and video rentals, and legislation
was passed aimed at protecting the privacy of children online (the
Children's Online Privacy Protection Act). Ongoing debate over sector-
specific protections attests to the importance attached to the protection of
certain kinds of personal information; the prospects for generalizing that
importance remain uncertain, however, although a number of cross-
sectoral issues are getting more attention (e.g., the privacy of employees
vis-à-vis their employers). The appointment in the late 1990s of a Chief
Counselor for Privacy at the Office of Management and Budget has at
least symbolic value and may be the beginning of a more comprehensive
consideration of protecting information about individuals collected by
the government as well as the private sector.

    Some other countries have acted more broadly or directly to protect
privacy. In particular, the European Union (EU) has adopted a more

---

[19]A set of principles resembling those adopted for privacy protection is contained in the
Fair Credit Reporting Act (*Fair Credit Reporting Act (FCRA)*, 15 U.S.C. § 1681 et seq.) as
amended by the Consumer Credit Reporting Reform Act of 1996 (Public Law 104-208, the
Omnibus Consolidated Appropriations Act for Fiscal Year 1997, Title II, Subtitle D, Chapter
1), Section 311 of the Intelligence Authorization for Fiscal Year 1998 (Public Law 105-107),
and the Consumer Reporting Employment Clarification Act of 1998 (Public Law 105-347);
see the discussion and full legislative text, available online at <http://www.ftc.gov/os/
statutes/fcra.htm>). The FCRA requires consumer credit reporting agencies to inform
individuals when information is being collected about them and for what purpose, and
individuals have the right to see this information and to correct it if it is inaccurate. Moreover, credit issuers must let customers know they may opt out of information sharing,
which includes both using the data internally for cross-marketing and selling the data to
third parties.

inclusive, government-led regulatory framework for privacy protection. The EU Directive on Data Protection, which took effect in October 1998, permits EU members to block the transfer of personal information about EU citizens to other countries that do not offer adequate protection of privacy. To pass the threshold, organizations must fulfill a number of requirements: among other things, they must tell individuals when they collect information about them, disclose how it will be used, and provide individual access to the information. Individuals must provide informed consent before a company or other organization can legally use the data. Thus, the EU directive mandates opt-in usage policies rather than the opt-out policies common in the United States, Japan, and many other countries. Each EU member nation must enact its own laws to implement the directive. The United States is one of the nations whose privacy protections have not met the EU threshold.[20] As a consequence, the United States and the European Commission (EC) of the EU have negotiated guidelines that would serve as a "safe harbor" for U.S. companies wanting to receive information from the EU.[21] The pressures to harmonize privacy policies on an international basis are a good example of the effect the Internet's global reach is having on national policies.[22]

---

[20]For example, the opt-out policies that are used by many U.S. firms, whereby customers must request that their personal information not be used or disclosed to others, do not meet the EU threshold of adequate privacy protection. U.S. firms also cite cases in which they use personal information obtained from others (e.g., mailing lists) and do not retain it, so that it would be impractical for them to give customers unconditional access to the information.

[21]The safe harbor guidelines state that U.S. organizations must inform individuals why they are collecting personal information, with whom they will share that information, and how individuals can limit its use and disclosure. Organizations must also offer individuals access to the information, as well as the opportunity to choose whether and how the personal information they provide is used or disclosed to third parties. In addition, organizations must take "reasonable measures to assure its [data] reliability for its intended use and reasonable precautions to protect it from loss, misuse, and unauthorized access, disclosure, alteration and destruction." The agreement also states that EU member states will be bound by the agreement; that it will be presumed that companies within the safe harbor provide data protection; that data flows to those companies will continue; that, generally, only the EC will be able to interrupt personal data flows; and that U.S. companies will have a grace period in which to implement the policies. See Electronic Commerce Task Force. 2000. "Safe Harbor Privacy Principles." Washington, D.C.: Electronic Commerce Task Force, International Trade Administration, U.S. Department of Commerce, Draft of June 9. Available online at <http://www.ita.doc.gov/td/ecom/menu.html>.

[22]The recent activity associated with the EU privacy directive builds on a history of concern for transborder data flow that preceded the commercialization of the Internet. It builds on different national traditions relating to social policy and rights and responsibilities in

A very different approach to privacy protection, advocated by some scholars more than 30 years ago, would have governments enact legislation giving individuals explicit property rights to their personal information.[23] Individuals would then be in a position to bargain with organizations over the price and other terms for using their personal information; and they could legally enforce such agreements if violated. Some firms (e.g., Microsoft and Privaseek) are investigating how they might profit from commercially implementing such a system. Proponents of this approach argue that, at least on the Internet, standardized agreements for the use of personal information, software technologies such as P3P, and agents acting for individuals could reduce transaction costs to a workable level—assuming sufficient ease of implementation. Privacy could then become a matter of consumer choice, backed by normal commercial and consumer protection laws, rather than a difficult and often intractable political issue. Opponents contend, among other arguments, that implementing individual property rights to personal information would be unworkable; that it would unnecessarily impede the development of electronic commerce; that those people most in need of privacy protection would be the least able to negotiate with large organizations; and that in any case, society should not let individuals bargain away their fundamental rights to privacy.[24]

Anonymity

Identification for the purpose of granting access to systems and information is a basic function of computer systems, and it has been an objective of mechanisms and procedures put in place by managers of large computer systems for decades. At the same time, technologies are being developed that make it difficult or impossible to identify the origin of computer-mediated communications.

---

general, and it also builds on the competitive posturing of nations. The EU's actions, for example, reflect concerns about privacy per se as well as European recognition of the competitive impact of U.S.-owned businesses that interact with Europeans.

[23]Alan Westin. 1967. *Privacy and Freedom.* New York: Atheneum, pp. 324-325; Arthur R. Miller. 1969. "Personal Privacy in the Computer Age: The Challenge of New Technology in an Information-Oriented Society," *Michigan Law Review* 67(April):1224-1225.

[24]Some argue that the "fundamental asymmetry between individuals and bureaucratic organizations all but guarantees the failure of the market for personal information." Oscar H. Gandy, Jr. 1996. "Legitimate Business Interests: No End in Sight? An Inquiry into the Status of Privacy in Cyberspace." *University of Chicago Legal Forum* 1996:77-137.

Individuals have a variety of reasons for wishing to be anonymous. [25] Anonymity is of particular importance for some types of political speech[26] and in other instances, such as when reporting certain kinds of incidents to the police or regulatory authorities. More generally, some people prefer to protect their privacy when they communicate or engage in commercial or other transactions in general or under certain circumstances.[27] A counterweight to individual interests in anonymity is the demand by individuals, organizations, and society in general that other individuals and organizations be accountable for their actions, often to protect against fraud and illicit or improper actions. Identity can be important if a commercial dispute arises, if a crime or tort is suspected, or for taxation and other legitimate government purposes. Anonymity is perceived as undesirable when it becomes an enabler of such activities as libel, distributing pornography to minors, or engaging in money laundering. The Internet amplifies these conflicting needs by simultaneously making it easier to track and monitor individuals (sometimes invisibly) and making it easier for people to act anonymously. For example, Web sites often allow or encourage users to adopt anonymous or pseudonymous identities when participating in chat rooms and other public meeting places. E-mail users are free to take on pseudonymous identities (e.g., JohnDoe@example.com, guesswho@example.com) when using many e-mail services. Some believe that the ease of assuming an anonymous identity on the Internet encourages unethical or illegal activities (such as spamming, harassment,

---

[25]For a recent examination of the role of anonymity online, see Al Teich, Mark S. Frankel, Rob Kling, and Ya-ching Lee. 1999. "Anonymous Communication Policies for the Internet: Results and Recommendations of the AAAS Conference." *The Information Society* 15(2).

[26]See, for example, *McIntyre v. Ohio Elections Commission*, 514 U.S. 334 (1995):

> . . . the interest in having anonymous works enter the marketplace of ideas unquestionably outweighs any public interest in requiring disclosure as a condition of entry. Accordingly, an author's decision to remain anonymous, like other decisions concerning omissions or additions to the content of a publication, is an aspect of the freedom of speech protected by the First Amendment.
>
> Under our Constitution, anonymous pamphleteering is not a pernicious, fraudulent practice, but an honorable tradition of advocacy and of dissent. . . . The State may, and does, punish fraud directly. But it cannot seek to punish fraud indirectly by indiscriminately outlawing a category of speech, based on its content, with no necessary relationship to the danger sought to be prevented.

[27]English and American law also recognize the legitimacy of cash transactions where either the buyer or seller, or both, prefer not to be identified. However, the right to anonymity in commercial transactions is not absolute—limits are imposed in the United States in instances such as hand gun purchases or, as a countermeasure to money laundering, cash deposits exceeding $10,000.

defamation, pirating of music or software, stalking, or exchanging child pornography) and thus poses additional risks to society that require greater government surveillance and action.[28] One area of particular concern because of its potential to damage an innocent third party without his knowledge or consent is masquerading, in which an anonymous entity transmits a libelous message or conducts a transaction that appears as if it came from another individual.[29]

The debate over anonymity on the Internet epitomizes the challenge posed by the sophisticated, complex, and poorly understood technology that underpins the Internet. People tend to act based on what they see and understand, and it appears that unless they have specialized technical knowledge, people may have false expectations of anonymity. Service providers cooperate with government authorities that are investigating suspected criminal activity and may choose to cooperate with efforts to control other forms of undesirable behavior online. Employers may monitor online conduct, a practice that is reportedly growing, with uneven notification of employees. Individuals seeking anonymity may use services that provide less of that quality than they think, just as they may adopt information security measures such as encryption or firewalls that, because of their design or implementation details, are less effective than they think. Given that concerted efforts to identify an individual will only be made in particular circumstances, imperfect protections of anonymity may well have a silver lining. With experience, users may become more aware of what does and does not provide them the anonymity they desire, but this awareness may only come through bad experiences.

Technology can significantly increase anonymity. E-mail senders can take measures to further hide their identities by using anonymous remailers, which strip off header information about the sender before forwarding the message to its destination.[30] More sophisticated services

---

[28]This point was echoed in the report of a government task force looking at unlawful online conduct. (See President's Working Group on Lawful Conduct on the Internet. 2000. "The Electronic Frontier: The Challenge of Unlawful Conduct Involving the Use of the Internet: A Report of the President's Working Group on Unlawful Conduct on the Internet." March. Available online from <http://www.usdoj.gov/criminal/cybercrime/unlawful.htm>.)

[29]This concern should be distinguished from issues related to anonymity in general. The names used for anonymous communications could, for example, be restricted to a special set reserved for just that purpose and thus not useful for masquerading; this is the approach taken in RFC 1422, which defines an approach for privacy-enhanced Internet e-mail. (S. Kent. 1993. *Privacy Enhancement for Internet Electronic Mail: Part II: Certificate-Based Key Management*, RFC 1422. Networking Working Group, Internet Engineering Task Force. Available online at <http://www.ietf.org/rfc/rfc1422.txt>.)

[30]A seminal paper on which practical designs have built is David L. Chaum. 1981. "Untraceable Electronic Mail, Return Addresses, and Digital Pseudonyms." *Communications of the ACM* 24(2).

make use of encryption and transmission through a series of anonymous remailers (perhaps located in several different countries), which make tracing the message very difficult even if some of the remailers are compromised.[31] Similar approaches can be used to anonymize Web transactions and the transmission of IP traffic across the Internet. These have progressed in status from being the subject of academic research to commercial deployment; Zero Knowledge Systems, for example, offers a commercial service called FreedomNet, which is designed to block the tracing of IP traffic back to its source and to provide tools that control other identifiers such as cookies.[32]

Meanwhile, e-mail software and Web-based e-mail services could allow users to filter out anonymous messages if they do not want to receive them—capabilities analogous to not accepting phone calls from callers who have disabled caller identification—if an infrastructure is in place to ascertain the identity of senders. While they are imperfect solutions and address only one class of problem associated with anonymity, such capabilities show that technology can respond to some of the concerns raised by online anonymity.

The legal status of anonymity on the Internet remains contentious and unresolved. Anonymity on the Internet has positive as well as negative social value, suggesting that a blanket prohibition is unlikely. It is not an absolute right in all circumstances, however, and society generally expects that individuals be held accountable for harmful or illegal actions, whether or not under the cloak of anonymity. Thus, abuses of anonymity undoubtedly will bring political pressures to shut down anonymous services or impose close monitoring or registration requirements on them. Existing laws and regulations that govern the behaviors and actions of concern may or may not be deemed adequate to cope with online anonymous behaviors.

Some recent legislative proposals would make certain anonymous actions illegal, holding providers of anonymous e-mail services, as well as

---

[31]For a good discussion of current battles to preserve or defeat anonymity, see David Mazieres and M. Frans Kaashoek. 1998. "The Design, Implementation and Operation of an Email Pseudonym Server." *Proceedings of the 5th ACM Conference on Computer and Communications Security.* Available online at <http://www.lcs.mit.edu/impact/perspect/9901.pdf>.

[32]Much of the design is traceable to research on onion routing. See P. Syverson, M. Reed, and D. Goldschlag. 1997. "Private Web Browsing." *Journal of Computer Security* 5(3):237-248; Michael G. Reed, Paul F. Syverson, and David M. Goldschlag. 1998. "Anonymous Connections and Onion Routing," *IEEE Journal on Selected Areas in Communication Special Issue on Copyright and Privacy Protection*; and David M. Goldschlag, Michael G. Reed, and Paul F. Syverson, "Onion Routing for Anonymous and Private Internet Connections," *Communications of the ACM* 42(2).

message originators, responsible for message contents or even prohibiting anonymous messages altogether. Anonymous online conduct has also been the subject of international discussions on how to address a perceived rise in "cyber crime." Law enforcement agencies, in particular, seek ways to pierce the veil of anonymous remailers when investigating suspected criminal activities. Such efforts are constrained by the global nature of the Internet; anonymizers can be located in other countries and messages can be passed through servers in multiple countries. Some people, in the interest of combating child pornography, drug trafficking, and other crimes, would prohibit anonymous e-mail altogether. Others point to the value attached to anonymity in U.S. legal tradition, such as a 1995 U.S. Supreme Court decision that upheld an individual's right to send anonymous political leaflets,[33] and argue that the same principles should apply to Internet communications as well.

An interesting, unresolved question is the extent to which specific solutions might alleviate the need for wholesale use of the more general anonymity services discussed here. For example, some of the need for anonymity would go away if satisfactory solutions were found for preserving individual privacy. And some other needs for anonymity, such as those occasioned by political expression or whistleblowing without fear of reprisal, might be accommodated by special anonymous forums (e.g., an anonymous posting site) established for those particular purposes.

Importantly, there are steps that the various interested parties can take to identify ways of resolving tensions associated with anonymous online communication. For instance, e-mail service providers, remailers, Web sites, and online communities can develop, publicize, and implement specific policies about appropriate and inappropriate use of anonymous or pseudonymous communications. Industry and user groups can work together to develop standard guidelines for such policies. Another useful step, in line with the practices of some services today, would be for such policies to clearly state the situations in which user identities may be disclosed to others.

Identity

Issues of privacy and anonymity ride on top of how we establish, manage, and even understand identity against a background of global networks and powerful databases. Controlling information about one's

---

[33]McIntyre v. Ohio Elections Commission, 514 U.S. 334 (1995).

identity and the links to data about that identity is one way that we can achieve privacy. Anonymity can be thought of as one extreme of identification, namely, the absence of any personal identification. In this section, the committee presents some basic principles of "digital identity" that may help reconcile the conflicts surrounding information disclosure, privacy, and accountability on the Internet. It hopes these principles will serve as a useful framework for future policy in the privacy area as well as for finding and implementing technical solutions in support of the various privacy requirements resulting from industry self-regulation and government legal and regulatory actions.

Individual identity is a complex concept. Each of us has different identities, with different roles and attributes, in different situations and at different times. A person can simultaneously be a parent, spouse, employee, consumer, auction buyer or seller, patient, and member of various organizations. People often try to keep these different identities separate. They may do this by providing more, less, or simply different information to different persons, government organizations, or commercial service providers. To the extent that people are able to do so, they make it difficult for third parties to link the actions and activities of their different identities and conclude they belong to a single individual.[34] The nature of Internet interactions and the explosive growth of electronic communities, sliced across a number of different geographic and demographic factors, amplify this need greatly and mean that more information is available from more sources and to more parties in a context that allows collecting pieces of information from disparate sources and matching them by technical means.

While the Internet indeed poses serious challenges related to identity, it also offers elegant and powerful tools for balancing individual and societal needs for privacy, anonymity, and accountability. Examples of the tools emerging include tools that allow the individual to manage and

---

[34]This is significantly easier to do in the United States, where the absence of a mandatory national identifier makes it easier for an individual to maintain separate identities that cannot be easily associated with one another. A number of other countries have measures in place that embrace a single, unique identifier for each person (e.g., a national ID card), and some are moving to implement this approach electronically (e.g., the "qualified certificate" concept expressed in a recent European Union directive on public key certificates and work in the IETF's Public-Key Infrastructure (X.509) working group). Not only does this run counter to U.S. practice and philosophy, it represents a more simplistic view of identity than the discussion here would argue for and enables the easy linking of one's various activities with a single individual profile. The widespread use of such common identifying information as the Social Security number does, however, limit the extent to which one can separate identities.

control "multiple identities," using one or more certifying authorities to validate various attributes where required. These tools also help the individual track and monitor what information is being collected and how this information is actually used. A caution, however, is that such tools depend in many cases on a foundation of effective security mechanisms and practices, including authentication capabilities that are not widely available (the exceptions being such instances as a merchant authenticating a customer's credit card account or two parties with prior relationship authenticating each other).

It is possible for individuals to have multiple digital identities on the Internet for use in different contexts and situations. Personal information—such as name, school, and job affiliations, home and business addresses, telephone and fax numbers, e-mail addresses, drivers' licenses, passports, credit cards, and other identifying records—can be stored and made selectively available on the Internet by the user, much as a person now physically takes out various cards from his or her wallet for different purposes. Today, users who make use of multiple services are likely to have established what effectively amounts to a portfolio of identities in which varying amounts of personal information have been provided, depending on the nature of the transaction, the information requested by the other party, and the type of information the user has chosen to provide. In many cases these different identities can be linked using either information provided by the user (e.g., name and address matching) or information gained from cookies that different Web content and service providers have placed on user machines. But in many other cases, correct identity information is needed for accountability. When a firm gives an employee an e-mail address (JohnDoe@example.com) it in effect certifies that the person is affiliated with that company. Cookies on users' computers often contain a mixture of self-reported information and information certified by a provider. Certification authorities exist to authenticate characteristics of identity (such as age, location, or ability to pay) that are necessary to engage in certain activities or complete certain transactions.[35]

It is also possible to provide mechanisms that allow users to create digital identities that provide explicit control over what personal information is disclosed under what circumstances. Discussion groups and chat rooms, like e-mail, often tolerate if not encourage pseudonyms, and some online interactions, such as multiuser domains, encourage creation of artificial, even fantastic, identities in the spirit of play. Even when a transaction needs to be authenticated, a user's name does not need to be

---

[35]For a discussion of this approach to public key infrastructure, see S. Kent. 1997. "How Many Certification Authorities Are Enough." *Proceedings of MILCOM 97 (unclassified papers)* 1 (November): 61-68.

disclosed; in a purchase transaction, it may be sufficient for a vendor to be able to associate an identity with a certification that the user has a valid credit card (or some other indication of ability to pay, such as an account at one of the new electronic money services).[36] For example, the user can choose to send only a reference to the needed information and can use encryption or other authentication tools to make sure that only the intended party receives the information and that the receiving party is who or what it represents it is. The user is then able to give general instructions to his or her digital identity agent about what information to release for which activities under what safeguards, or he or she can personally approve each use of data or each transaction. Such tools can provide distinct levels of digital identity on the Internet; these, in turn, can vary with the kind or degree of interaction and according to the stringency or authority with which the information about identity is established or attested to, ranging from the self-identified to private certification to government certification of identity.

A logical complement to relying on institutions with which one has established some relationship, such as a credit-card issuer, for identifying and certifying information is third-party repositories and/or certifiers. One approach may be user-controlled: the information making up one's digital identity can be stored in well-known places or managed by agents accessible to authorized parties on the Internet. Users of such a tool would be able to manage all components of their digital identity except for those that require certification, which will be controlled by the certifying entities. When organizations doing business on the Internet set out their privacy policies on their Web sites, users can instruct their digital identity agent to negotiate with the Web sites about release of personal data. This sort of automated process is, of course, only as good as the system and the user's choices. As described above, the P3P technology under development by the World Wide Web Consortium is one approach to facilitating the flow of necessary identifying information while still protecting individual privacy as defined by the user. An alternative is that, seeking greater convenience, people will choose not to maintain a high level of control over such information, electing instead to let third parties manage it for them. For example, users might use services that are less complex and less robust (e.g., there is no use of certifiers), relinquishing direct control over the use of their information. Examples of third-party systems now in the marketplace include Microsoft's Passport and Privaseek, online services that provide such features as password man-

---

[36]This is the approach used in the SET (secure electronic transactions) specification for payment card transactions over the Internet. See <http://www.setco.org/set_specifications. html>.

agement and automatic completion of online forms based on saved information. Other services, such as Yodlee.com and VerticalOne work on behalf of the user by gathering the private information that users provide to diverse Web sites and aggregating them to present the user with a single, integrated view. These services are new, and the merits and consumer acceptance of approaches ranging from tight user control to delegation of decisions to third parties remain to be proven. The prospect of third-party involvement in identity management begs the question of "identity portability"—the ability to easily switch between identity agent services in an analogous fashion to number portability among telephone carriers—meaning in this context that people's selected identities are not tied to a particular site or service.

The emergence of technical approaches that allow individuals to manage their online identities is a positive development. Such approaches depend on government and business cooperation. For example, responsible service providers will clearly state their privacy policies in digital form so that an individual's identity agent can readily determine whether or not to use the site. Privacy advocates argue that, in general, the amount of information required and revealed should be minimal for the purpose. It is also likely that we will see the emergence of tools and services that allow users to identify and document when privacy promises are violated; such tools and services may be another alternative to regulation as a remedy. If digital identity is to become widely accepted, there will also need to be a legal framework for behaviors with respect to identity technologies: Who, for instance, would be expected to decide who controls what about identity, and under what circumstances would they make this decision? How would conflicts be resolved?

Some basic principles for such a framework include the following:

• The information associated with each identity should be under the user's control.

• The holder of a digital identity should not be compelled to reveal elements of that identity against his or her will except to the extent and under the circumstances dictated by law for a similar transaction offline.

• An identity holder should be allowed to modify its elements as needed.

• The theft or unauthorized modification of the elements of someone else's digital identity should be subject to appropriate penalties under either civil or criminal law.

• Government-created or -certified identities need not be the default, although it may be necessary for governments to recognize certain certifications as authoritative for official purposes. Such official certifications exist today, such as passports and drivers' licenses; these are issued for particular purposes and have specific regulatory criteria associated with them.

AUTHENTICATION ON THE INTERNET

Authentication—the process of establishing that a particular claim about an entity's (e.g., a person's or organization's) identity is, in fact, valid—is needed for many transactions, including electronic buying and selling, voting, access to health records, and so forth, and it is an essential element of the processes that bear on privacy and anonymity. But identity authentication is a complex issue, not least owing to the multifaceted nature of identity. For example, e-commerce may not necessarily require verifying the identity of an individual but may instead require verifying whether an individual possesses certain properties relevant to a purchase (e.g., whether the individual is above a certain age, is authorized to make purchases using a particular payment mechanism, or is trusted to maintain privacy/confidentiality). A related additional service, nonrepudiation, allows the receiver of a message to not only authenticate the sender but also be able to prove that the sender in fact originated the message.

Authentication technology and practice build on a history of work in computer and communications security, including experience with people who have sought unauthorized access to information and systems, sometimes by hiding or misrepresenting who they are. Because perfect security is a chimera, e-commerce security, like security in other domains, is generally thought of as a risk management process, whereby stronger and more costly technologies are introduced in response to the dynamics and magnitude of the risk. Issues such as buyer authentication and recourse for nonpayment arise in other commercial transactions, just as in e-commerce, and are dealt with in those contexts through a combination of technology, business practices, and sound risk management principles. Therefore the processes that are required to implement buyer protection, transaction enforceability, and dispute resolution for e-commerce can rely primarily on existing business risk management and legal frameworks. However, we do not yet have a large enough base of experience in types of risk and the legal and regulatory challenges a business faces when providing these authentication services over the Internet to fully understand what changes in business risk management and legal frameworks will be necessary, including clearly establishing the liabilities of authentication providers.

Support for authentication over the Internet is fragmented today. There is no standardized, widely accessible, cheap, and easy approach— in short, there is no single best-technology solution. Multiple technologies for authenticating the identity or related attributes of individuals and organizations are in use and/or development. These range from simple solutions that make use of exchanging shared secrets (e.g., passwords) over secured communications links to more sophisticated systems that rely on the exchange of credentials or certificates that attest to the authenticity of an individual's identity or other attributes. User authentication mechanisms can be characterized as relying on something an individual knows (such as a password), something an individual has, and/or something an individual is (an innate biological property). None of these is without shortcomings.

To illustrate, a simple authentication mechanism is to challenge the other party with questions about a shared secret, such as a password, that only the intended recipient should know the correct answer to. This is what is generally used today in transactions with consumers over the Internet, typically in conjunction with secure sockets layer-based (SSL) encryption that makes it difficult for eavesdroppers to steal the consumer's password by monitoring network communications. Shared secret mechanisms such as passwords have a number of weaknesses; for instance, passwords chosen by users are often relatively easy to guess. The mechanisms can be strengthened by making the secrets dynamic, such as by using information contained in recent transactions or communications (e.g., asking the customer what the amount of the first purchase listed on his most recent statement is). Because users are likely to make use of multiple services, there are ease-of-use issues when they have to manage multiple passwords—potentially a separate password for each Internet account or service they use. Such considerations have led to commercial interest in services that offer to manage these passwords for consumers; several of these were discussed above in the section on identity. And, more fundamentally, mechanisms that rely on shared secrets require that a relationship has already been established between the parties. The exception would be when the two parties do not know each other but do know and trust a third, neutral party who can use shared secrets with each to authenticate and vouch for each party on behalf of the other. Note, however, that third-party verification of individual identity is only as good as the verification conducted by the certifying authority— for example, How did it verify the identity of the individual? How much information has it certified?[37] What guarantees and recourse does it provide if the certified information proves false?[38]

---

[37]For example, if the certifying authority is not the same entity as the individual's agent in that arena (e.g., the credit card issuer) can it responsibly perform that authorization (e.g., authenticate that the individual is the rightful and authorized user of the card)?

[38]There is an important distinction between authoritative certification authorities and

Public key cryptography[39] is commonly used to provide authentication and nonrepudiation services. A major challenge in public key cryptography work is distributing the public keys in a secure manner so that, for example, an individual cannot be misled into using the public key of someone who wishes to impersonate that individual by substituting the impersonator's public key for the correct public key. Transacting parties that have a prior relationship can make use of already exchanged and validated public keys to validate the received digital signature. Otherwise, each could ask the other party to provide some sort of credential, such as one provided by a trusted third party that attests to the authenticity of their identity or some set of attributes including their public keys.[40]

The term public key infrastructure (PKI) is frequently used as a label for the technology, processes, and policies that underlie public key management. PKI makes used of certificates that allow the identity of users to be authoritatively associated with their public key. One PKI model makes use of trusted third parties, known as certification authorities, who themselves use public key cryptography to digitally sign certificates that bind the identity of subscribers to a public key.[41] PKI is a complex undertaking that requires the implementation of technical mechanisms, the establishment of procedures for the issuance and revocation of certificates, possibly updating directories, certificate revocation lists, and so forth. The complicated nature of certificate management (e.g., registering, revoking, and updating certificates) is one hindrance to PKI's widespread use.[42]

---

trusted certification authorities. No one questions, for example, whether a company is trusted to identify its employees, because the company is understood to be the source of authoritative information on this subject. In contrast, an arbitrary third party does not have the same authoritative status.

[39]Public key cryptography also provides the basis for more robust encryption and authentication. The technique relies on a public, freely published key that is used to encrypt messages together with another, private key that is used for decryption. Importantly, the decryption key cannot be derived from the encryption key. This allows secret communications where the only one who can decrypt a message is the holder of the private key that matches the public key that the message was encrypted in.

[40]Much of this discussion is based on the discussion of public key cryptography in Computer Science and Telecommunications Board (CSTB), National Research Council. 1998. *Trust in Cyberspace.* Washington, D.C.: National Academy Press, pp. 121-132.

[41]There are other PKI models; for example, Pretty Good Privacy (or PGP) makes use of a "web of trust" in which any user with a public key can issue a certificate for any other user.

[42]Specific difficulties include root and cross certifications, certificate revocation, and certificate management. See Computer Science and Telecommunications Board (CSTB), National Research Council. 1998. *Trust in Cyberspace.* Washington, D.C.: National Academy Press, pp. 130-132. There are also questions as to when certificates need to be exchanged

Lack of compatibility among different implementations is another obstacle. While there are base standards for PKI, they are not always followed, in part because some of today's systems were designed to be stand-alone systems. The technology is also still relatively costly, and its use incurs significant performance penalties; thus its use today requires sufficient transaction risk to justify the investment and some inconvenience in use.

Biometrics, which is based on measurement of such physical characteristics as fingerprints, hand geometry, or iris shape, is also being used for identity authentication. Biometrics at first appears ideal because of its dependence on a physical feature that is unique to a person. However, its use of pattern matching carries the risk that an unauthorized user will be accepted or that an authorized user will be rejected and/or that the identifying information will be misappropriated.[43]

The selection of an authentication technology entails trade-offs. For example, exchanging shared secrets has the disadvantage that these secrets must be remembered and can be guessed or stolen, whereas more sophisticated authentication approaches, such as those that rely on PKI, often require certificate management, rely on sophisticated software and/or hardware components, and cost more to deploy, along with other drawbacks. Biometrics technologies have issues with performance, such as user acceptance, the impact of compromise, and the risks of false rejection or acceptance. The use of two or more of these technologies (often called two-factor authentication) makes for stronger (harder to spoof) authentication than the use of a single one but generally increases the cost and inconvenience. The ideal combination of authentication technologies for a given class of applications has yet to be agreed upon.

Another set of tradeoffs must be made between the strength of the cryptographic algorithms required and the risk exposure associated with selecting lower strengths to reduce cost and system performance penalties. In addition, all systems, even those assumed to be strong, are susceptible to vulnerabilities associated with flaws in their implementation.[44]

---

and whether they can be stored and accessed via directories. For example, directory-based solutions have been proposed for simplifying some of the certificate management and public key distribution issues, but this is still relatively new and just emerging and not completely compatible with current implementations. It is also important to distinguish between when one needs certificates and when authentication can take place without certificates (where public keys are previously known or exchanged by other means).

[43]See Computer Science and Telecommunications Board (CSTB), National Research Council. 1998. *Trust in Cyberspace*. Washington, D.C.: National Academy Press, pp. 123-124.

[44]History has also shown that the adequacy of cryptographic algorithms is continually being challenged by inevitable advances in computer processor performance that makes code-breaking easier as well as by advances in code-breaking techniques and growth in the number of people who attempt to break cryptosystems.

Deployed systems may not be as strong as they might at first glance appear. For example, in many implementations of digital signatures and certificates for authentication, the digital-signing software can itself be accessed through a simple password. Also, the strength of software-only systems is tied to the strength of the security mechanisms in the computers on which they run; systems that run on personal computers are subject to all of the well-known security limitations of these platforms. Additionally, the vulnerability of a cryptographic algorithm will change over time with advances in computing and power cryptanalysis techniques (and key lengths will be increased in response). Special-purpose hardware and token-based mechanisms, which rely on closed hardware devices such as smart cards or PC cards in place of software running on a user's PC, can offer greater security. The greater costs associated with hardware-based solutions may, however, make such solutions impractical for many applications. These systems have their vulnerabilities as well, especially if they lack built-in displays and input devices, and one must rely on the PC for interaction with the user.[45] The relation between these trade-offs and the various security technology options is poorly understood.

It appears likely that, despite their many limitations, shared secrets (e.g., passwords) will continue to be used for consumer authentication for the foreseeable future and that stronger authentication technologies will first begin to be deployed in corporate and commercial applications where the larger risk exposure warrants the introduction of stronger, but more costly and intrusive, authentication approaches and where these approaches can be implemented over a more limited and manageable number of players and covered by contract law. Unfortunately, these solutions are likely to be deployed initially as proprietary islands, optimized to particular applications by competing service providers. This could forestall the emergence of a widespread standard approach sufficiently open and minimalist that interoperability can be enabled without innovation being stifled.

Two challenges—the chicken-and-egg challenge associated with deployment of authentication infrastructures, whereby authentication providers and potential users wait for each other to make the first investments in authentication, and the challenge of increasing the potential

---

[45]Another open question is what the right sort of dedicated authentication hardware would be: should one use a smart card, which offers a limited amount of data storage and processing power, or should one use a much simpler device such as a radio frequency identification (RFID) tag or, alternatively, a more powerful one such as a personal digital assistant?

demand from a range of different users and uses—suggest that widespread deployment awaits one or more first movers making significant investments. Both private and government actors can play a role in propelling online authentication. Authentication is an area where governments can and do intervene: at state, national, and international levels there has been support for a legal framework, for technology development, and for the implementation of specific authentication technologies such as biometrics and PKI.

In their efforts to establish an enabling framework for authentication and nonrepudiation, Congress and state legislatures have moved forward with attempts to legitimize electronic signatures. Most notably, the Electronic Signatures in Global and National Commerce Act was enacted in 2000. And, there are encouraging signs of moves to harmonize state laws, to eliminate the current inconsistencies among them. Other laws, such as the Government Paperwork Elimination Act and government programs that promote electronic transactions, especially over the Internet, within a government and between a government and its citizens, promote greater use of authentication. (They also raise new questions about the interaction of authentication, privacy, and anonymity considerations.) Efforts are also under way in such international forums as the ITU and the European Union.

Various online federal and state government initiatives have been launched that involve the widespread government deployment of authentication and nonrepudiation services. They include initiatives for online government purchase (by, for example, the General Services Administration), electronic voting (by, for example, the Department of Defense), and online electronic tax filing. These initiatives are expected not just to satisfy government needs but also, it is hoped, to demonstrate technologies and practices in ways that make discussion of PKI less abstract. They could also lead to the transfer of knowledge to private industry and could serve as a critical mass for an authentication infrastructure.

But, important as they are, legislative action and government investment alone cannot address the many technical and business issues discussed in this section that are the root causes for the lack of widespread acceptance of authentication technologies. The complexity of these issues and the range of relevant stakeholders across all levels of government, industry, and the population at large suggest that an in-depth inquiry by a joint industry-government advisory panel would be appropriate. The Congress, the Department of Commerce, and other federal agencies, as well as state and local agencies, would all benefit from an examination of the factors that are impeding the early introduction of authentication services and from an identification of the factors that might accelerate investment in these services and—ultimately—their deployment.

TAXATION OF INTERNET-BASED COMMERCE

Taxation of commerce conducted over the Internet has emerged as a controversial, high-profile policy issue. Unlike other policy issues related to e-commerce, taxation is a nonmarket objective for which it may be harder to assume that voluntary action and self-interest by individuals and organizations can offer adequate solutions. It involves information and mechanisms that may bear on privacy and anonymity and it is likely to involve authentication at some point. The taxation issue is not only important in its own right, it also illustrates a large class of issues that are location- and identity-dependent. E-commerce benefits from its independence of geography, which allows retailers to offer both specialty and mass-market products to a wide variety of customers without regard to where they live. In contrast, commerce in the physical world has been mostly governed by relatively independent, discrete geographic domains, and tax obligations have been enforced based on physical presence. Problems arise, however, for governments that seek to impose laws determined by geography, such as state or city sales tax, on e-commerce transactions.[46] Any resolution of how to tax e-commerce transactions will have to take into account the inherent difficulties of verifying the location, identity, and residence of a seller or purchaser over the Internet. In the United States alone, considering the intersection of the various levels of local, state, and national government, there are a very large number of separate geopolitical regions with differing tax structures. Presently, local governments in 34 states are authorized to impose local sales taxes; approximately 7,600 jurisdictions have chosen to do so, and this number could grow significantly if other local governments choose to exercise this option.[47] International e-commerce, of course, raises an additional set of

---

[46]Existing U.S. sales tax law treats goods sold over the Internet the same way it treats goods sold from catalogs using mail or phone orders. A company without a physical presence in a state (known as nexus) cannot be required to collect that state's sales tax even if the customer lives in the state. The purchaser is nonetheless responsible for remitting a "use tax" to his state of residence. For example, if a buyer in Boston orders a book from an online retailer located in Washington State that has no physical presence in Massachusetts, then Massachusetts cannot require the retailer to collect the use tax, even though the purchaser owes this use tax to Massachusetts. Instead, states must rely on self-reporting and payment by the customers. Compliance is, of course, harder to ensure with a use tax paid by the individual purchaser than it is with a sales tax collected by the merchant. See, for example, Austan Goolsbee and Jonathan Zittrain. 1999. "Evaluating the Costs and Benefits of Taxing Internet Commerce." *National Tax Journal* 52(3):413-428.

[47]National Tax Association (NTA). 1999. *Communications and Electronic Commerce Tax Project: Final Report*. Washington, D.C.: NTA, September 7, p. 12. Available online at <http://www.ntanet.org/ecommerce/final_report_cover.htm>.

complications associated with the different tax rates and rules. There are different tax structures (e.g., national or state/regional) and different approaches to taxation (e.g., a sales tax versus a value-added tax[48]). Potentially taxable transactions can cross even national borders without there being any traceability other than that contained in transaction audit trails on vendors' systems. Additionally, the Internet environment has been conducive to creating new forms of value, both nonmonetary (e.g., online barter exchanges) and monetary (new forms of currency such as flooz, beenz, and RocketCash), that portend further strains on tax structures at least until they become widespread and commonplace enough to be monetized.

On the issue of taxing online transactions, governments have competing interests. Many state and local government leaders do not want to lose sales tax revenue when purchases are made from companies without nexus in that state, while other policy makers are interested in not retarding the growth of commerce over the Internet. Another consideration is that changing the current tax policy could affect the volume and distribution of commerce that is conducted over the Internet, which could in turn affect the way in which the Internet is used.

There is a lot of ambiguity and uncertainty as to how a change in tax policy would affect tax revenues or, directly, the growth of the Internet. Work by Goolsbee[49] gives empirical support to the idea that taxes (and other price differences) will have significant effects on the purchasing behavior of individuals living in a "world without borders." He projects that the price impact of applying existing sales taxes to Internet commerce might reduce the number of online buyers by up to 24 percent. To the extent that e-commerce is an important driver of investment in Internet infrastructure (and supports other Internet services via advertising), the outcome would affect the Internet's future development and growth.

Forecasts of the volume of tax revenue at stake vary. The National Governors Association has quoted forecasts that by 2002 there may be more than $300 billion in commerce over the Web or through mail order and concluded that this would result in up to $20 billion in lost tax revenue,[50] and similar numbers are often cited by advocates of Internet taxation. Goolsbee and Zittrain[51] offer a different perspective. They observe

---

[48]In June 2000, for example, the EU considered imposing a broad VAT obligation.

[49]Austan Goolsbee. 2000. "In a World Without Borders: The Impact of Taxes on Internet Commerce." *The Quarterly Journal of Economics* 115(2):561-576.

[50]Juliana Gruenwald. 1998. "Vote Bodes Ill for Internet Tax Agreement." *Congressional Quarterly This Week*, August 3.

[51]Austan Goolsbee and Jonathan Zittrain. 1999. "Evaluating the Costs and Benefits of Taxing Internet Commerce." *National Tax Journal* 52 (3):413-428. Available online at <http://papers.ssrn.com/paper.taf?ABSTRACT_ID=175666>.

that the previously predicted amounts seem to include business-to-business as well as business-to-commerce sales; that they ignore the possibility of trade creation; and that the calculations fail to account for the types of products being sold. They find that for the next several years, there is little tax revenue to be gained from enforcing taxes on Internet sales.

When confronted with the issue of how to collect sales taxes for transactions conducted over the Internet, given that states and local municipalities are the ones that levy sales tax, Congress passed the Internet Tax Freedom Act (ITFA), which put in place a 3-year moratorium on imposing new taxes associated with Internet transactions and established a congressional Advisory Commission on Electronic Commerce to study the question of sales tax revenue.[52] This action was motivated by not wanting to do anything that could adversely impact the growth of commerce over the Internet and by the ambiguity resulting from the inherently borderless nature of the Internet. The ITFA, however, does not restrict the right of states to apply sales and use taxes to online commerce (these are not, after all, new taxes). Instead it primarily prevents states from applying new taxes to Internet access. The commission completed its work in April 2000 without the mandated supermajority of the committee reaching consensus. Resolution of the tensions between retaining a tax revenue base and fostering e-commerce are likely to remain a contentious political issue for some time.[53]

The difficulty of knowing the identity and location of parties to an e-commerce transaction is exacerbated by several factors. As discussed in an earlier section, the Internet enables a range of anonymous transactions, making it difficult to ascertain the identity of a purchaser let alone his or her location. The location capabilities that are offered by emerging wireless data services may prove an exception, although they would be enabled by mechanisms provided as part of the wireless service rather than conventional Internet connectivity provided through the wireless link. Also, digital systems acting on behalf of people or organizations, rather than the people or organizations themselves, can be the actors responsible for buying and distributing a product or service over the Internet. Of course in some instances location could still be established based on the delivery address. However, many goods are electronic (e.g., downloaded software or music) and many services can be delivered via communications over the Internet, so these goods and services can be delivered to a

---

[52]Title XI of Public Law 105-277.

[53]Intel leader Andrew Grove's June 2000 statement supporting taxation of Internet-based commerce indicates that the high-tech industry does not have a uniform position on these issues.

computer attached to the Internet without any physical goods being delivered to a verifiable physical address. The recipient computer sits in a physical location, but associating a physical location with that computer's network address cannot be done with certainty in today's Internet. And internationally, even if there were agreements to collect taxes, enforcement of tax collection for physical goods shipped across national boundaries would depend on customs agencies to block shipments or collect duty.

One suggested remedy is to build into the Internet's infrastructure itself the ability to provide the location and/or identity of the parties to a transaction. However, efforts to embed solutions to the taxation problem at the network level would have far-reaching consequences for the Internet, which currently has no concept of locality in a geographical or geopolitical sense. As discussed in Chapter 1, a central design tenet of the Internet is the placing of applications and intelligence in the end systems rather than within the network. A solution to the taxation issue that relied on building into the network mechanisms that provide knowledge of the geographical location of a network element would violate this principle, as it would require a new, intelligent capability within that network that determines, and on request provides, the physical location of a device or some surrogate, which is not easy to do in any case. Such a solution could also have adverse privacy implications. It would, in contrast, be possible to build such knowledge into end systems or higher-layer authentication infrastructures. It might, for example, be more productive to try to derive location information from authenticated information about a party to a transaction. Because Internet technology and e-commerce technology are evolving so rapidly, it is clearly preferable for solutions to avoid placing requirements on the Internet infrastructure that are dependent on a specific e-commerce technology.

Given that the Internet generally ignores geography and makes it difficult for vendors or third parties to assure identification of a purchaser, there are significant difficulties associated with solutions that depend on ascertaining the location of the purchaser. This suggests, first, that if taxation policy relating to e-commerce must be changed, the changes should be as unspecific to geopolitical region as possible and, second, that today's sales tax system, which involves many thousands of distinct jurisdictions, would need to be simplified. And, in order to reflect the Internet's architecture, including the dynamic nature of its routing, taxation schemes should be based on the end points only and not on mechanisms embedded in intermediate points within the network.

There are a number of solutions that avoid these problems. Some tax structures would not require a complex knowledge of geography to be built into the technology. A flat e-commerce sales tax collected by the

seller at the time of payment would not be locality-sensitive, would require no technology changes at the buyer's end, and would be easier for
the vendor to implement. The collection of taxes would be simpler if they
were added to each transaction at the point of sale, much as is done with
a cash transaction at the physical point of sale today. (Such a scheme
would also enable the appropriate tax to be collected even if the transaction were conducted anonymously.) Another simplification would be to
separate the means of tax collection from the distribution and allocation
of tax revenues. The issue of which governmental bodies get some of the
tax collected and what portion of it they get could then be addressed
separately by the respective governmental bodies. It would be easier to
allocate revenue if such allocation did not depend on knowing the location of the purchaser. Of course other simplifying schemes could be
devised that would not be such a radical departure from today's sales tax
system. These approaches would help reconcile the tensions between
those who want to preserve the tax revenue base for state and local governments and those who want to foster the growth of e-commerce, but
striking a balance between these interests is likely to remain a contentious
political issue for some time.

UNIVERSAL SERVICE

Equity in access to and use of the Internet is a matter of values and
social policy. Such policy has been reflected in universal service for telephony, with access provided to people across all income classes.[54] Universal service programs fall into two general classes—setting rates that
benefit particular classes of customers (e.g., residential or rural users)
who might otherwise face considerably higher rates and offering subsidized lifeline rates to low-income subscribers to expand the number of
households with access to basic telephone service, thereby expanding
opportunities for economic, community, and political participation and
emergency (911) service.

Universal service has long been an element of U.S. telecommunications policy.[55] Indeed, whether or not one agrees that universal service

---

[54]Universal service policies go beyond establishing uniform rates for service: they create
subsidized "lifeline" rates for basic service at prices low enough to permit the poorest
families to have access to the telephone network.

[55]Basic telephone service has long been regarded as a social good, universal access to
which required a deliberate policy effort to achieve. However, the history of universal
service policies can support a different interpretation. Milton Mueller argues that, given
today's rates, universal access would easily have been achieved even without subsidiza-
tion. See Milton Mueller. 1997. "Universal Service and the Telecommunications Act: Myth
Made Law," *Communications of the ACM* 40(3):39-48.

for networks is an appropriate objective of public policy, it is worth pointing out that extension of universal service policies to new communications networks has always enjoyed popular support. Historically, the government intervened to establish universal service at uniform rates for postal services as well as telephone service and to extend to remote areas and impoverished areas the benefits of such infrastructure as electrification and highway construction. Given the rapid pace at which Internet-based applications and services are being deployed in both the private and public sectors, social and political demands for expanded access to Internet-based communications services, which are increasingly seen as essential for commerce, education, employment, or political participation, can be expected to increase.[56]

There are several geography-related factors associated with Internet access. These geographical considerations are, of course, closely linked to economic factors. Places with less access will generally be those where the remoteness, the lower density of potential customers, or the lower ability (or willingness) of the population to pay make the provision of service a higher-cost undertaking or a less attractive investment. There are differences in the availability and price of dial-up access that depend on (1) the number of carriers that have established local access points (whereby dial-up access is via a local, typically flat-rate billed call) in a given location and (2) the availability of dial-up Internet access service providers. A recent study by Downes and Greenstein[57] found that, as of the spring of 1998, most of the U.S. population had access to competitive dial-up Internet service. According to this research, more than 90 percent of the population lived in areas served by more than 10 ISPs, while fewer than 1 percent lived in areas without any dial-up service.[58]

---

[56]Concerns about universal access to the Internet are not new. For example, in the fall of 1993, they were featured in an Administration policy statement (William Jefferson Clinton and Albert Gore. 1993. *The National Information Infrastructure: Agenda for Action.* Washington, D.C., September 15. Available online at <http://metalab.unc.edu/nii/toc.html>). The state of access to Internet and related services has also been the subject of a series of National Telecommunications and Information Administration (NTIA) reports from 1995 to the present. (NTIA, Department of Commerce. 1995. *Falling Through the Net: A Survey of the "Have Nots" in Rural and Urban America.* Washington, D.C.: NTIA, July. Available online at <http://www.ntia.doc.gov/ntiahome/fttn99/contents.html>.)

[57]Thomas A. Downes and Shane M. Greenstein. 1998. "Do Commercial ISPs Provide Universal Access?" *Competition, Regulation, and Convergence: Current Trends in Telecommunications Policy Research.* Sharon Gillet and Ingo Vogelsang, eds. Mahwah, N.J.: Lawrence Erlbaum. Available online at <http://skew2.kellogg.nwu.edu/~greenste/research/papers/tprcbook.pdf>.

[58]Even in unserved areas, the upper bound on the cost of dial-up Internet is set by the roughly $4 to $5 hourly rate offered by a number of ISPs for access via toll-free numbers.

High-speed (broadband) access is less widespread than lower-speed dial-up service.[59] Constraints include technical factors (e.g., DSL services are limited to locations within a given distance from a local exchange, with the exact distance depending on the variant of DSL technology employed, the bandwidth, and the condition of the phone lines); the extent to which the necessary telecommunications infrastructure is present (e.g., cable modem service is limited to locations passed by cable service, which is less prevalent in rural areas), and the pace at which investment is made in service deployment, including the associated required infrastructure improvements. With deployment of such services in its early stages, a few communities have both DSL and cable service and many have no high-speed services at all. Higher bandwidth services require investment in upgraded facilities (e.g., deployment of DSL facilities in the telephone local exchange or upgraded cable plants) and so are more likely to occur, at least in the earlier phases of deployment, in wealthier communities, where more customers are likely to purchase service as a result of an upgrade. Whether physical access to high-speed services will begin to approach the near-universal level seen for dial-up service as deployment continues remains to be seen. It is the subject of political and regulatory debate.

Access to a service does not mean that it will be used; this can be seen in the history of telephone and television use. There have been a variety of studies conducted by both government and market research firms to monitor and describe patterns of Internet access and use. One such effort culminated in a series of reports from the National Telecommunications and Information Administration (NTIA). For example, a July 1999 NTIA report based on U.S. Census Bureau data from December 1998[60] indicates that, of the households able to access the Internet, the fraction that actually subscribe to an ISP is far from 100 percent—41.1 percent of U.S. households owned computers and roughly 25 percent had Internet service. Such studies point not only to the persistence of disparities but also to their instability: whole groups can increase their use of the Internet between studies, and the implications of the findings are hard to pin down. A number of efforts have been made to understand the extent of

---

[59]Broadband last-mile technologies and local access are the concerns of a separate CSTB study, to be completed in 2001.

[60]National Telecommunications and Information Administration (NTIA), U.S. Department of Commerce. July 1999. *Falling Through the Net: Defining the Digital Divide: A Report on the Telecommunications and Information Technology Gap in America.* Washington, D.C.: NTIA. Available online at <http://www.ntia.doc.gov/ntiahome/digitaldivide/>.

disparities in service, including those between high- and low-income households and between urban and rural status and those based on education or race. The situation is volatile, with a panoply of data showing both persistent disparities as well as instances where disparities have decreased over time.

To what extent is the fraction of the population that has Internet access likely to broaden? Recent years have seen a drop in the cost of computer equipment required to access the Internet; relatively inexpensive PCs and a range of Internet access appliances have entered the market. Also, various new businesses are offering free Internet access or even free PCs along with Internet service in exchange for viewing advertising. Complementing home-based access, kiosks operated by public institutions and commercial enterprises make Internet access available in a number of public places. One motivation for the federal e-rate program that provides subsidies to schools, libraries, and hospitals is to increase the number of public access points. Free e-mail services allow people unable to afford Internet service to maintain private e-mail accounts that are accessible from public locations. However, the long-term viability of new schemes and business models for providing Internet service remains to be proven. Pricing schemes and bundling are in flux as new business models emerge. Declining costs and increasing utility may result in universal or nearly universal access to the Internet without any government action, but this outcome is neither certain nor guaranteed.

Universal service programs applied to Internet-based services raise a number of social and political questions, including who should receive universal service benefits, what value judgments underlie these choices, whether funds should be obtained from service-specific sources or from general funds, what constitutes universal service (e.g., which collection of services, from personal/household access to access through public facilities), and even whether universal service programs should be implemented at all. In this section, the committee briefly reviews what is known about Internet penetration in the United States and then addresses some issues that would arise if one were to try to implement universal service policies for the Internet. It does not take a position on whether universal service programs *should* be extended to the Internet or on how they should be funded and managed, because to do so adequately would require full consideration of the costs and benefits over time, a complex matter well beyond the scope of this report.

Universal service policies have, at their core, sought to ensure that price or geographical location is not a barrier to use. These policies combine two distinct elements—universality of physical access and universality of financial access. In the case of the Internet, the cost is the sum of several elements. First, there is the price of the Internet service itself.

Second, there is the cost of access to the Internet (e.g., via cable modem, DSL, or dial-up services), which is frequently bundled together with the cost of Internet service or, in the case of dial-up access, already paid for as part of local telephone service. Third, there is the cost of the associated hardware (computer and modem or other connection device) and the communications software (generally available at little or no cost or bundled with a PC's operating system or with the Internet service). Finally, there are additional costs associated with the use of particular online services, such as subscription fees for accessing particular content.

The traditional universal service obligation applied to telecommunications carriers was a bundle of obligations that users, service providers, and regulators experienced as a single package. The characteristics of universal telephone service—such as expectations for quality and access to callers within the local area, to interexchange carriers, and to operator and emergency services—were well defined and had been developed over the course of many years. Internet services stand in marked contrast. For the Internet user, service translates into a set of Internet applications (e.g., Web browsing, listening to audio programming, video conferencing, or banking online). What the user experiences as "service" depends on the software running on both his and an application provider's computer as well as the characteristics of the network links over which the communication passes. The notion of guaranteeing a particular service to a broad class of potential subscribers needs to be revised, since service in the end-to-end model is in the control of applications running on machines at the edges of the network as well as the capacity and explicit quality of service mechanisms offered by a network operator.[61] In some cases these applications and services are offered as part of a bundle from the Internet service provider, but in general they are provided separately. The desired applications will vary from user to user, and the available mix will change over time as new Internet applications emerge and old ones fall out of favor (few, for example, make use of "gopher" today). Which services and applications (e.g., e-mail, Web, chat, telephony, or streaming video)

---

[61]Moreover, even in the telephony model, no single service was adequate to provide equivalent network access for all users. Users with disabilities, for example, were not well-served under the traditional universal service schemes. Interface and access issues were explored by the CSTB (Computer Science and Telecommunications Board (CSTB), National Research Council. 1997. *More Than Screen Deep: Toward Every-Citizen Interfaces to the Nation's Information Infrastructure.* Washington, D.C.: National Academy Press). Implementing provisions of section 255 of the 1996 Telecommunications Act and section 251(a)(2) of the Communications Act of 1934, the FCC issued rules on July 15, 1999, aimed increasing access to such telecommunications hardware as telephones and to services such as call-waiting and operator service.

should be included in a universal service package, and at what performance level (e.g., speed of download) and quality level (e.g., reliability)?

The emergence of alternatives to dial-up access for residential Internet access means there are more choices with respect to bandwidth and service quality as well a range of service and price options. Also, the Internet's default best-effort service quality allows no guarantees that adequate capacity and quality will be provided to support particular applications. Approaches for providing explicit quality of service are emerging, but there is neither broad agreement on which approaches to use nor widespread deployment, particularly for the home users who are the target of universal service policies. Also, while some applications would be provided by a customer's ISP directly, most require communications across Internet provider boundaries. In the case of the Internet, termination would, at a minimum, mean that any Internet user could access any other user. By virtue of the arrangements that interlink the Internet's constituent networks, basic best-effort connectivity is provided to all network users. However, especially in the case of residential customers, there is generally no service level agreement nor are explicit quality-of-service mechanisms supported. One concern expressed by consumer activists is that people with subsidized or lowest-cost access might not receive service that supports explicit quality of service and might therefore experience a significantly degraded Internet service or be unable to use certain demanding applications.

Efforts have been made to define classes of Internet services. For instance, several years ago the Cross-Industry Working Team project led to the concept of "NII Class Profiles" for characterizing end-to-end performance.[62] Such classification schemes are intended, for example, to simplify specification of the requirements of an application and the ability of equipment and services to meet those requirements. While such a classification might be useful to consumers for evaluating the technology options available to them, its use to define fixed bundles of service in a universal service policy would be too limiting. Because Internet technologies are immature and still in the early stages of deployment, it would be premature to embody them in regulation.

Even the application that was the basic element of traditional universal service, voice telephony, presents difficulties from a universal service standpoint when it is offered as an Internet service. As the discussion in Chapter 4 indicates, there are many approaches to providing IP or Internet telephony, complicating efforts to define a standard service. There are

---

[62]Cross-Industry Working Team (XIWT). 1997. *Class Profiles for the Current and Emerging NII.* White paper. Reston, Va.: XIWT, Corporation for National Research Initiatives. Available online from <http://www.xiwt.org/documents/ClassProfiles.html>.

multiple tiers of service quality, some of which offer consumers a lower price in exchange for reduced guarantees of service quality. Moreover, the issue of guaranteed access to critical services such as 911 service, which is an element of telephony universal service obligations, is an especially difficult one in an Internet context. While it can be anticipated that future obligations will build on those associated with today's 911 service, it is difficult to predict how expectations for critical services will evolve, how they will be shaped by new Internet capabilities, or how they will be implemented.

In telephony, universal service programs, whether aimed at addressing financial or geographical disadvantages, generally involve setting rates and fees so as to achieve a particular objective, whether it is to benefit particular subscribers, extend the telephone network, or increase the total number of subscribers. A number of mechanisms can be employed, including cross-subsidies among service offerings (e.g., subsidizing local calling at the expense of long-distance calling), different rates for different classes of users (e.g., lower rates for residential—as opposed to business—users), the establishment of particular service obligations in exchange for other regulatory relief, or, more recently, explicit fees.[63]

The Internet, by contrast, has a much richer assortment of service providers, ranging from single-niche service providers to full, vertically integrated service providers. Therefore, if it is decided that a universal service program aimed at households is warranted, a range of options for achieving this aim should be considered. The rapid change in Internet services and service offerings would argue for a technology-neutral approach—one that does not rely on mandates to service providers that specific types of service be made available at regulated, possibly subsidized rates. A recent example of this approach is the e-rate program, which has used a fee levied on telephone service to establish a fund to help schools, libraries, and hospitals to pay for Internet access. It is not necessary to transfer resources through cross-subsidies among classes of customer. Other options include subsidies funded by general tax revenue and used by needy citizens to purchase services of their choosing (within established guidelines)—something more akin to food stamp programs.

---

[63]The committee has been careful to avoid labeling these mechanisms as cross-subsidies as there are arguments refuting the idea. For example, there are data that suggest—and a number of state public utility commissions have accepted this viewpoint—that residential rates fully cover the costs of providing that service, which suggests that there is not a transfer between business and residential customers. Also, since universal service programs have network extension as one goal, it can be argued that what might appear to be a transfer of money is, in fact, the regulatory apparatus positioning subscribers to capture the network externality. In other words, if new subscribers come on the network, then there may or may not be a subsidy of the new user.

APPENDIX

Biographies of Committee Members

Eric Schmidt, Chair, joined Novell in April 1997 as chairman of the board of directors and chief executive officer. At Novell, Schmidt is involved in all significant operating and strategic decisions for the company and plays a central role in the technical development and management of the company. Dr. Schmidt came to Novell from Sun Microsystems, Inc., where he was chief technology officer and corporate executive officer. In his 14 years at Sun, Dr. Schmidt held a range of progressively more responsible executive positions, earning international recognition as an Internet pioneer. He was also instrumental in the widespread acceptance of Java, Sun's platform-independent programming language. Prior to joining Sun, Dr. Schmidt was a member of the research staff at the Computer Science Lab at Xerox Palo Alto Research Center (PARC). He also held positions at Bell Laboratories and Zilog. Dr. Schmidt has a B.S. degree in electrical engineering from Princeton University and an M.S. in electrical engineering and a Ph.D. in computer science from the University of California at Berkeley.

Terrence McGarty, Vice Chair, is the chairman of the Telmarc Group, LLC, a company he founded in 1984 that invests in and manages several high-tech start-up ventures. He is currently chairman and CEO of Zephyr Telecommunications, an international record carrier, and managing director of CROSSCONNECT, a venture capital company.

Dr. McGarty has been active in the telecommunications industry for over 30 years. He was until 1992 a senior vice president at NYNEX and the chief operating officer of NYNEX Mobile, a cellular carrier. Prior to that he was the first head of R&D for NYNEX, during which time he created the organization and conceived and developed one of the first multimedia communications systems and the first network management system using the manager of managers concept. All developments were successfully commercialized. Dr. McGarty also spent 5 years in the CATV business, as group president at Warner Communications, and 6 years in the satellite communications business as a division director and general manager of COMSAT's first nonregulated businesses. While at Warner Communications, Dr. McGarty developed and implemented the first video-on-demand cable-telco videotex system in the United States, which is the predecessor of all interactive multimedia cable/telco systems. His early career was as a faculty member and research staff member at the Massachusetts Institute of Technology, where he was involved in research in communications and imaging systems as well as microeconomic policy development.

Dr. McGarty is also very active in the ongoing development of telecommunications policy and is internationally known for his policy development work in this area. He has served in many government advisory roles, specifically as senior advisor to the U.S. negotiating team on the Comprehensive Test Ban Treaty during the Carter Administration. He has also advised the Defense Department, the Energy Department, the State Department, and the Transportation Department.

Dr. McGarty holds a Ph.D. from MIT in electrical engineering as well as his two other degrees and also studied medicine in the joint Harvard/MIT program. He is the author of four books on random process theory, business planning, and telecommunications policy and over 75 professional papers in areas from telecommunications to law to radiology and medical imaging. He sits on the boards of several companies, including MDSI, a publicly traded company.

Anthony S. Acampora is a professor of electrical and computer engineering at the University of California at San Diego, which he joined in 1995. There he is involved in numerous research projects addressing various issues at the cutting edge of telecommunication networks, including the Internet, ATM, broadband wireless access, network management, and dense wavelength division multiplexing. From 1995 through 1999, he was director of UCSD's Center for Wireless Communications, responsible for an industrially funded research effort that included circuits, signal processing, smart antennas, basic communication theory, wireless telecommunications networks, infrastructure for wireless communications, and software for mobility.

Before that, Prof. Acampora taught electrical engineering at Columbia University, which he joined in 1988, and was director of its Center for Telecommunications Research, a national engineering research facility. He was involved in research and education programs on broadband networks, wireless access networks, network management, optical networks, and multimedia applications.

For 20 years before that he was at AT&T Bell Laboratories, most of the time in basic research, where his interests included radio and satellite communications, local and metropolitan area networks, packet switching, wireless access systems, and light-wave networks. His last position at Bell Labs was as director of the Transmission Technology Laboratory, where he was responsible for a wide range of projects, including broadband networks, image communications, and digital signal processing.

He received his Ph.D. in electrical engineering from the Polytechnic Institute of Brooklyn and is a fellow of the Institute of Electrical and Electronics Engineers (IEEE) and a former member of the IEEE Communication Society Board of Governors. Prof. Acampora has published over 160 papers, holds 30 patents, and has authored a textbook entitled "An Introduction to Broadband Networks: MANs, ATM, B-ISDN, Self Routing Switches, Optical Networks, and Network Control for Voice, Data, Image and HDTV Telecommunications." He sits on numerous telecommunications advisory committees and frequently serves as a consultant to government and industry.

Walter S. Baer is a senior policy analyst at the RAND Corporation, Santa Monica, California. He directs research on interactive media, telecommunications, and information infrastructure developments, as well as on the public policy and business implications of new communications, information, and educational technologies. Dr. Baer was appointed in 1994 to the Governor's Council on Information Technology for the state of California. He currently chairs the Telecommunications Policy Research Conference and serves on the IEEE Committee on Communications and Information Policy and the editorial board of *Telecommunications Policy*, as well as on the advisory boards of the U.S. Committee for the International Institute of Applied Systems Analysis, the Columbia University Institute for Tele-Information, the Los Angeles Learning Center Network Project, and the Children's Partnership. He holds a B.S. from the California Institute of Technology and a Ph.D. in physics from the University of Wisconsin.

Fred Baker has worked in the telecommunications industry since 1978, building statistical multiplexors, terminal servers, bridges, and routers. At Cisco Systems, his primary interest is the management of congestion for best-effort and real-time traffic. In addition to product development, as a Cisco fellow he advises senior management of industry directions and appropriate corporate strategies. His principal standards contributions have been to the Internet Engineering Task Force (IETF), but he has contributed to the International Telecommunication Union's H.323 and to such industry consortia as WINSOCK II and the ATM Forum. In the IETF, he has contributed to Network Management, Routing, PPP, and Frame Relay, the int-serv and diff-serv architectures, and the RSVP signaling protocol. In addition to being a technical contributor, he currently serves as the IETF chair.

Andrew Blau is a program designer and strategist working with foundations and other organizations developing programs at the intersection of technology and society. Building on 15 years as a policy analyst focused on the social and policy impacts of the Internet, telecommunications networks, and digital media, he launched Flanerie Works in 2000 to help foundations better incorporate these technologies and their effects into their work. Current or recent clients include the Ford Foundation, the Rockefeller Foundation, the Paul G. Allen Foundation, the Surdna Foundation, and the Carnegie Corporation.

Previously, Mr. Blau was program director at the Markle Foundation, and prior to that he directed the Benton Foundation's program in communications policy and practice. He also analyzed federal and state telecommunications and Internet policy for leading public interest groups including the Electronic Frontier Foundation and the United Church of Christ's communications policy program. In 1991, he spent a year as a senior member of the research staff at the Columbia Institute for Tele-Information (CITI).

At the request of the Clinton Administration, Mr. Blau was the principal organizer of the first national meeting to bring together leaders from nonprofits, foundations, and the White House to discuss public interest policies in communications. He has testified before Congress about the role of nonprofits in the information age, participated in scores of regulatory proceedings before federal and state regulatory agencies, and published and lectured internationally on developments in U.S. telecommunications policy. He is a member of the Program Committee for the 2001 Telecommunications Policy Research Conference and has been an advisor on technology projects to many organizations, including the U.S. Department of Health and Human Services, the National Endowment for the Humanities, the City of Seattle, and the Microsoft Corporation.

Deborah Estrin is a professor of computer science at the University of California at Los Angeles. From 1986 to 2000, she was on the faculty of the University of Southern California in Los Angeles. In 1987, Dr. Estrin received the National Science Foundation's (NSF's) Presidential Young Investigator Award. She is a codesigner of the PIM and RSVP protocols, and her current research interests include multicast, self-configuring systems, and scaling issues in general. Dr. Estrin received her Ph.D. (1985) and M.S. (1982) from the Massachusetts Institute of Technology and her B.S. (1980) from the University of California at Berkeley. She is a member of the Association for Computing Machinery, IEEE, and the American Association for the Advancement of Science. She has served on several panels for the National Science Foundation, on the National Research Council's Computer Science and Telecommunications Board (CSTB), and as a member of DARPA's Information Science and Technology Study Group (ISAT). She currently chairs a CSTB study on networked embedded computing.

Christian Huitema is the architect in the Windows Networking & Communications group at Microsoft, a group responsible for networking support for Windows. From 1996 to 2000, he was the chief scientist in Telcordia's Internet Architecture research laboratory, where he worked on Internet telephony and Internet quality of service. Before joining Telcordia, he was a senior scientist at INRIA in France, leading a networking research project that investigated innovative applications, such as video on the Internet, and innovative technologies, from directories to protocol compilers. He is the author of several books (among them, *Routing on the Internet* and *IPV6: The New Internet Protocol*), a former member of the Internet Architecture Board, which he chaired from April 1993 to July 1995, and a trustee of the Internet Society.

Edward Jung is copresident of Intellectual Ventures. Prior to that he was general manager of the Web platforms group in the Interactive Media Group and a Microsoft chief architect, serving as a technical strategy advisor to the executive staff on advanced technology. He also led object-oriented and end-user interface technologies in the Advanced Systems division for Microsoft's future-generation operating systems products, now part of Windows NT. He also served as software architect in Applications Architecture, where he codeveloped COM and OLE, and as Information at Your Fingertips (IAYF) coordinator, where he developed and deployed the IAYF technical strategy.

Before joining Microsoft in 1990, Dr. Jung ran several start-up companies and was a biophysicist investigating protein structure-function relationships. His research has been published in *Proceedings of the National Academy of Sciences, Biophysics Journal*, and the *Journal of Biological Chemistry*.

David A. Kettler is vice president for BellSouth and is in charge of the Science & Technology organization and chief architect for the BellSouth Network. His responsibilities include applied research, systems engineering, software application development, network architecture, technical analysis and support, technical standards, network fundamental planning, technology deployment directives, and infrastructure planning.

Dr. Kettler joined BellSouth in 1987 to form the new Science & Technology organization. Prior to that he was employed by AT&T Bell Laboratories for over 15 years and managed departments in network architecture, signaling, and network management. In addition, he led system architecture activities in strategic planning at AT&T corporate headquarters. Dr. Kettler has led and continues to lead major technology thrusts, including data networking services, residential broadband, fiber-in-the-loop, advanced intelligent networks (AINs), and emerging wireless and video technologies. Dr. Kettler has been a world leader in the introduction of AIN, high-speed packet switching (ATM) for information highways, ADSL for high-speed data access, and optical-fiber distribution systems such as fiber-to-the-home. Presently, Dr. Kettler is leading activities in the transformation of BellSouth's Network to a data-centric architecture.

Dr. Kettler received his B.E.E., M.S.E.E.., and Ph.D.E.E. from the University of Virginia. Dr. Kettler is an IEEE fellow. He has served on numerous technical and scientific committees, has organized and chaired conferences and technical sessions, and has presented talks at conferences around the world.

John C. Klensin is vice president for Internet Architecture at AT&T. Prior to joining AT&T in 2000, he was Distinguished Engineering Fellow at MCI and then MCI WorldCom. Outside his corporate commitments, he has had significant responsibility for the present generation of Internet applications standards. His involvement with what is now the Internet began in 1969 and 1970, when he participated in the working group that created the file transfer protocol and that made the decision to include electronic mail capability in the network's design. Dr. Klensin was on the permanent research staff at MIT for about 25 years, participating in or directing a wide variety of projects, many of them involving the application or development of computer networking or related technologies. Dr. Klensin has also been involved with international development work with a United Nations University project on food composition data, archives of images in Islamic architecture, and the Network Startup Resource Center.

Milo Medin is the chief technology officer of Excite@Home, where he oversees the development of the company's high-speed backbone. @Home's performance-engineered scalable network removes Internet "traffic jams" and enables true end-to-end management. In addition, the network employs replication and caching technologies that dramatically improve network efficiency.

Prior to joining Excite@Home, Mr. Medin served as project manager at NASA Ames Research Center. During his tenure, he directed the NASA National Research and Education Network project that, in combination with partners at the Lawrence Livermore National Laboratory, deployed a high-speed national ATM infrastructure connecting major supercomputing and data archiving centers. He also supervised the primary West Coast Internet interconnect network. In addition, he pioneered the global NASA Science Internet project, providing network infrastructure for science at more than 200 sites in 16 countries and 5 continents, including Antarctica, and helped establish the TCP/IP protocol as an industry standard.

Before NASA, Mr. Medin held various positions at Science Applications Inc., programming supercomputers for defense program activities at the Lawrence Livermore National Laboratory and the Los Alamos National Laboratory, under contract to the Defense Nuclear Agency. He has a B.S. in computer science from the University of California at Berkeley.

Craig Partridge is a chief scientist at BBN Technologies (a part of Verizon Communications), where he leads a variety of Internet-related research projects. His most recent major projects involved building an experimental multigigabit router and developing a next-generation routing protocol. Dr. Partridge is the chairman of the Association for Computing Machinery's Special Interest Group in Data Communication (one of the two major professional societies in data communications) and a part-time professor at Stanford University. He is the former editor in chief of both ACM's *Computer Communication Review* and *IEEE Network Magazine* and a consulting editor for Addison-Wesley's professional computing series. He is a fellow of the IEEE and holds his A.B., M.Sc., and Ph.D. degrees from Harvard University.

Daniel Schutzer is vice president and Director of External Standards and Advanced Technology in the Advanced Development Group at Citibank. He is responsible for interfacing with external organizations and standards bodies and for representing Citibank. This includes coordinating technology with business goals and priorities and keeping Citibank up-to-date with the latest technology and standards advances. Projects include electronic banking and electronic commerce, bill presentment and payment, risk management, customer behavioral modeling and mathematical marketing, and new product design. Advanced technologies under investigation include agent technology, machine learning, multimedia, biometrics, image and voice processing, and high-performance computing.

His previous positions included Technical Director for Naval Intelligence; Technical Director for Navy Command, Control and Communications; and program manager at Sperry Rand. He also worked at Bell Labs, Syracuse University, and IBM. He currently teaches part time at Iona College in New Rochelle, New York, and George Washington University in Washington, D.C. He is the author of over 65 publications and 7 books: *Parallel and Distributed Processing, Application of Emerging Technologies in Business, Applied Artificial Intelligence, Military Communications, Command and Control*, a chapter on financial risk management in a financial management handbook, and a chapter in a book on electronic commerce. Forthcoming books are on electronic payment and electronic commerce. He is a board member of the Financial Services Technology Consortium Board and chairman of ISO Subcommittee 2. He received his B.S.E.E. from the College of the City of New York and M.S.E.E. and Ph.D. from Syracuse University.

Index

Internet Protocol. *See* IP
Internet revolution, 1-2
Internet service providers (ISPs)
  free, 111
  growth and diversification of markets
    for, 46-48
  hosting providers, 112
  interconnecting, 108
  interpositioning, 144
  mergers among, 109
  policies for filtering or prioritizing IP
    traffic, 25
  role of, 3, 6-7
  structure of the industry for
    interconnection through multiple
    providers, 109-112
  tier 1, 12-13, 110-111, 119, 122-124
  value-stratification of customers by, 9,
    105
Internet Society (ISOC), 135
Internet Software Consortium, 73
Internet Tax Freedom Act (ITFA), 207
Internet telephony, 15-16, 27, 118
Interoperation between IP telephony and
  the PSTN, 165-170
  addressing and number portability,
    167-168
  groups addressing, 165-166
  robustness considerations, 169-170
  signaling and control and service
    creation, 168-169
Interpositioning, ISP, 144
Intervention, triggers for Internet, 26
Investment, in deployment of IPv6
  technology, 24
IOPS, 91, 94
IP-addressability, 74
IP-layer encryption, 15
IP technology, 31
IP telephony
  architectural contrasts with today's
    PSTN, 161-162
  architectures for, 155-159
  defined, 15-16, 152-154
  groups addressing interoperation
    involving, 165-166
  implications for telephony regulation,
    170-175
  interoperation with the PSTN, 165-170
IPng. *See* IPv6 technology
IPSec protocol, 15, 142

IPv6 technology
  for addressing and configuration, 77-79
  deploying, 7-8, 53, 70, 79-81
  recommendations for investing in, 24
ISO. *See* International Organization for
  Standardization
ISOC. *See* Internet Society
ISPs. *See* Internet service providers
ITFA. *See* Internet Tax Freedom Act
ITU. *See* International Telecommunication
  Union

J

Jitter, 99
  reducing, 100-101

K

Keeping the Internet interconnected and
  open, 10-15
  access to the local loop, 11
  innovation and transparency, 13-15
  interconnection, 11-13

L

Large customers, requirements of, 120n
Latency, 99
  end-to-end, 103
Latency-sensitive traffic, 104
Laws and regulations
  recommendations for creating, 27-28
  recommendations for focusing on
    concerns identified, 27
Layering principle, 36n
Level 3, 163
Links
  failures of, 86
  point-to-point, 108
  wireless, 104
Local access infrastructure, 154
  trends in upgrading, 49-50
Local area networks, wireless, 74
Local loop, access to, 11
Logical (routing) interconnection, 114-115
Long-term benefits, of open IP service, 24-25
Lowering barriers, to entry, for innovation,
  42